IMAGES
of America

DAYTONA BEACH LIFEGUARDS

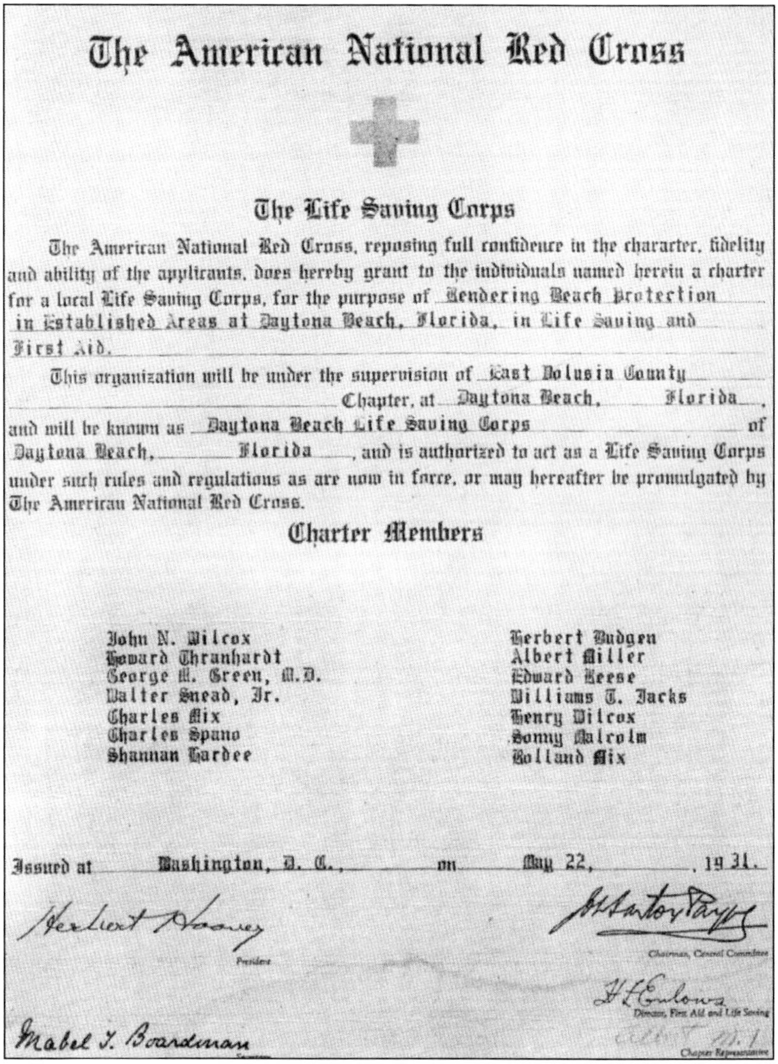

The American National Red Cross

The Life Saving Corps

The American National Red Cross, reposing full confidence in the character, fidelity and ability of the applicants, does hereby grant to the individuals named herein a charter for a local Life Saving Corps, for the purpose of Rendering Beach Protection in Established Areas at Daytona Beach, Florida, in Life Saving and First Aid.

This organization will be under the supervision of East Volusia County Chapter, at Daytona Beach, Florida, and will be known as Daytona Beach Life Saving Corps of Daytona Beach, Florida, and is authorized to act as a Life Saving Corps under such rules and regulations as are now in force, or may hereafter be promulgated by The American National Red Cross.

Charter Members

John N. Wilcox	Herbert Budgen
Howard Thranhardt	Albert Miller
George M. Green, M.D.	Edward Reese
Walter Snead, Jr.	Williams T. Jacks
Charles Mix	Henry Wilcox
Charles Spano	Sonny Malcolm
Shannan Hardee	Rolland Mix

Issued at Washington, D. C., on May 22, 1931.

Herbert Hoover
President

Chairman, Central Committee

Director, First Aid and Life Saving

Mabel T. Boardman

Chapter Representative

The American Red Cross had an influence on lifeguard corps across the country, but this was the second charter granted to a surf lifesaving organization. Pres. Herbert Hoover executed the document on May 22, 1931, naming 14 charter members and signifying the Daytona Beach Life Saving Corps as an official Red Cross Life Preserving Corps. (Courtesy of Volusia County Beach Patrol.)

On the Cover: In 1947, the Daytona Beach Life Saving Corps monitored the waters and guarded the lives of thousands of residents and visitors annually. Their equipment consisted of a metal buoy, a first aid kit, and some rope. There was one station housed under the band shell at the boardwalk, and they monitored 3 miles of beach within the city limits. The dory (rescue boat) in the background was a four-oar lapstrake boat built by the carpenters at the Mary Karl Vocational School on Seabreeze Boulevard. Under the leadership of legendary captain Don Kirkwood, these men were trained in surf lifesaving technique, first aid, and water safety. Since that time, this corps of lifeguards, now a part of Volusia County Beach Patrol, has grown to employ 65 lifeguards full-time, with up to 250 guards at peak season patrolling 47 miles of beach. (Courtesy of Volusia County Beach Patrol.)

IMAGES
of America

DAYTONA BEACH LIFEGUARDS

Patti Light

ARCADIA PUBLISHING

ISBN 978-0-7385-6621-4

Published by Arcadia Publishing
Charleston, South Carolina

Printed in the United States of America

Library of Congress Control Number: 2009925608

For all general information contact Arcadia Publishing at:
Telephone 843-853-2070
Fax 843-853-0044
E-mail sales@arcadiapublishing.com
For customer service and orders:
Toll-Free 1-888-313-2665

Visit us on the Internet at www.arcadiapublishing.com

For those who dedicate their lives to making Daytona Beach and Volusia County beaches a safe playground for millions. I thank you for the privilege of writing your story.

Contents

Acknowledgments		6
Introduction		7
1.	The World's Most Famous Beach	9
2.	Daytona Beach Red Cross Life Saving Corps	21
3.	World War II and WAACs	51
4.	Ormond Beach, New Smyrna Beach, and Volusia County Lifeguards	63
5.	Volusia County Beach Patrol	79
6.	Training, Drills, and Rescues	103
7.	Surf Lifesaving Now and Beyond	113

ACKNOWLEDGMENTS

This book was made possible by the help of many, many people and organizations. First and foremost, I want to thank the personnel of the Volusia County Beach Patrol, who generously shared their archives and their expertise. In particular, thanks to Scott Petersohn, Tami Andrasco, Mike Hensler, Tony Sopotnik, Kathy Martin, Chris Nowviskie, Chris Dembinski, and Art Condon for their assistance. Unless otherwise noted, all images appear courtesy of the Volusia County Beach Patrol.

Retired guards and officers Ray Hutton, Bob Wheeler, Andy Romano, Dick Every, Jim Montgomery, and Jim Willits provided images (both somatic and mental) that gave this book its texture and authenticity. The family of Bert Powell donated to the beach patrol numerous pages from his meticulously kept and notated scrapbook, from which the images of the 1930s and 1940s are drawn almost in their entirety. And a very special thanks goes to Joe Wooden, the quintessential authority on "all things lifeguard" as it pertains to Daytona Beach and Volusia County—past and present—for his tireless answers, referrals, and efforts in providing people, pictures, and facts.

The Halifax Historical Museum, Joy McMahon, Phil Brennen, Jeff Thorla, Russ McCarthy, the New Smyrna Museum of History, Charlie Baldwin, Bud Wright, Gary Luther, and Toni and Joe's Cocktail Lounge were invaluable in providing images, research, and memories. This book was a group effort, and it was quite a large group by the time it drew to a close. If I have left anyone out—and I fear that is inevitable since there were so many—I apologize. This could not have been done without you all.

Luke Cunningham and Arcadia Publishing believed this was a story worth telling and preserving, but without my editor Lindsay Harris's encouragement and hand holding, it would not have come to fruition.

On a personal level, I forever credit my dear friend Gaulden Reed for sharing with me his many friends and his knowledge of surfing, the sea, and Daytona Beach. And on the home front, Don Heal kept me focused and stood by me with carrot juice, hugs, and encouragement. I love you, Don.

Introduction

From the beginning, the need for organized, trained, and equipped people whose mission was to provide rescue from the sea has been recognized. Although the roots of surf lifesaving are documented in China as early as 1708, in the United States the first bastion of organized efforts to revive drowning victims, as well as rescuing others from the perils of the sea, is the Massachusetts Humane Society (also called the Humane Society of the Commonwealth of Massachusetts), established in 1785. In 1787, the society had begun to construct small huts as "houses of refuge." Should a shipwrecked mariner make his way to shore and find such a safe house, he would have a store of food, candles, kindling, fuel, and a tinderbox.

By 1803, the idea of providing boats for rescue purposes had evolved, and in October 1807, the first American lifeboat was launched and America's first lifeboat station established near Boston in Cohasset, Massachusetts.

The beaches of Volusia County have always been a premier vacation destination thanks to their wide stretches of white "sugar" sand. But the extreme fluctuation of high and low tides brings an abundance of rip currents, which creates a dangerous situation for swimmers, particularly visitors. Clearly there was a need for organized efforts to safeguard bathers unaccustomed to the tides and currents of the ocean.

As early as the 1900s, there were volunteer surf lifesavers in Daytona Beach, and by the 1920s, the communities of Volusia County had begun to organize their efforts and form individual surf lifesaving corps. In the spring of 1930, the American Red Cross, under the direction of A. M. (Al) Boland, director of first aid and lifesaving, East Volusia County Chapter of the American Red Cross, organized the Daytona Beach Red Cross Life Saving Corps. The members of this volunteer corps, aged 17 to 26, were required to pass the American Red Cross senior lifesaving and standard first aid tests. Other requirements included 100 hours of volunteer service each season (Thursdays, Sundays, and holidays were not compensated), plus drill and attendance at one meeting per week. Manning 12 towers equipped with first aid kits, two buoys, one blanket, an umbrella, and 200 feet of rope, these 30 guards boasted a record of only four deaths in 1,000 rescues.

On May 22, 1931, the American Red Cross Life Saving Corps (1929–1956) issued its second charter, signed by Pres. Herbert Hoover, to the lifesaving corps of Daytona Beach. Along with regular beach monitoring duties, each guard compiled a daily record of the number of bathers, rescues, first aid cases, weather, water currents, station, and hours worked and noted general remarks along with his name and number.

At this time, each of the cities along the 47 miles of shoreline that fell within the confines of Volusia County were manned by their own respective lifesaving forces, and the history of the Daytona Beach lifeguards cannot be told without including the stories of the lifeguards of the surrounding communities and their ultimate merger into one unified, county-wide beach patrol. Ormond Beach (District 4) spanned the city limits from the Harvard approach north to Neptune. Daytona Beach (District 1) took up at the southern edge of Ormond Beach and ran 3 miles to

Daytona Beach Shores. New Smyrna Beach was a separate corps, controlling the shoreline within the city limits. All remaining territory was monitored by Volusia County.

In 1962, Daytona Beach and Volusia County combined forces, becoming Volusia County Beach Patrol (VCBP). In 1971 and 1972, Ormond Beach and New Smyrna Beach, respectively, joined the VCBP. This beach patrol now has 65 full-time officers, but its seasonal total reaches between 225 and 250 beach safety officials, including tower guards. Today Volusia County Beach Patrol is a premier agency worldwide, encompassing law enforcement, EMT, and lifesaving in a class with beach patrols of New Zealand, Australia, and Los Angeles County. In 2007, Volusia County, one of 25 beach patrols in the state of Florida, accounted for an average of 3,000 rescues out of 5,600 total rescues statewide.

For Daytona Beach lifeguards, much has changed since the days of a single control tower, one truck, a scooter, and two bicycles. State-of-the-art lifesaving techniques and technology have evolved over the near-100 years of this organization. The percentage of lifeguards who have gone on to become outstanding citizens is impressive: judges, physicians, police chiefs, government officials, surgeons, fire and safety officers, and decorated officers of the armed forces, along with teachers and coaches, are just a few of the noble careers occupied by former and current lifeguards. They all cite the training, discipline, and self-confidence instilled during their time as a lifeguard as a major contributor to their success.

In the words of 39-year veteran Tony Sopotnik, describing his forerunners, "They were men of character, of principle, of unparalleled inner strength. They took boys and inspired them to be men. I feel it is my personal duty, out of respect for these men and anyone who ever sat a tower with distinction, to maintain the same approach to being a Volusia County lifeguards as they did."

And in the words of the bumper sticker that inspired this book: "Only the Lord saves more than the beach patrol."

One

The World's Most Famous Beach

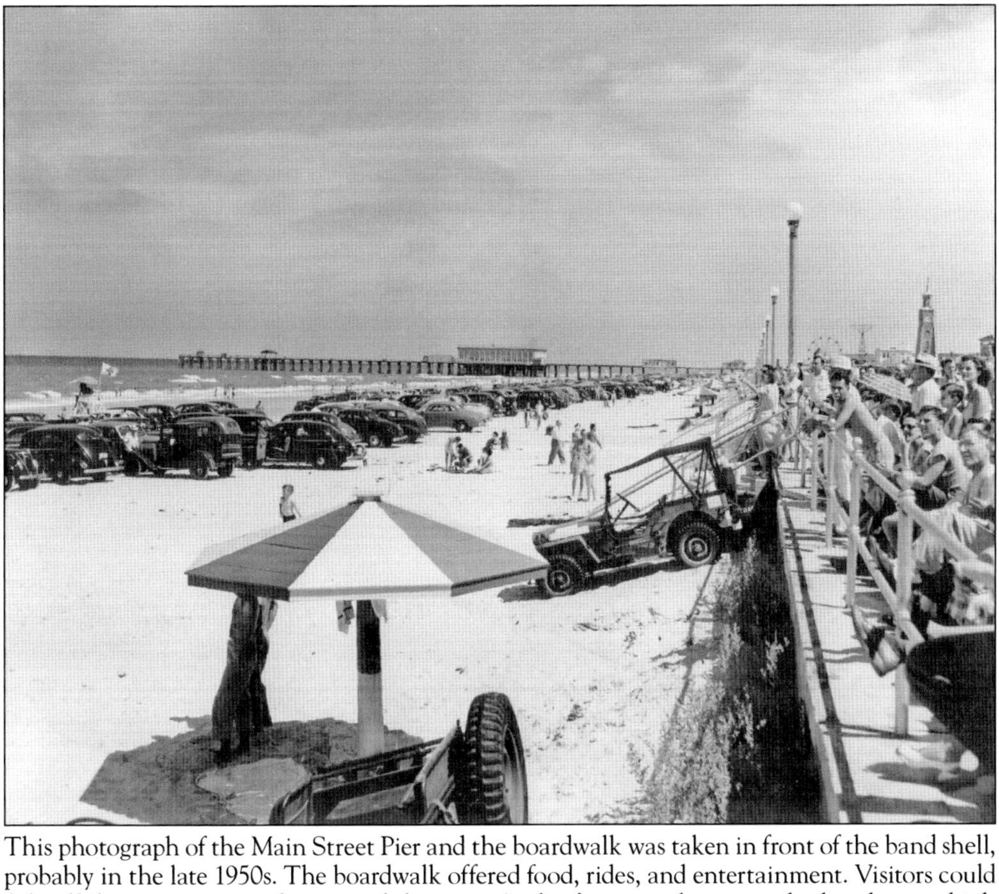

This photograph of the Main Street Pier and the boardwalk was taken in front of the band shell, probably in the late 1950s. The boardwalk offered food, rides, and entertainment. Visitors could fish off the pier or enjoy dinner and dancing. And, of course, there was the beach, on which visitors could drive their cars.

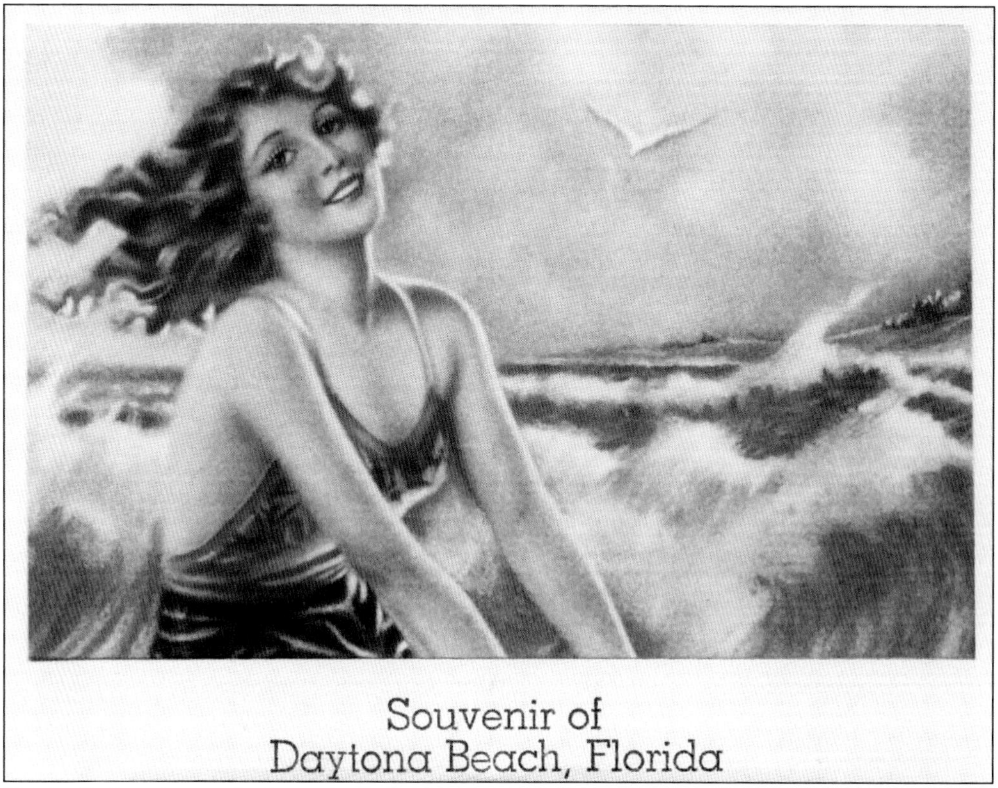

Originally done in pastels, this quintessential image of the beach beauty was used on souvenir postcards in the 1930s. Mabel Rollins Harris was the illustrator, and her work appeared extensively in calendars and advertisements from the late 1920s until the end of the 1930s. (Courtesy of John McSwain.)

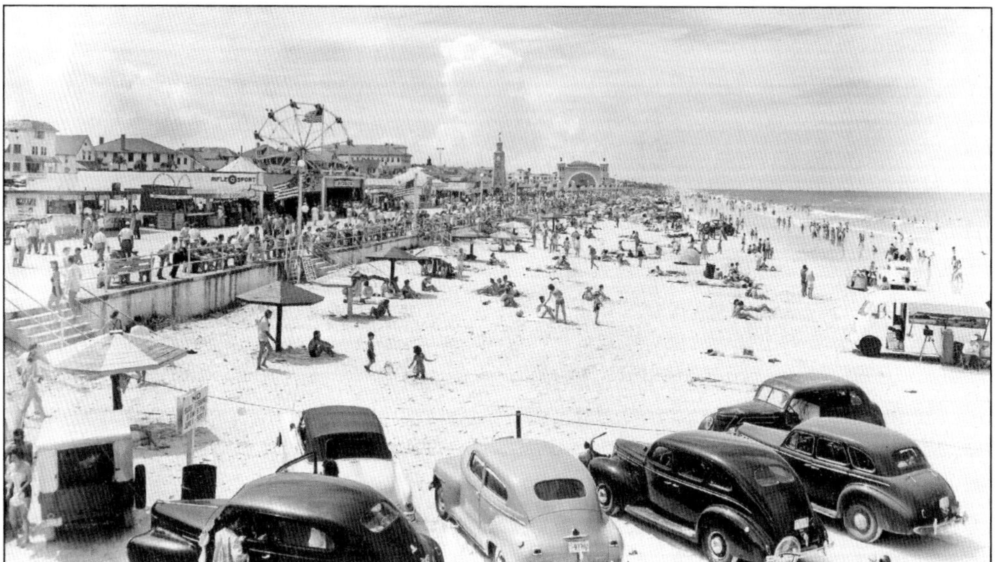

In 1949, the boardwalk was a major attraction in Daytona Beach. Vacationing families could rent umbrellas and floats from beach concessionaires, enjoy snacks from beach vendors and the merchants on the boardwalk, and even ride the Ferris wheel. (Courtesy of State Archives of Florida.)

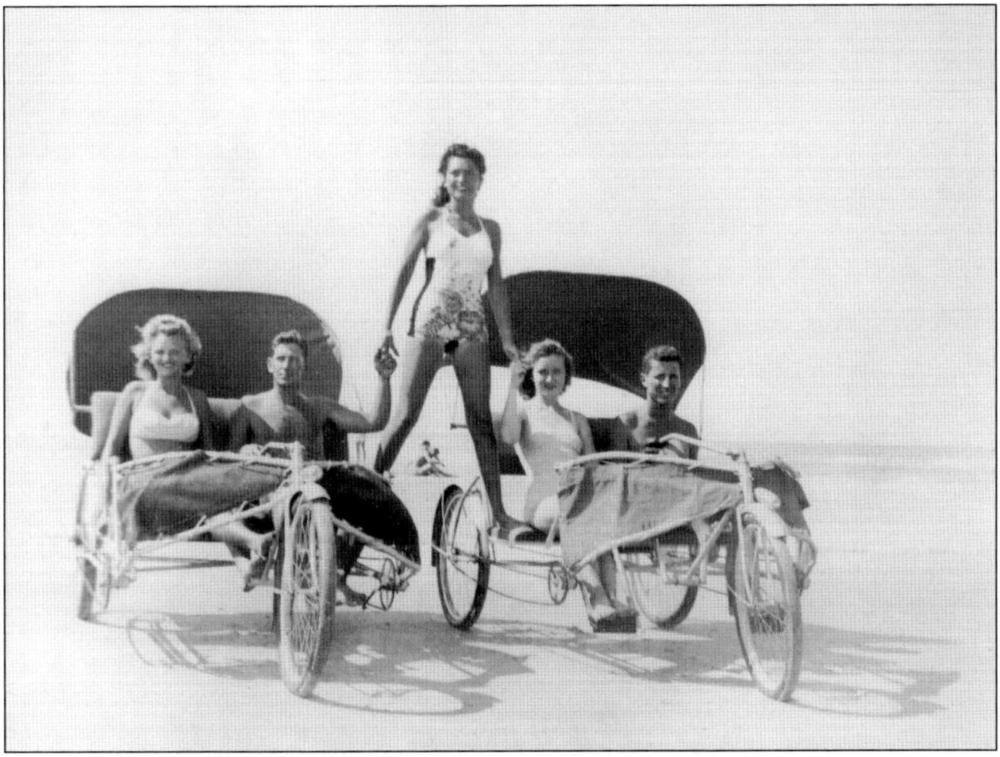

The sun surrey was the newest beach fad, as shown in these 1946 beach publicity pictures for Associated Press. Pedaled by both drivers, the surrey featured a seat umbrella and a locker in the back. Both these photographs came from the scrapbook of Bert Powell, former lifeguard captain, and carried the caption, "Helping make beach buggy ads." In the above photograph, pictured from left to right are Betty Kirkwood, Bud Smith, Barbara ?, unidentified, and Dick Stanier. In the photograph below are, from left to right, Betty Kirkwood, Bud Smith, unidentified girl, Dick Stanier, Barbara ?, Bert Powell, unidentified girl, Jimmy Heinemann, unidentified girl, and George Linton.

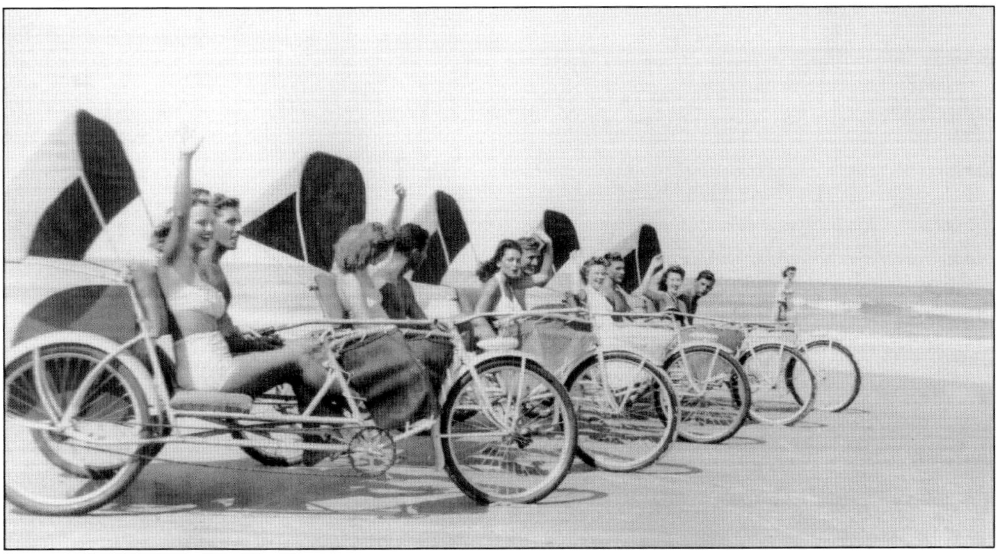

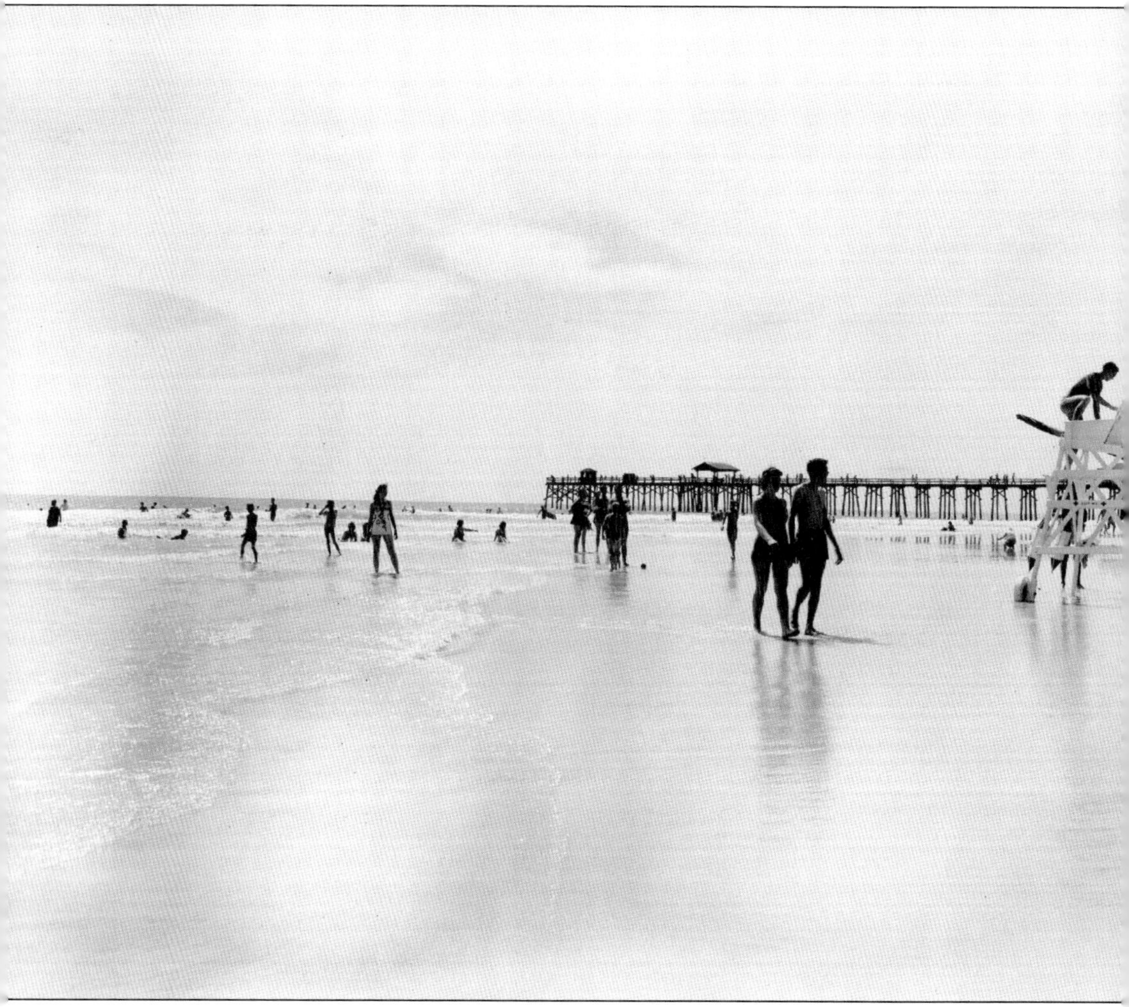

In 1949, members of the Daytona Beach American Red Cross Life Saving Corps were required to work holidays (as well as other days, a minimum of 100 per year) without pay as a form of contribution to the American Red Cross. This morning photograph shows a dedicated guard taking his place on his tower on the Fourth of July.

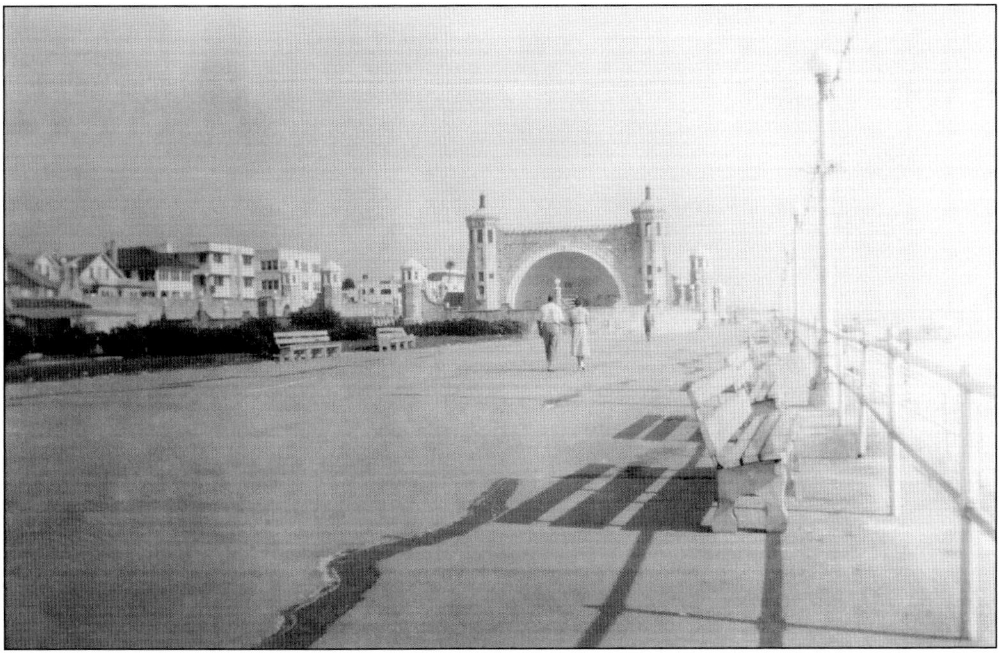

In 1950, the band shell on the boardwalk was billed as the "World's Largest Open Air Theater." (Courtesy of State Archives of Florida.)

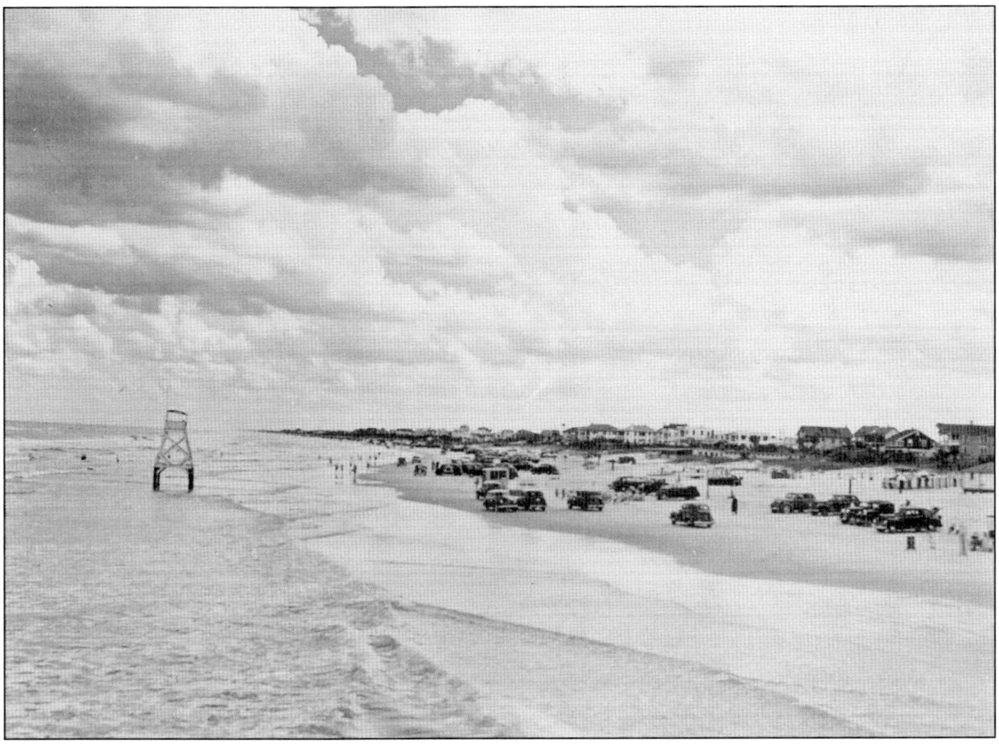

The lifeguard tower afforded the guard on duty a view of miles of open beach. This 1950s photograph shows a time when the lifeguard corps was limited to communications via flags, hand and body signals, and whistles. (Courtesy of State Archives of Florida.)

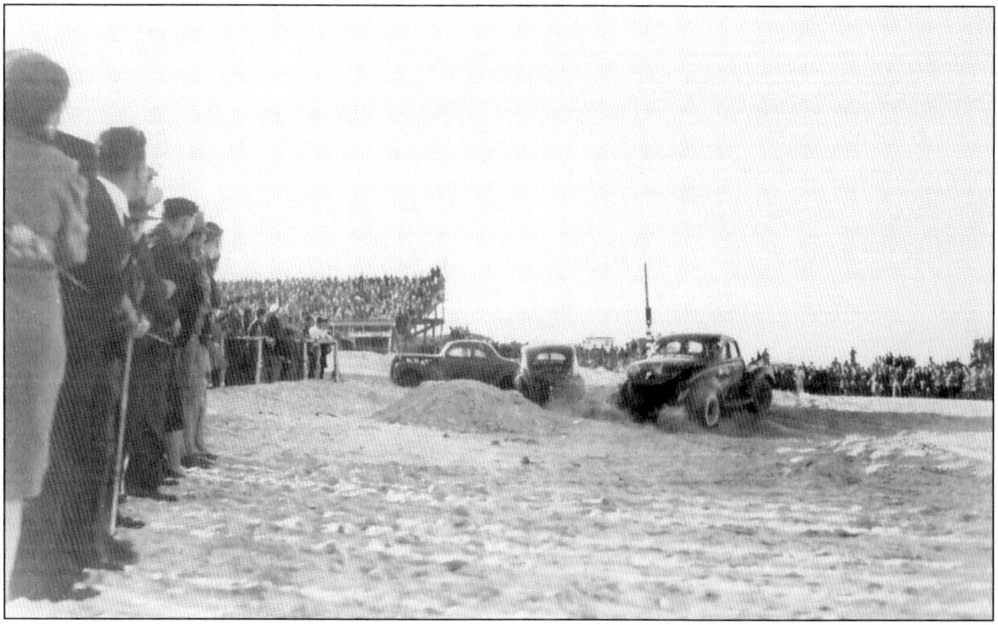

In 1952, people flocked to the beach to watch the races, which often ended in disaster. With crowds like this one lining up for a stock car race, it is easy to see why Bill France predicted there was a future in automobile racing.

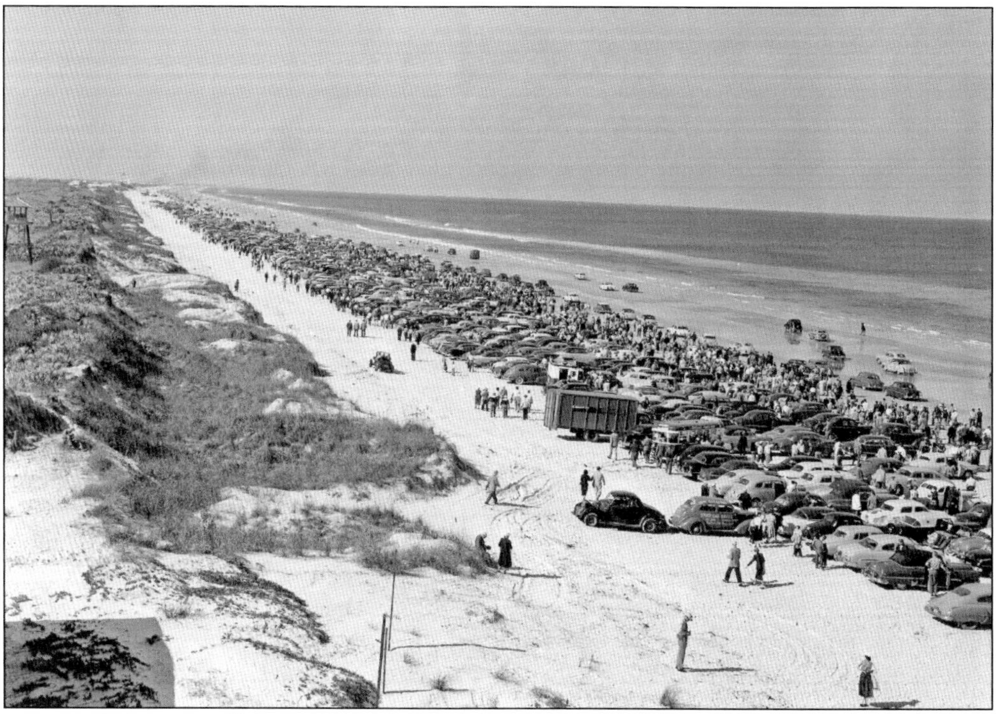

Daytona Beach is also known as the "Birthplace of Speed." Drivers came here to set speed records on the "Measured Mile," which ran from the Main Street Pier southward. Here spectators witness a pileup in a 1942 race. Lifeguards assisted with race casualties and related casualties, such as the time a tire flew off and hit someone in the crowd. Lifeguard Dick Every was on hand to provide first aid.

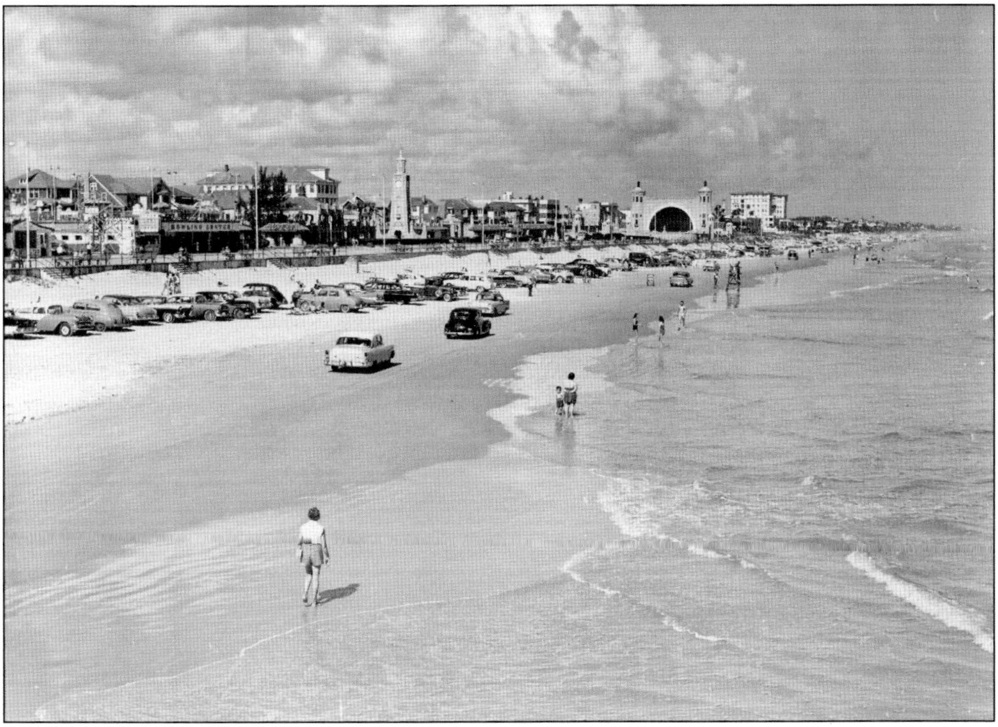

The flat, packed sands of Daytona Beach were always a draw, allowing cars to drive for miles along the shoreline. This 1957 photograph shows automobiles parked along the main stretch of the city limits.

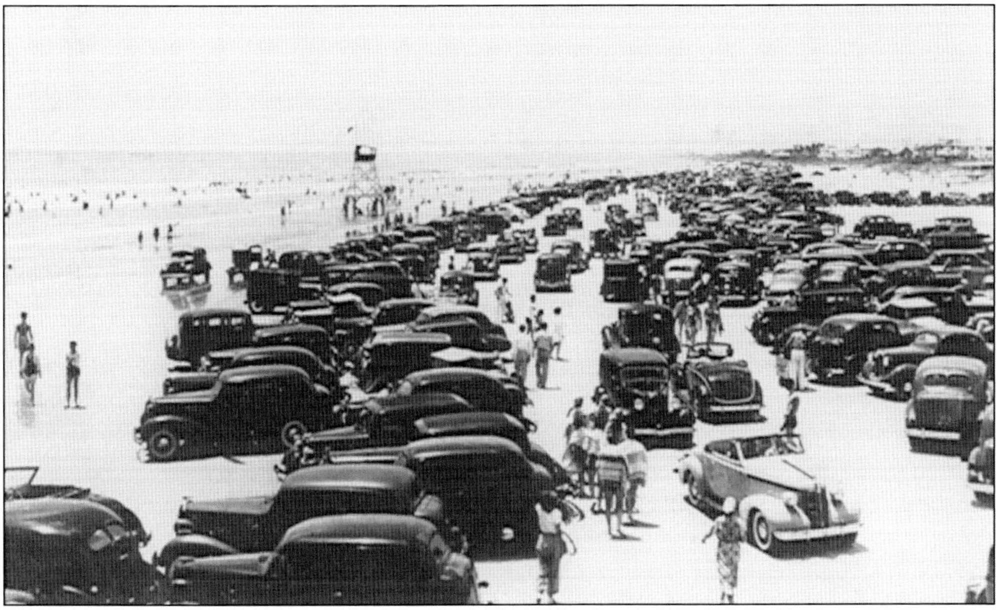

The official turf of the Daytona Beach lifeguards was within the city limits, running 3 miles between Daytona Beach Shores and the southern border of Ormond Beach. The Harvey Avenue approach (shown here) lies between Main Street and International Speedway Boulevard. Today this part of the beach is a traffic-free zone.

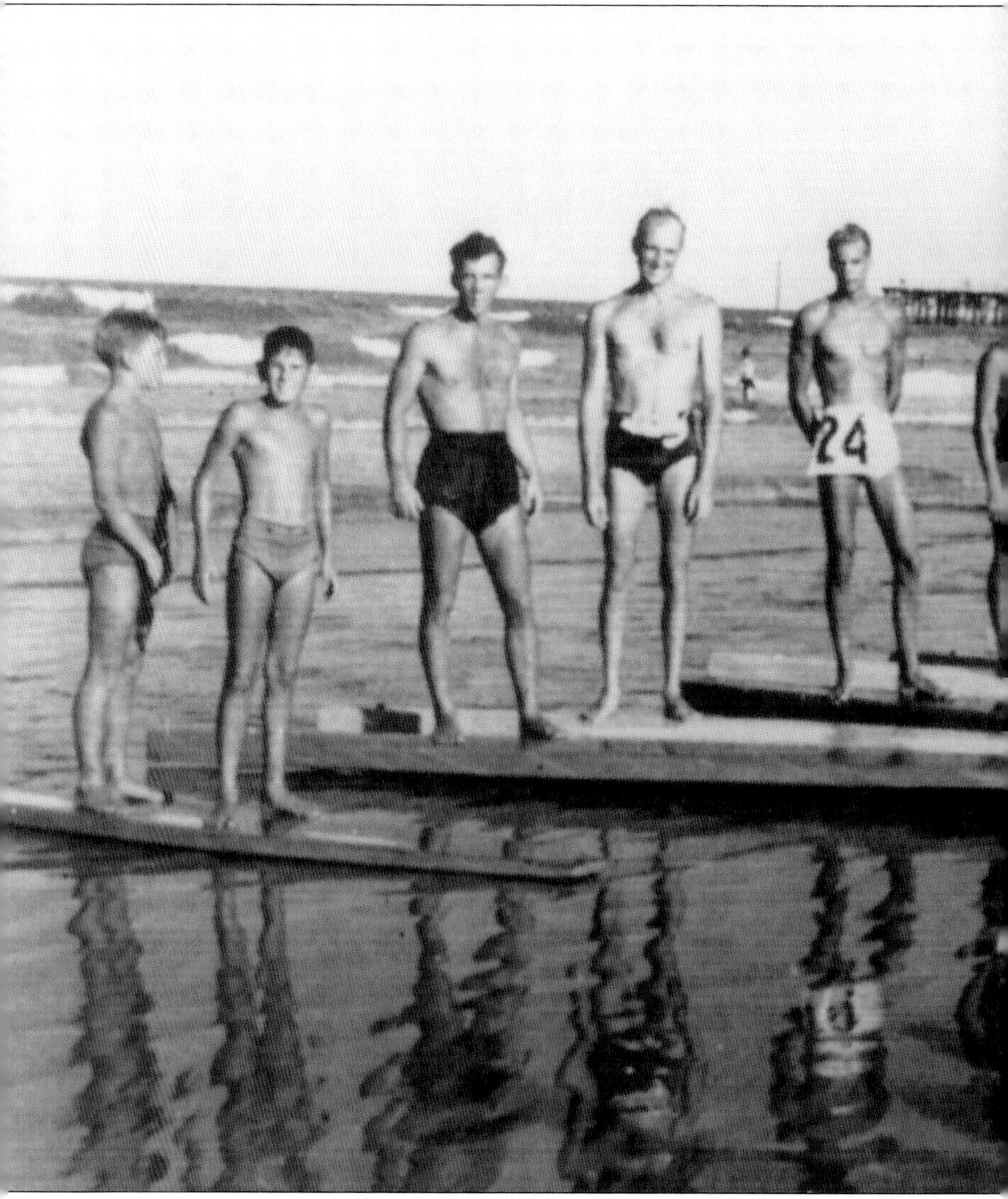

Surfing has deep roots in Volusia County as well, with international champions Frieda Zamba, Lisa Andersen, and Mimi Munro hailing from the Ormond and Flagler Beach areas. East Coast Surfing Hall of Fame members include the above mentioned, along with Flea Shaw and surfing pioneer Gaulden Reed. Hall of fame members Bill and Dudley Whitman (and Dudley's daughter Renee) came to Daytona Beach as a favorite surf destination. This 1930s photograph, taken near

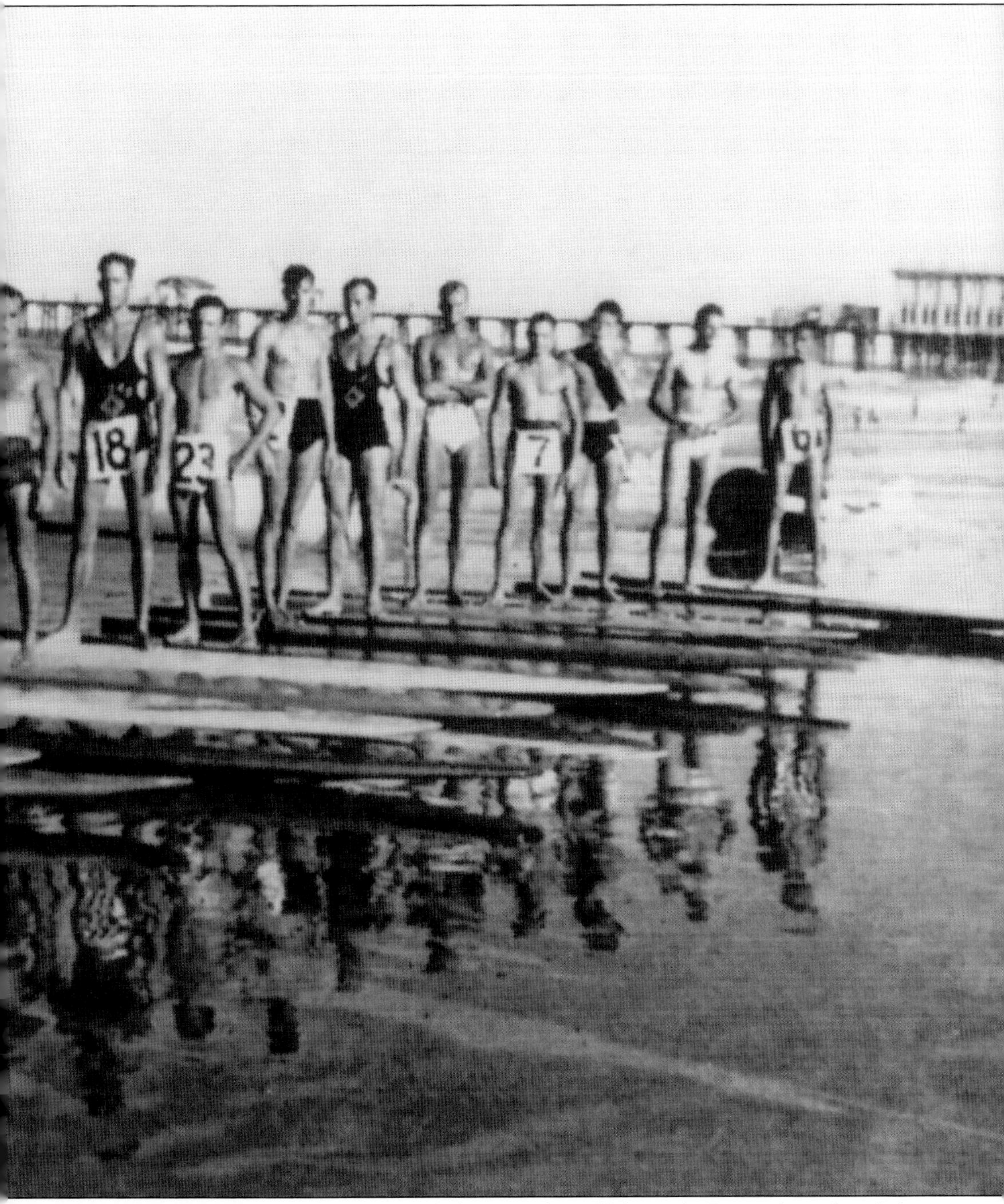

the Main Street Pier after a surf contest, includes a number of lifeguards. Pictured are, from left to right, unidentified, Barney Barnhart Jr., unidentified, Comdr. Al Bushman, Dudley Whitman, Dick Every, Donald Every, Donald Gunn, Bitsy Hart, Gaulden Reed, Floyd Graves, Bill Whitman, three unidentified people, and Earl Blank.

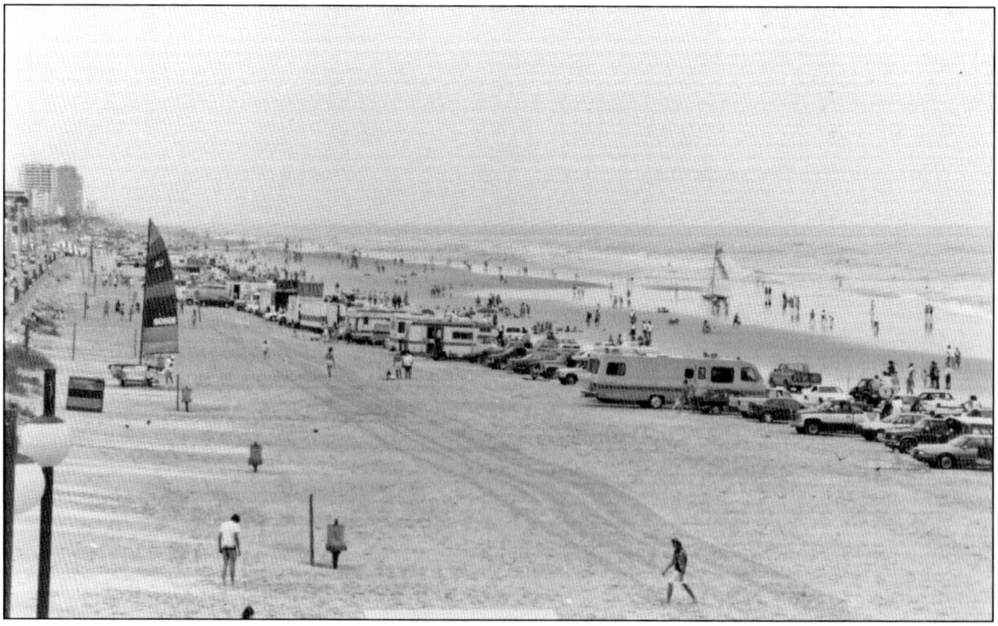

These 1961 photographs depict the continued popularity of Daytona Beach as a favorite vacation spot and show cars, both parked and moving, as far as the eye can see. Surfing and sailing were becoming popular pastimes, and there was always something happening at the beach. (Both photographs courtesy of Jim Willits.)

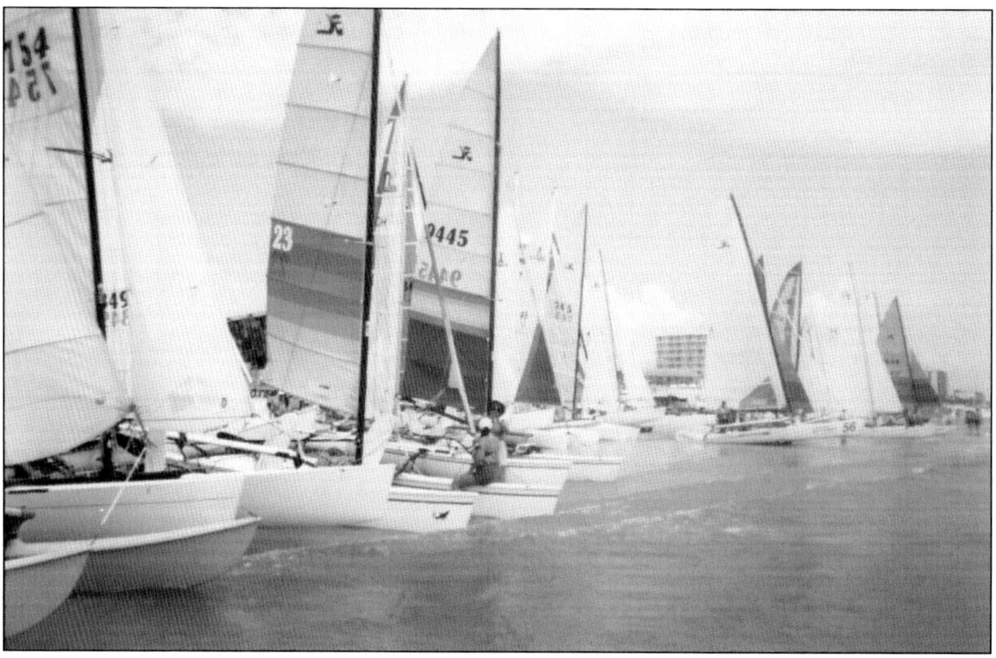

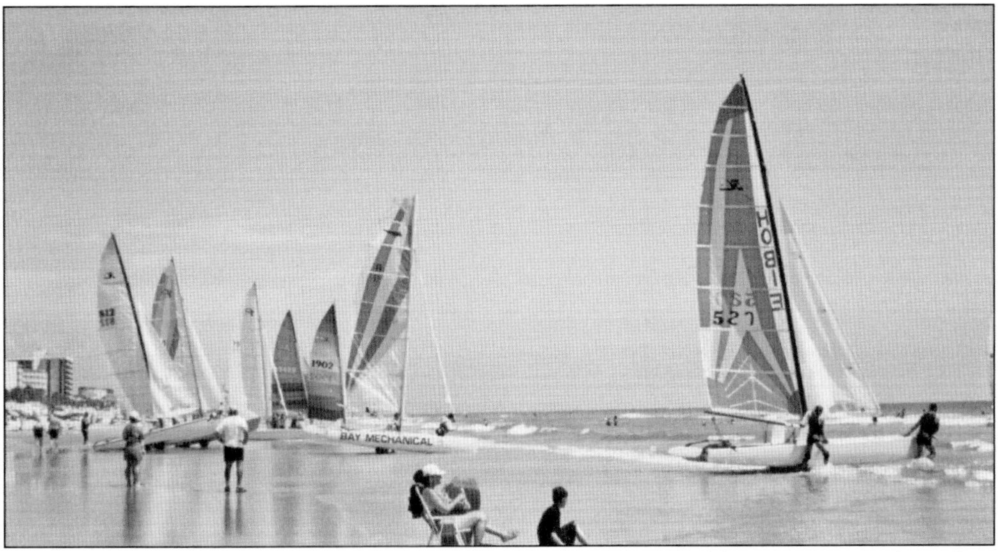

The Gaulden Reed Summer Sizzler, a national Hobie-cat race named for Daytona Beach resident Gaulden Reed, began in 1993 and continues as of this writing. This photograph, taken April 10, 1991, by Jim Willits, shows the crowd gathering as one catamaran launches and another prepares for the race. Beach events such as this one rely heavily on the Beach Safety Division to coordinate designated launch spaces, crowd management, and increased rescue ability. (Courtesy of Jim Willits.)

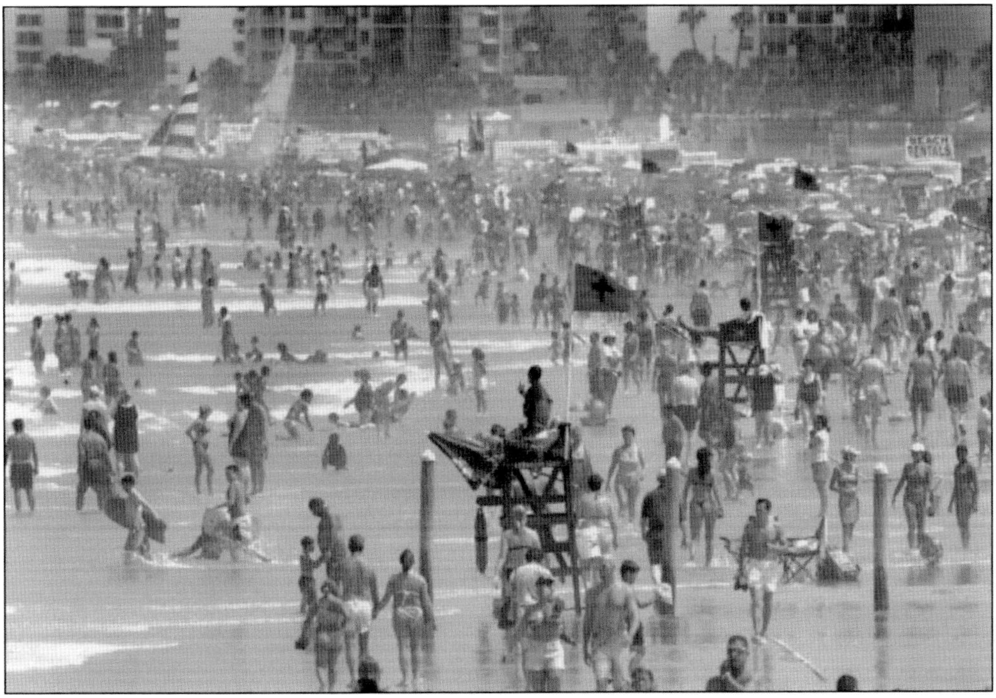

These heavy crowds mean an increased threat of injury and drownings. Here one sees three towers within yards of one another as the corps does whatever it takes to keep the crowds safe on a busy weekend.

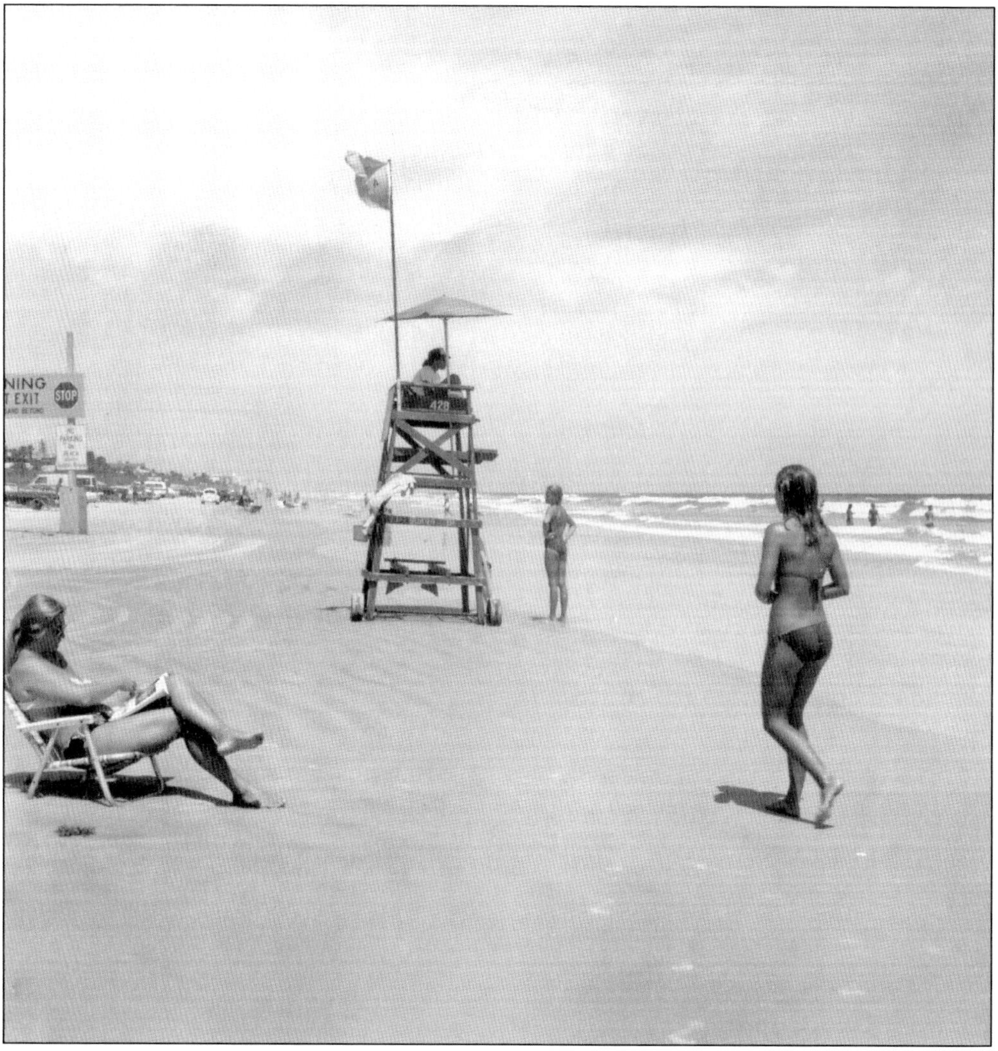

By the 1970s, society was changing. Surf, sun, and sand had become a way of life, and the beach was gaining in popularity. The role of lifeguard took on a luster that attracted many to the profession—and many more to the guards themselves. But ask anyone who has ever been on a rescue and pulled someone to safety, and they will say it is not about the glory. It is a real job, and it is about saving lives.

Two

Daytona Beach Red Cross Life Saving Corps

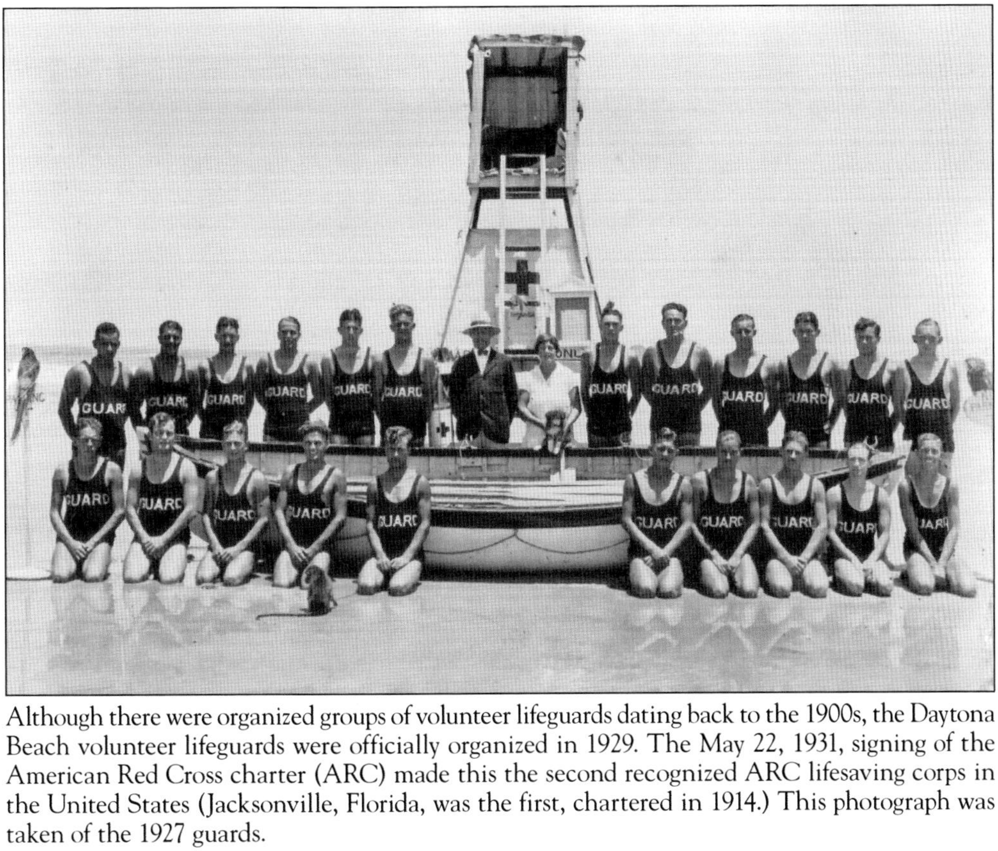

Although there were organized groups of volunteer lifeguards dating back to the 1900s, the Daytona Beach volunteer lifeguards were officially organized in 1929. The May 22, 1931, signing of the American Red Cross charter (ARC) made this the second recognized ARC lifesaving corps in the United States (Jacksonville, Florida, was the first, chartered in 1914.) This photograph was taken of the 1927 guards.

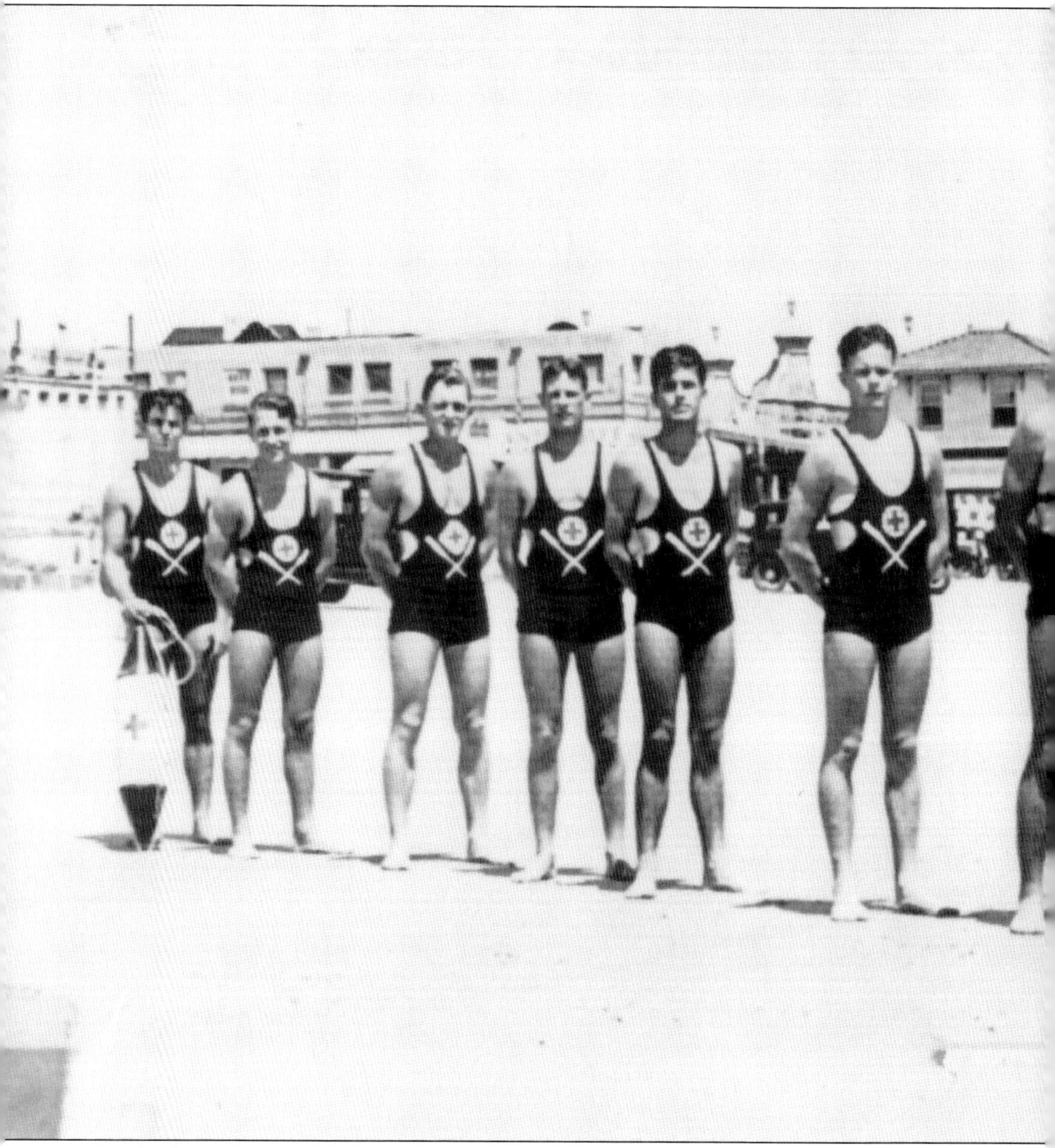

Under the charter of the ARC, lifeguards were provided a uniform and a first aid kit. The kit was a white metal box with the Red Cross emblem containing bandages, antiseptic, and ammonia to neutralize stings. Every lifeguard was required to work one day per week without compensation and to attend one meeting and drill per week. The first corps is pictured here, with the Main Street Pier in the background. Members are, from left to right, Sonny Malcolm, Shannon Hardy, Rollan

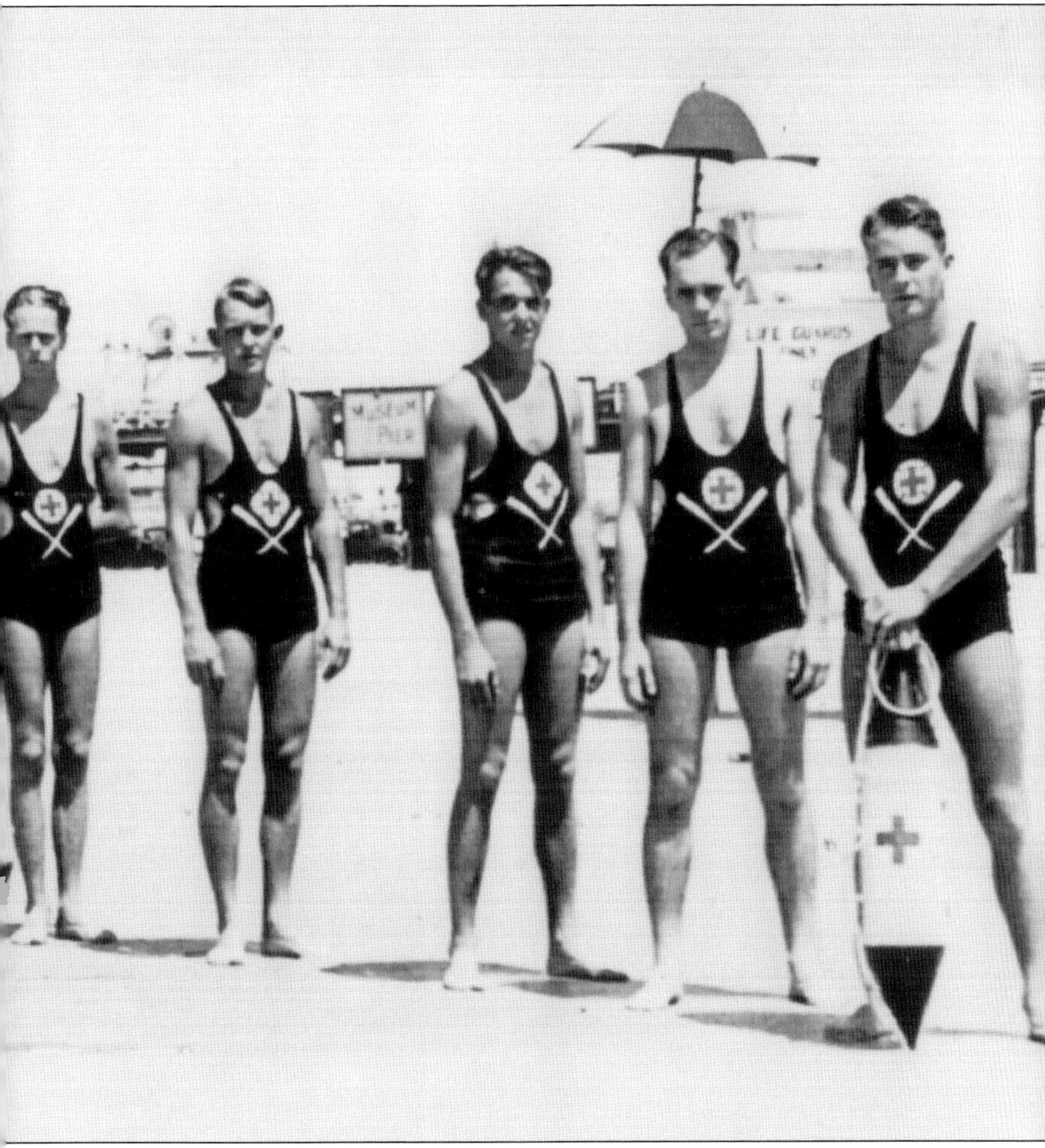

Mix, Howard "Nappy" Thranhardt, Hubert Budgen, Ed Reese, Nutter Wilcox, William "Bill" Jack (captain), Chuck Mix (the first paid captain), Walter Sneed, Henry Wilcox Sr., and Charles "Chuck" Spano. Spano, Thranhardt, and Budgen were the last surviving members of this original corps. A note of interest is that Reese's son, Eddie Reese, became three-time U.S. Olympic men's head coach in swimming and is the swimming coach at the University of Texas, Austin.

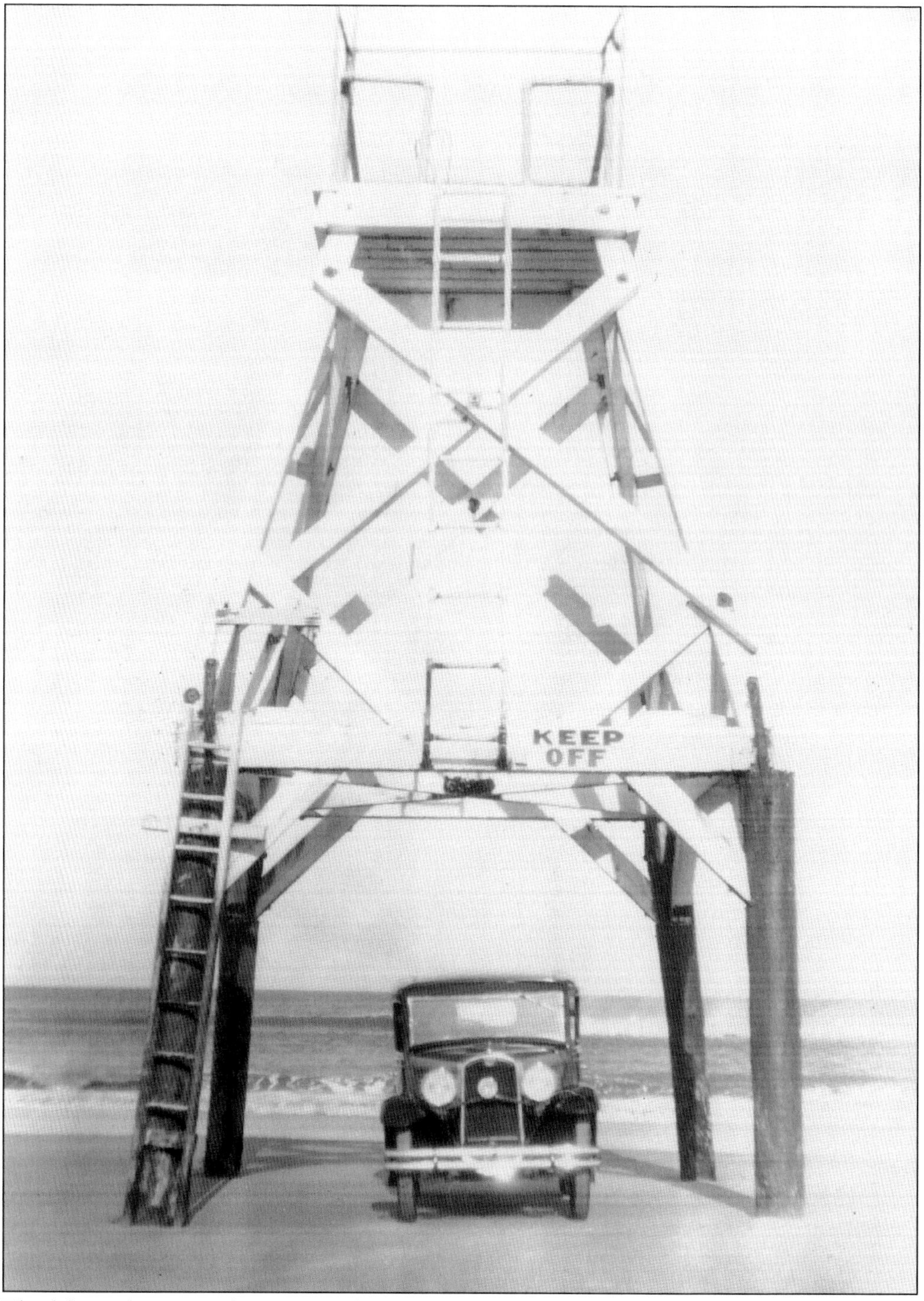

This lifeguard tower sat about 100 yards south of the Main Street Pier and featured a hand-cranked siren. At the time, the only methods of communication were hand signals, whistles, and these sirens. The tower was built by the City of Daytona Beach in the surf, and when the tide came in the guards would ride the waves under it. The Model A parked beneath provides a perspective of the size of the tower, which was eventually destroyed by a hurricane.

Jack Coleman stands in front of his tower in 1933. Each tower was equipped with a first aid kit, two metal buoys, one umbrella, one blanket, and 200 feet of rope. Guards kept daily records of the number of bathers, surf and weather conditions, rescues, first aid, and other observations.

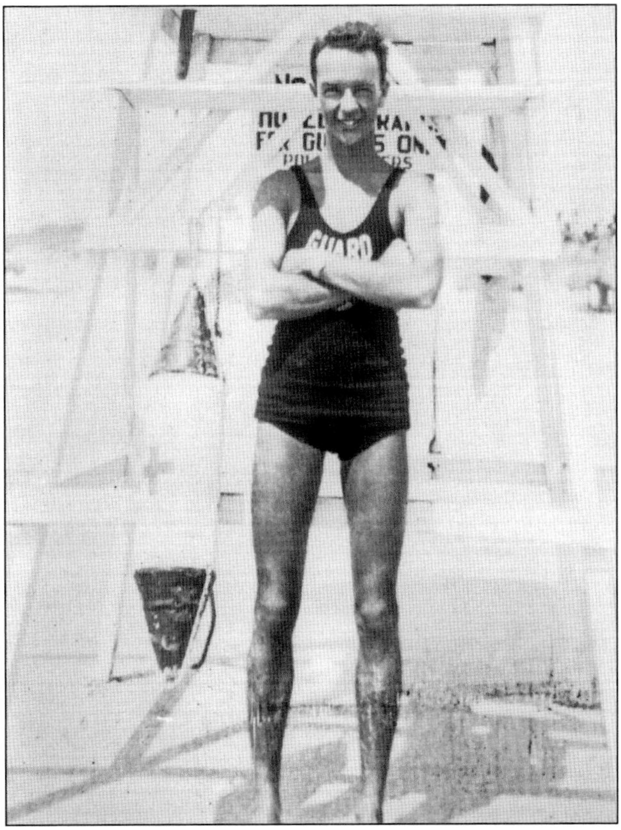

The lapstrake boat was used for rescues and bore the emblem of the American Red Cross as well as the American flag. This boat was equipped with four 8-foot-long oars and was normally manned by a crew of five—one man per oar plus one to steer.

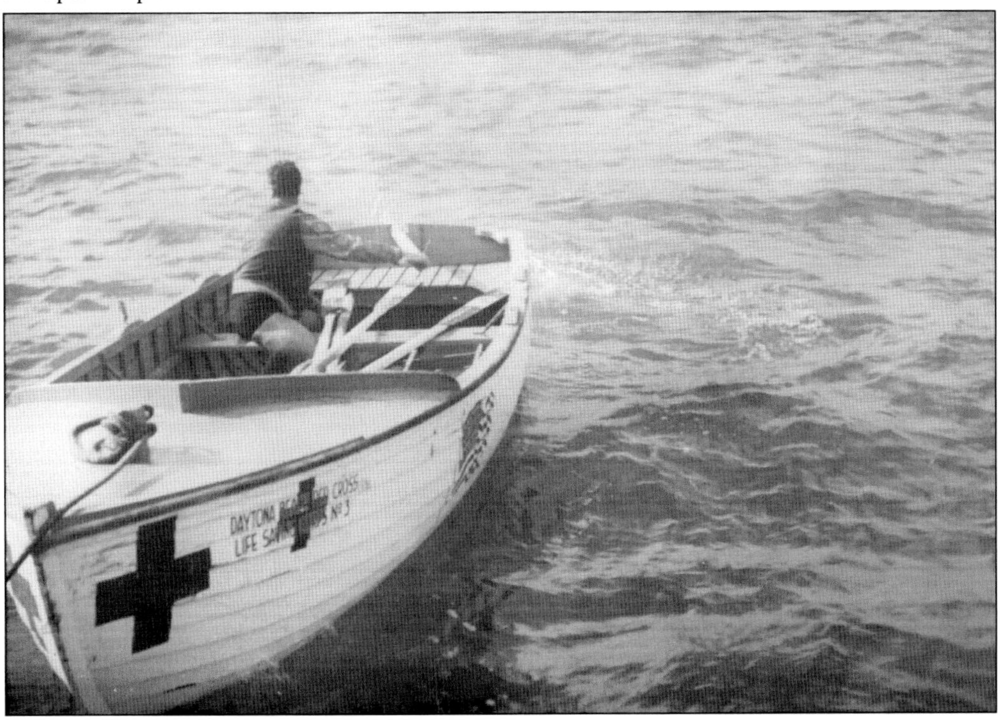

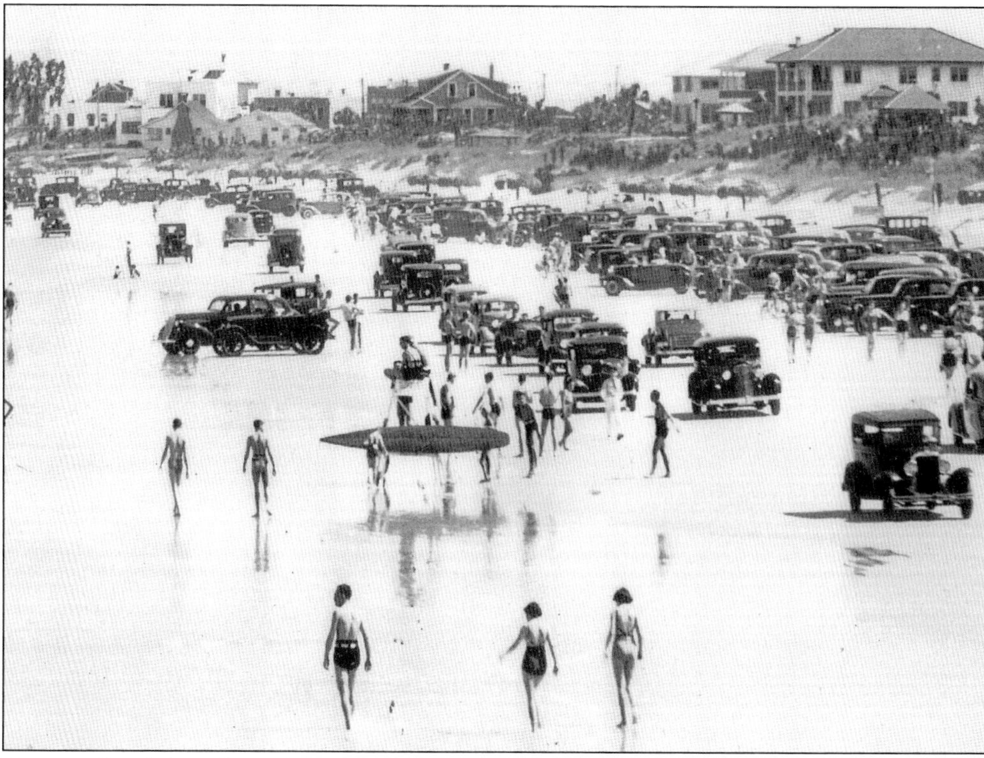

Daytona Beach has always been a popular recreation area, with tourists and residents flocking to drive on the packed sand and enjoy the beaches. With the intense rip currents, also called run-outs, providing lifeguards was a prime concern for the city, thus ensuring the safety of the public. In this photograph, lifeguard Gaulden Reed keeps a careful eye from his spot on the tower, to which a paddleboard is attached for rescue use.

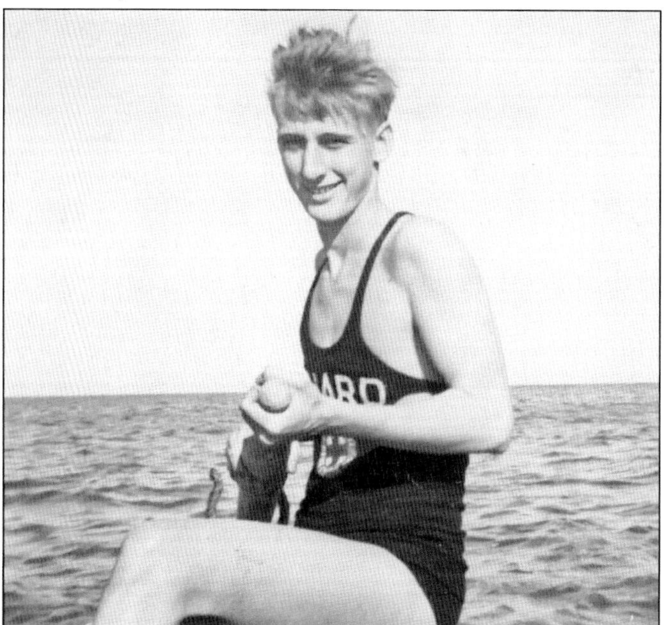

Bert Powell played a major role in the development of the corps, serving as captain and also training the WAACs (Womens Army Auxiliary Corps) during World War II. The caption on this photograph from his personal scrapbook, which was donated to the beach patrol, read: "Steering the guard boat at Christmas 1939."

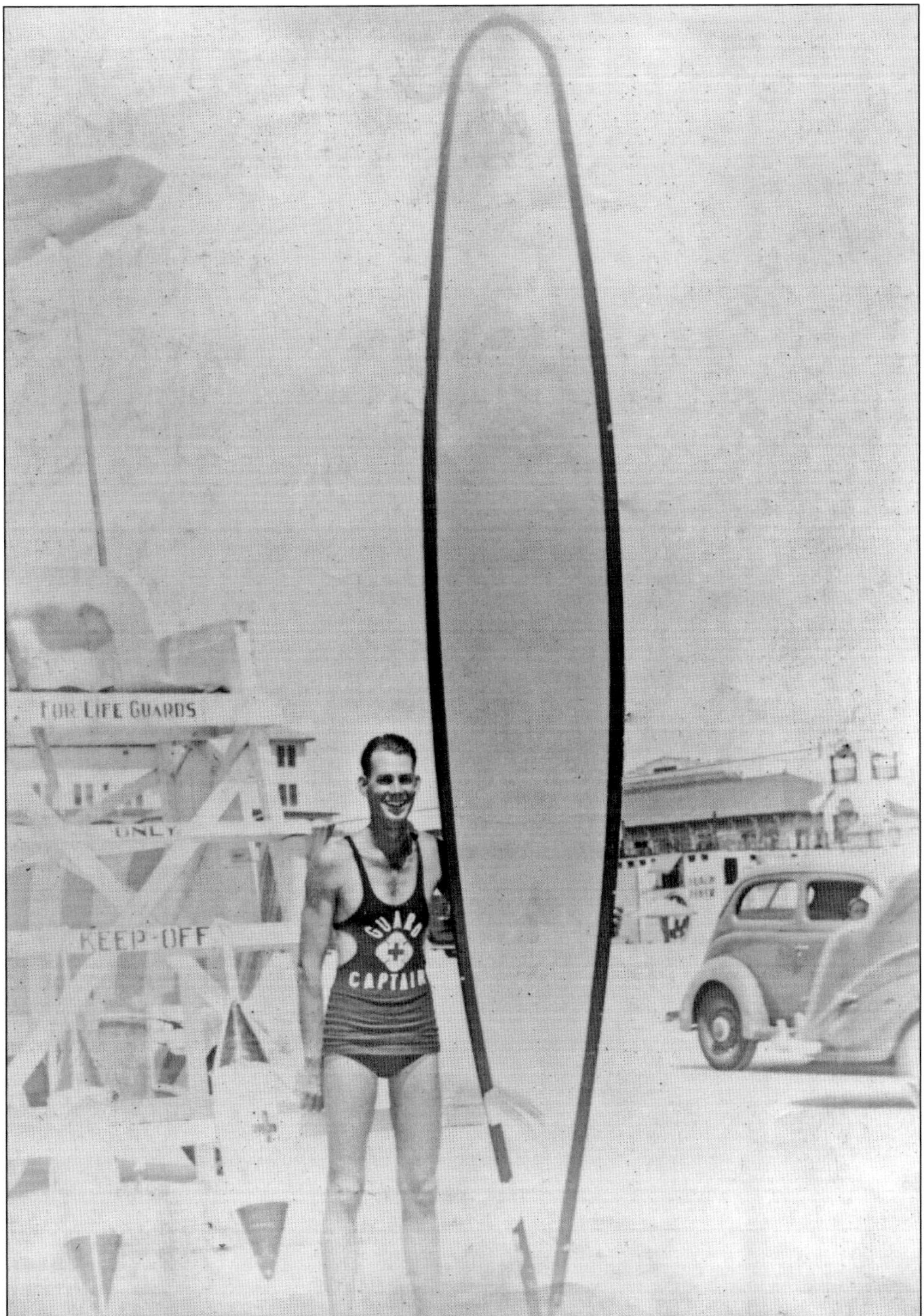

George Boone was captain of the lifeguards, running a tight ship until 1937, when Don Kirkwood became captain. This 1939 photograph shows him holding the enormous paddleboard in front of his tower.

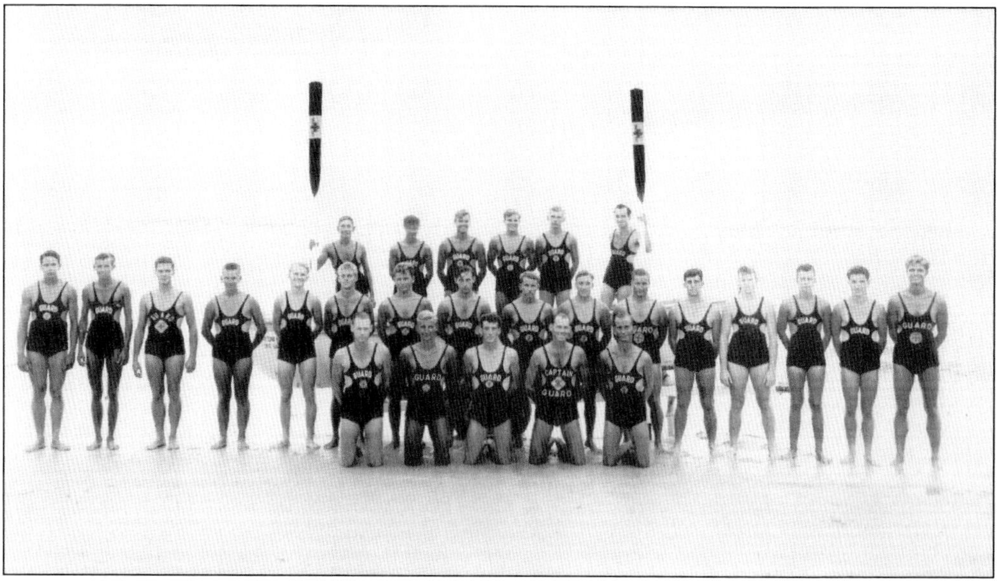

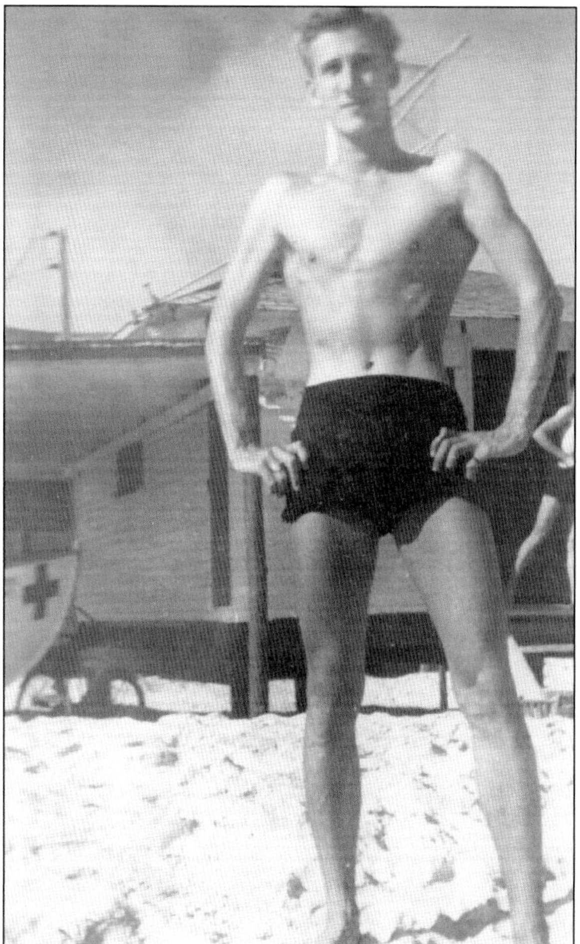

By 1941, the number of guards was increasing to keep up with the growing number of tourists crowding to the beaches. Pictured are, from left to right, (first row) Freddie Tranhart, Bert Powell, William "Itchy" Purcell, George Boone, and "Bubba" Atkins; (second row) John Crane, Mac Bailey, Tommy Willis, Dick Every, Billy May, "Cocoa" Gibert, Marvin Roth, Warner McIntosh, Bill Russell, John "Bird-dog" Peardon, Floyd Odum, "Skip" Eichholz, Henry "Red" Duffett, Ralph ?, Dick Stanier, and Pierce Timberlake; (third row) Bud Smith, Nick Triantefallu, Eddie Thompson, unidentified, Charlie Merry, and unidentified.

Bert Powell was captain and president of the corps during the early part of World War II. But he also served his country, leading a bomber squadron out of England on D-Day. Powell was shot down and spent two years as a prisoner of war in Germany. Standing in front of the lifeguard station in 1941, Powell enjoys happy times.

Dick Every was recruited for the lifeguards in 1937, and he served as a guard from 1938 to 1953. Eventually he became an examiner, teaching swimming and lifesaving technique. In the late 1940s, the drills consisted of running 1 mile, swimming the length of the boardwalk, and running the mile back in under 40 minutes. A day in the life of a guard went from 7:00 a.m. until dark during peak season, and the pay was $3.25 a day. Additionally, the guards were required to spend one day weekly as a volunteer.

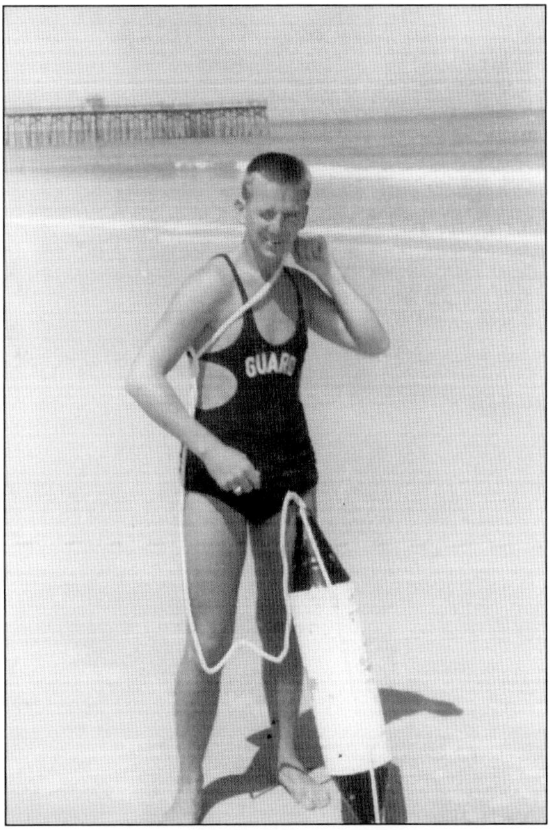

Here George Boone and Dick Every manage to enjoy one of the perks of the job—being on the beach and surfing.

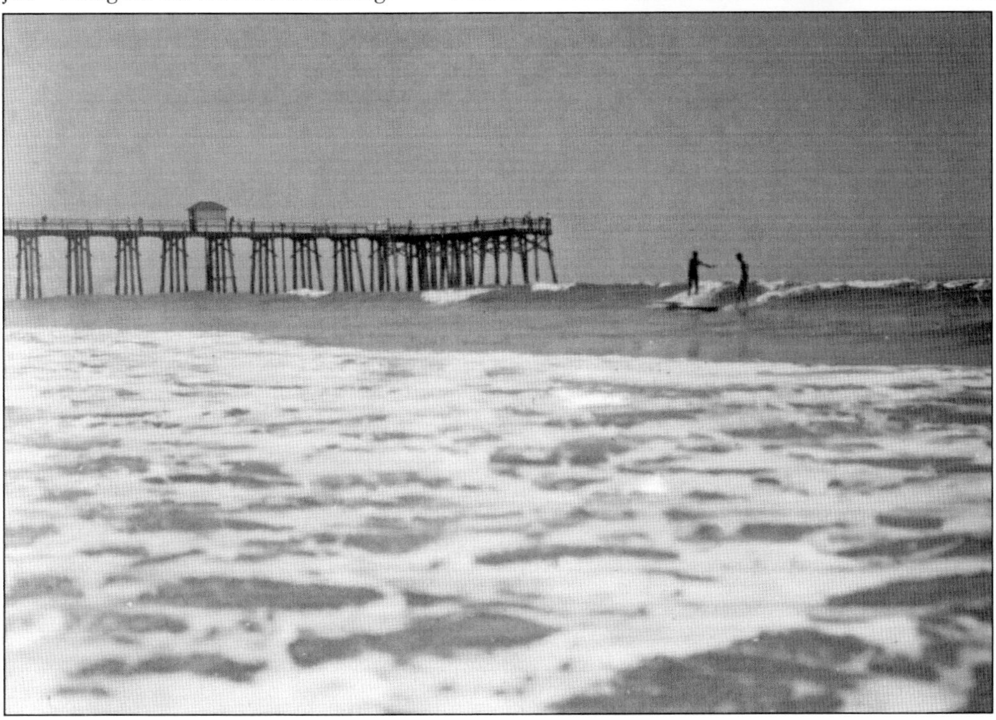

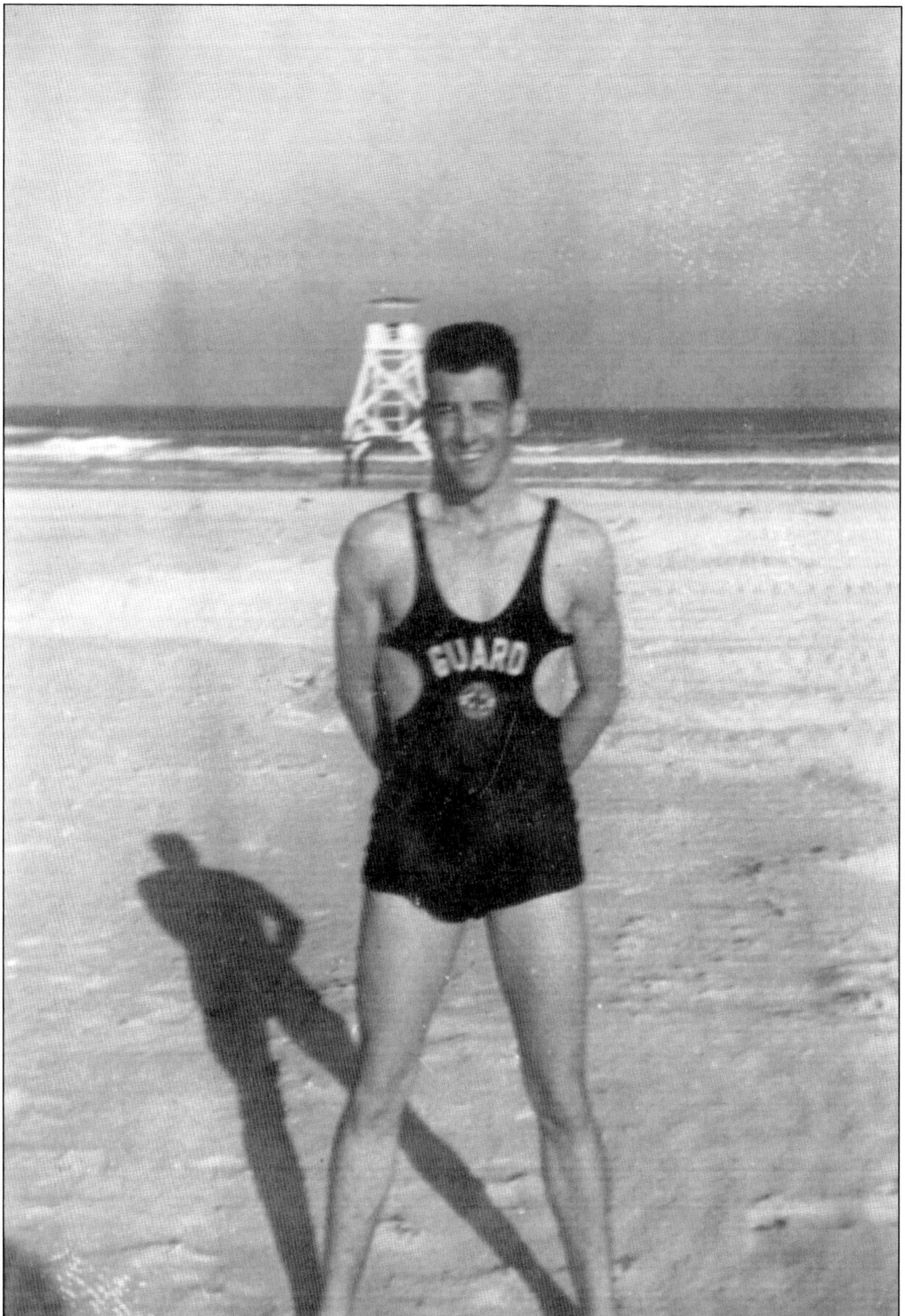

The uniforms of the day were one piece and made of 100 percent wool, and they were notorious for being itchy. That explains how William "Itchy" Purcell, pictured here in 1941, got his nickname.

After his career as a lifeguard, Ernie Johnson opened a fishing, tackle, and key shop on Main Street and later moved it to the corner of Ballough Road and Dunn Avenue.

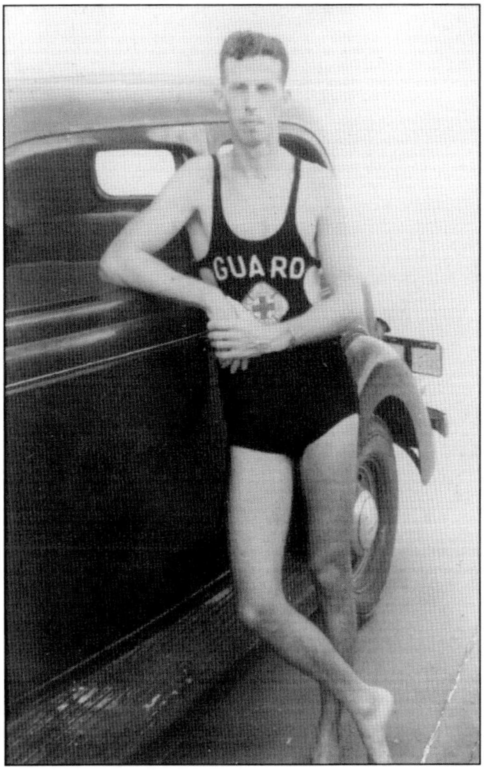

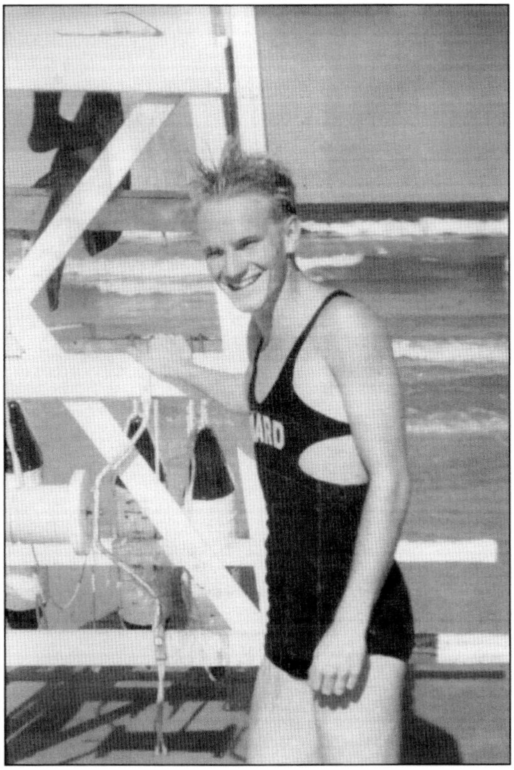

William "Billy" May, shown here in 1941, entered the military and by 1946 had become one of the Blue Angels.

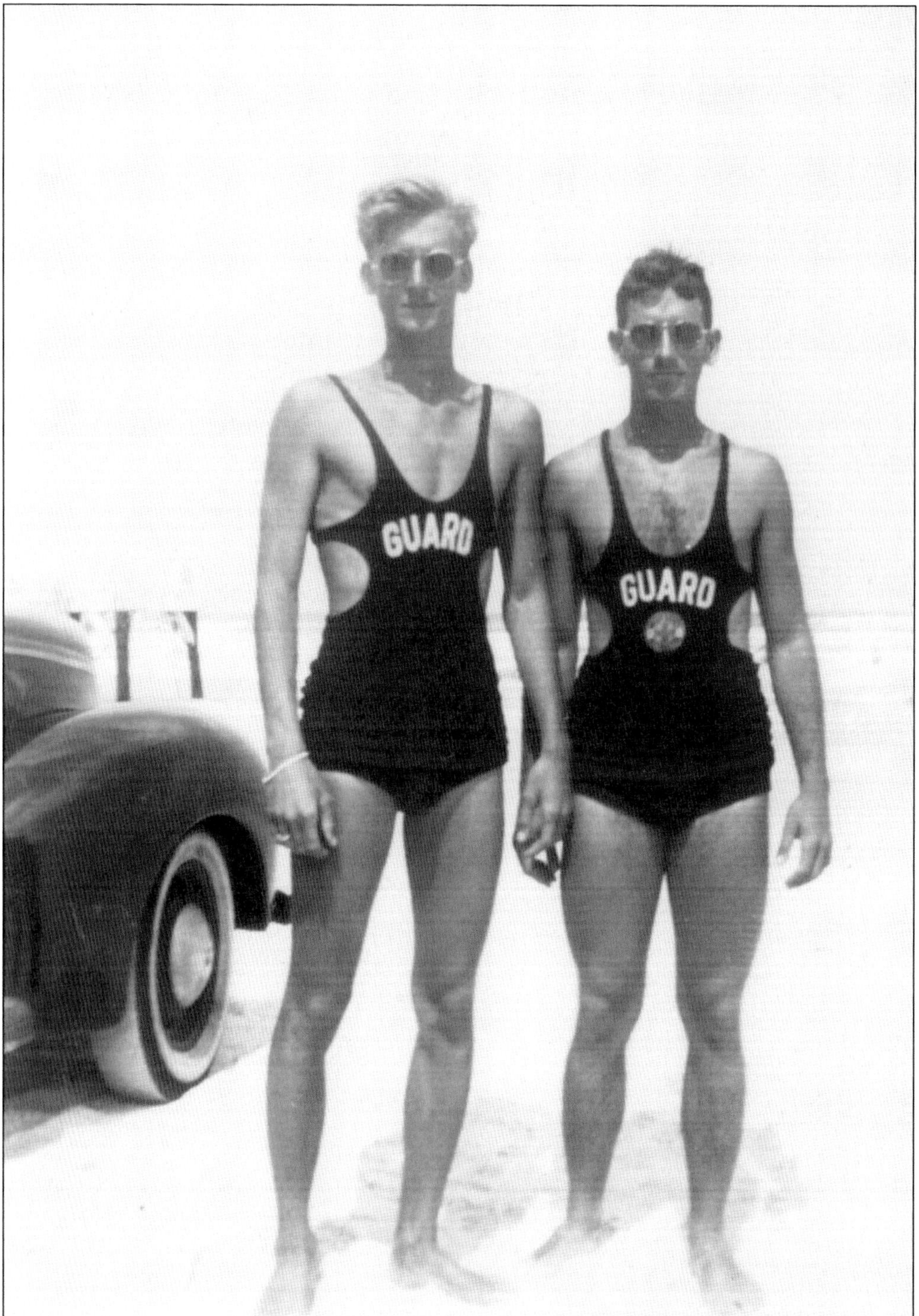

Bert Powell (left) and Bud Smith pose in front of the tower in the early 1940s. Powell not only trained the WAACs when they were stationed here, but he also wrote the first safety booklet on first aid and lifesaving for them.

Enjoying an unofficial boating excursion in January 1943 are, from left to right, (first row) Marvin Roth and Sonny Keating; (second row) Don Kirkwood, Toni Lynch, and Walter Lally.

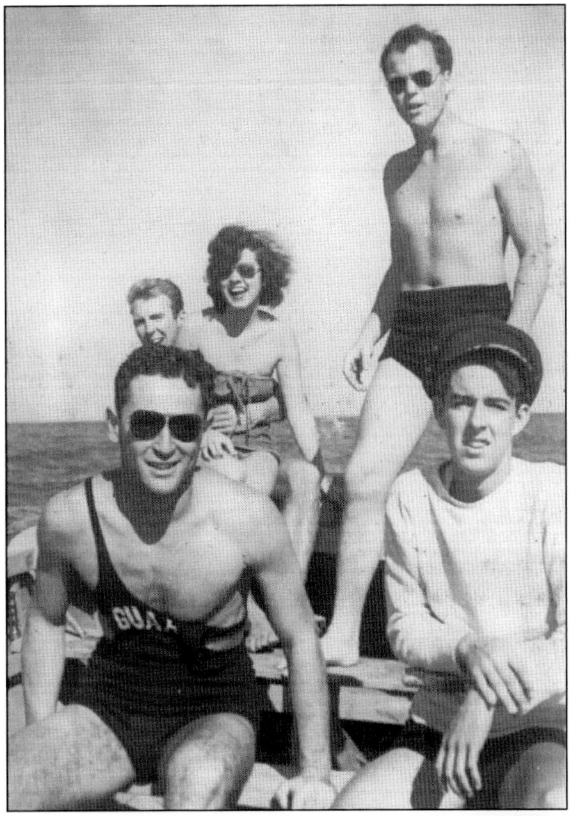

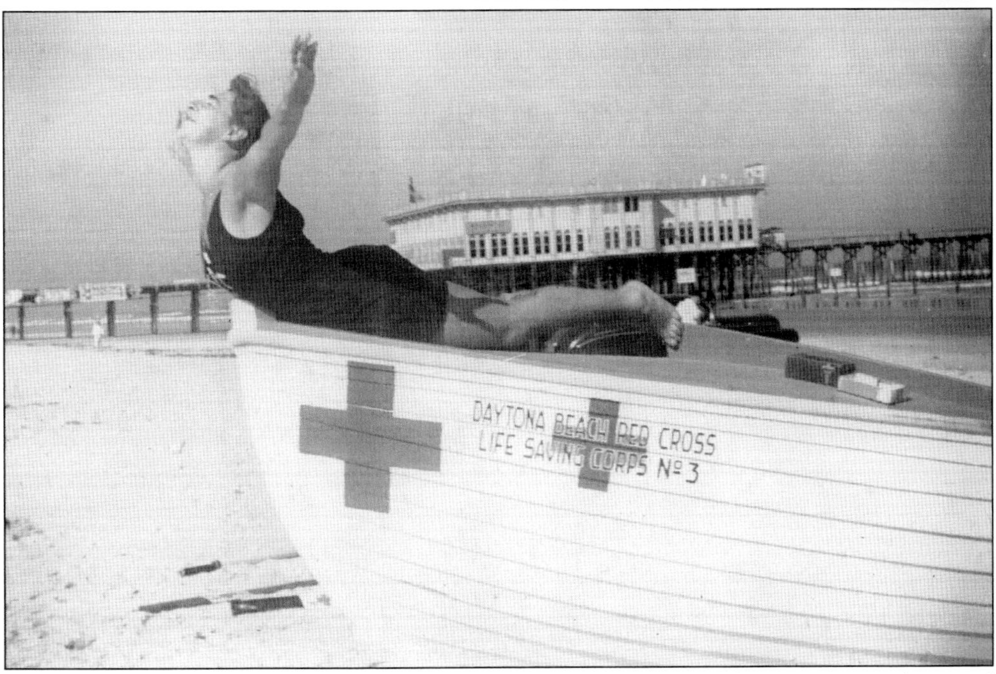

This early 1940s photograph shows the Daytona Beach Red Cross Life Saving Corps boat and the Main Street Pier. The caption simply reads, "Sternstein the Figurehead."

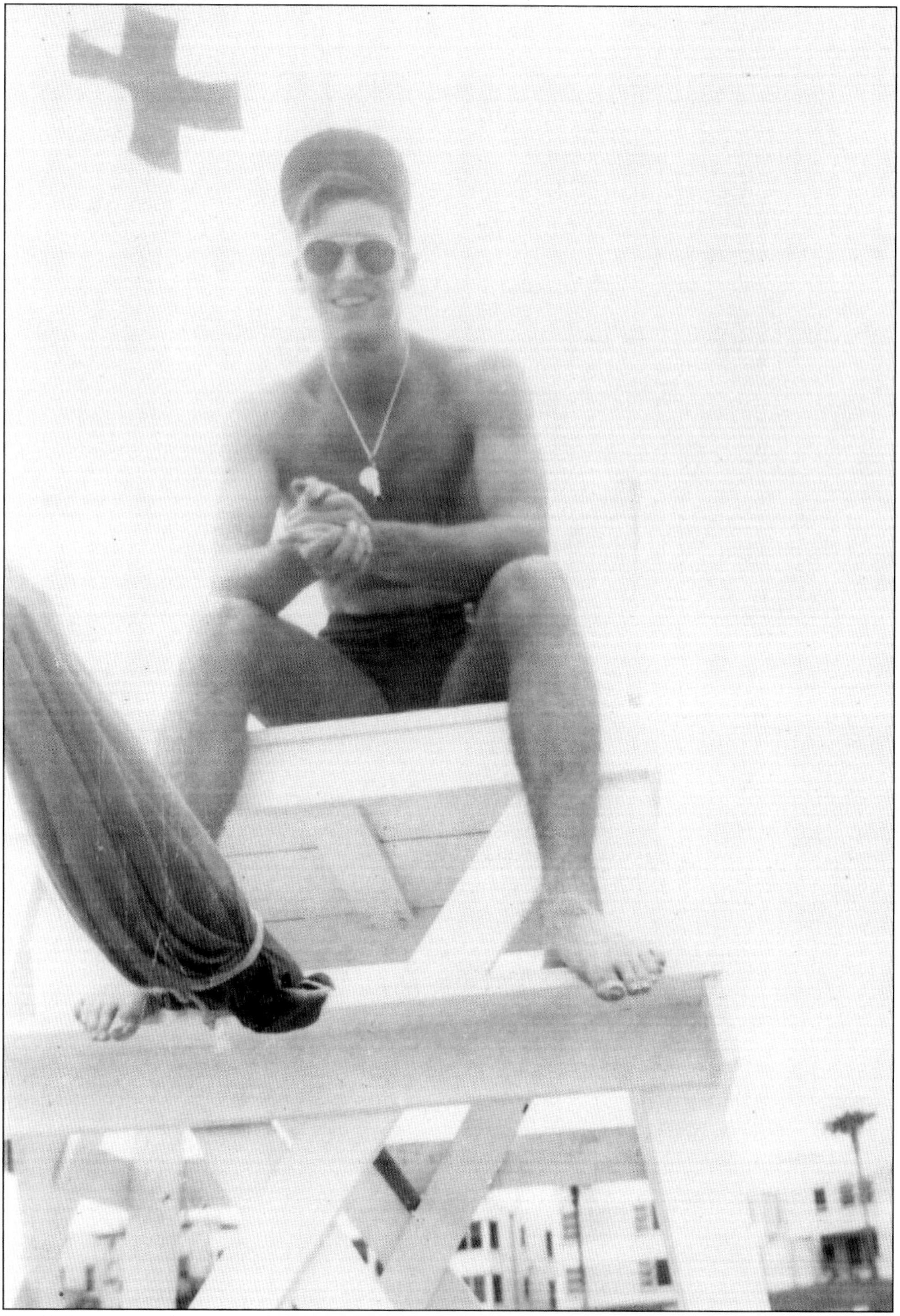

Fred Honour sits his tower at Main Street in 1947, when it was a privilege to be a lifeguard. Qualifications for the post included being a strong swimmer, having lived in Daytona Beach for at least a year, and being "of good character."

Sponsors for the 1945 lifeguard dance were Jeanne Trainor (left) and Ordy Taprell. Trainor was a graduate of Mainland High School in 1944, and Taprell was a junior at Seabreeze High School.

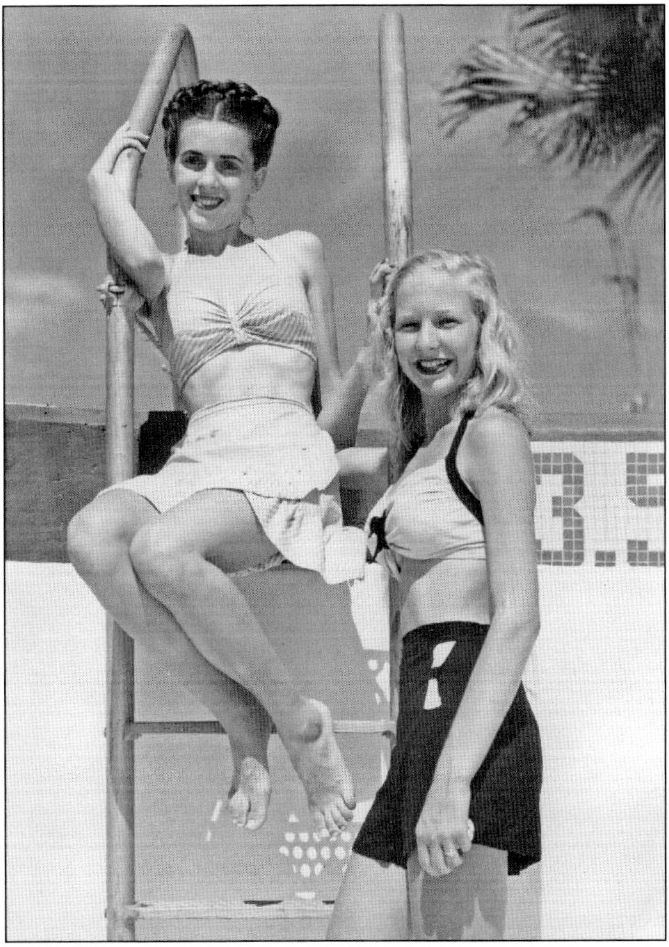

Anyone who had become a lifeguard was eligible to join the lifeguard social club and would remain a member in good standing as long as dues were kept current. Dances were held monthly, with a local girl named as sweetheart. An annual ball was held at the Pier Casino, a fund-raiser where the queen of the lifeguard corps would be announced. Attended by several hundred people, this was a major social event. The 13th ball cost 55¢ to attend.

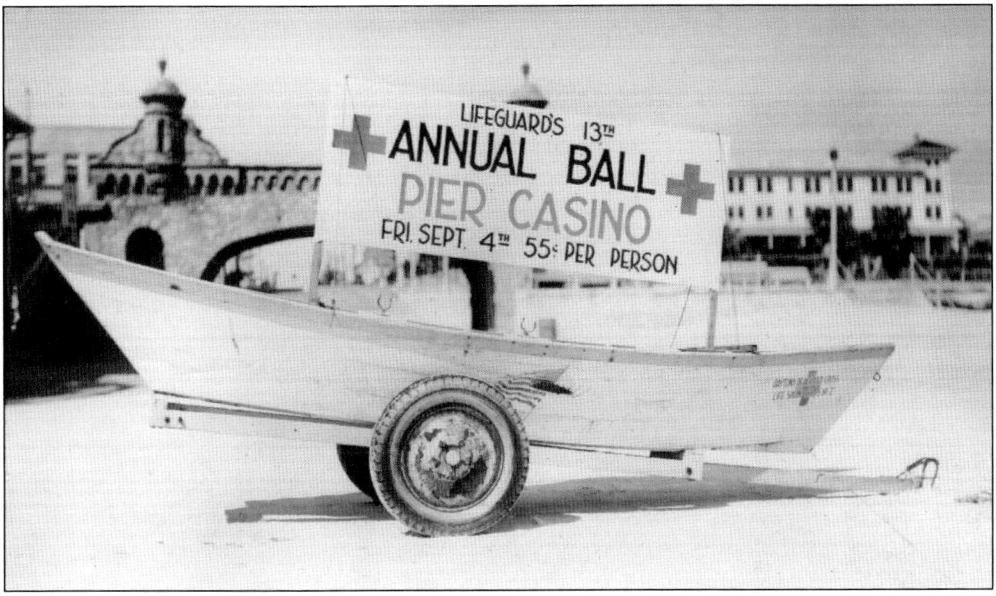

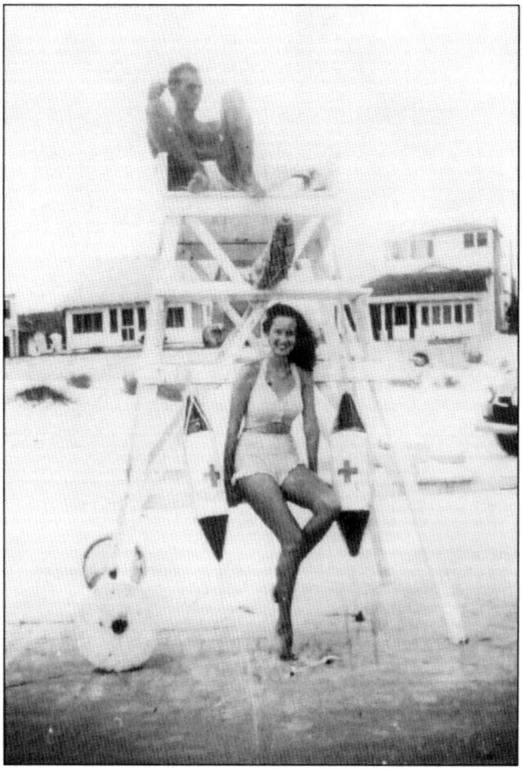

Ellen Cash, lifeguard sweetheart, poses before the tower while the lifeguard behind her keeps a watchful eye on the beach. (Courtesy of Joy McMahon.)

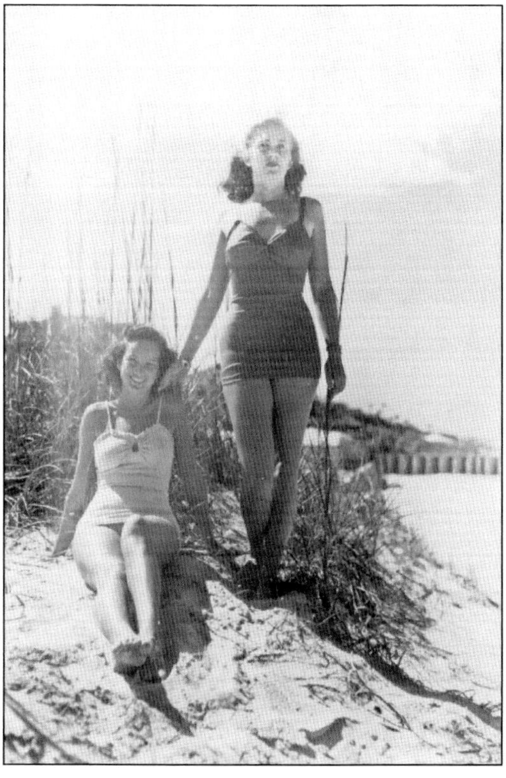

This 1946 photograph shows sweethearts Ellen (Cash) Toomer, left, and Jean (Lowe) Thomas. Jean Lowe was chosen queen of the lifeguards in 1943. Her father, L. E. Lowe, owned the Ormond garage where many young dreamers prepared their cars to race on "the World's Most Famous Beach." Lowe later married lifeguard Bill Thomas. (Courtesy of Joy McMahon.)

These unidentified guards were in a festive spirit, providing entertainment at one of the lifeguard balls.

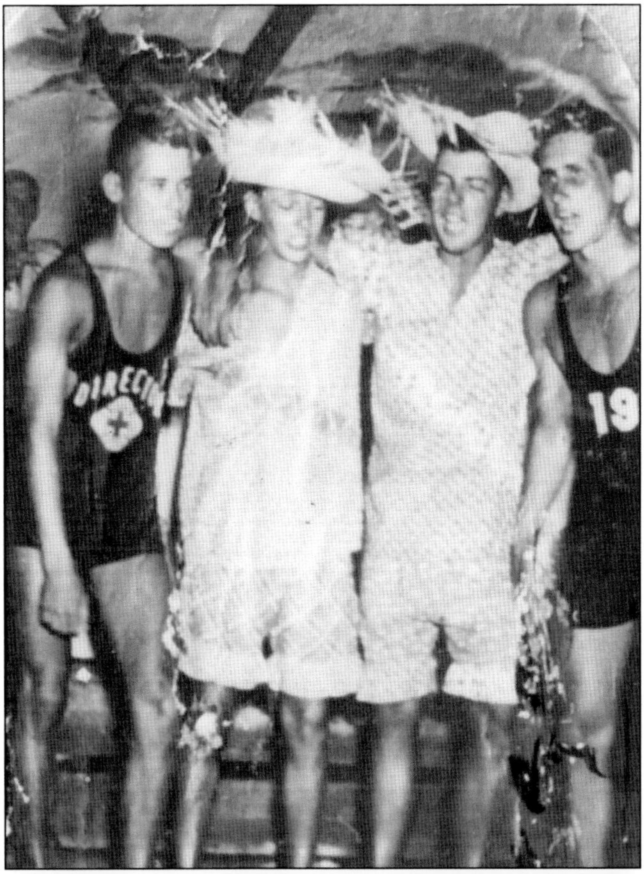

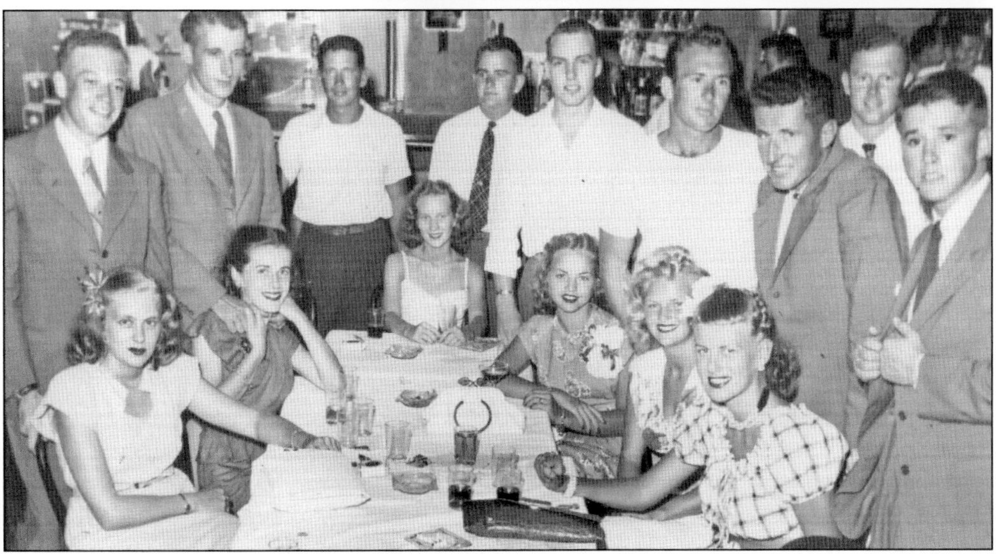

Attending the 1946 lifeguard dance were, from left to right, Bill Thomas, Jean Lowe, Bert Powell, Jeanne Trainor, Bud Smith, unidentified, Shirley Haigler, Barry Graves, Peggy Mordt, Don Kirkwood (captain), Betty Kirkwood, Richard "Dick" Stanier, Marge Stanier, Henry Duffett, and Bill Turnbull.

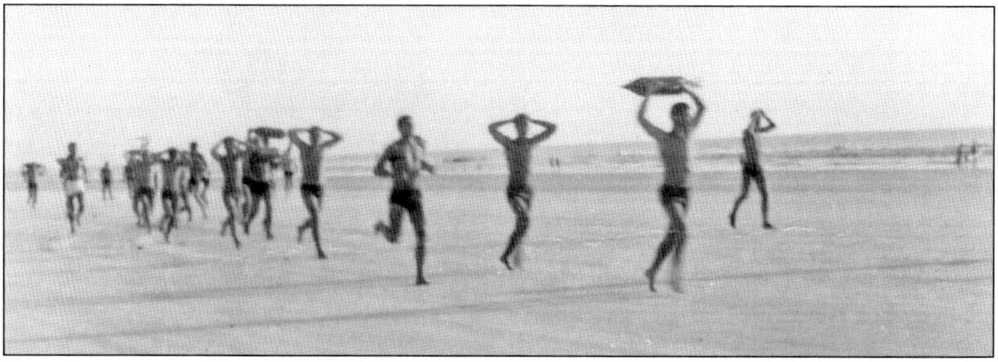

Part of becoming a Daytona Beach lifeguard was a training exercise known as the water cure. This involved maneuvers such as running 4 miles carrying a buoy overhead (above photograph) and other strenuous exercises designed to test the physical and mental limits of the recruits. As with any senior lifesaving course, it also included breaking holds and rescuing victims in a simulated drowning. The water cure, however, was at sea. All contenders for lifeguard positions were taken a mile offshore in a boat, then dropped in the water. Under the supervision of the president and captain, they were then grabbed by other lifeguards and would have to break the hold and "rescue" the lifeguard by taking him back to the boat, then return to their position in the water. This went on until all but the number of men required to fill the openings had been eliminated. There was a "pinch" code, which meant the trainee had had enough and was released. However, since that meant failure and loss of the job, most would nearly drown rather than pinch. The water cure was discontinued in 1964, when George Beers died during the exercise. Charges were brought but later dropped. The lifeguards who "took the water cure" are an elite group who, to this day, do not recognize anyone who did not undergo the procedure as a true lifeguard.

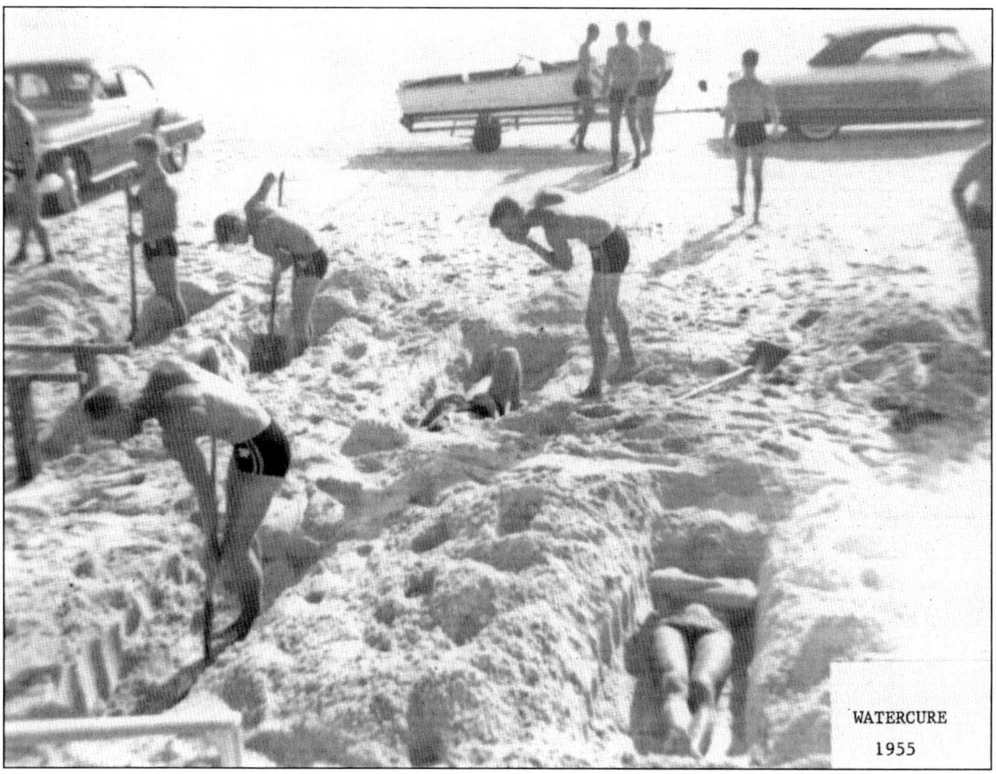

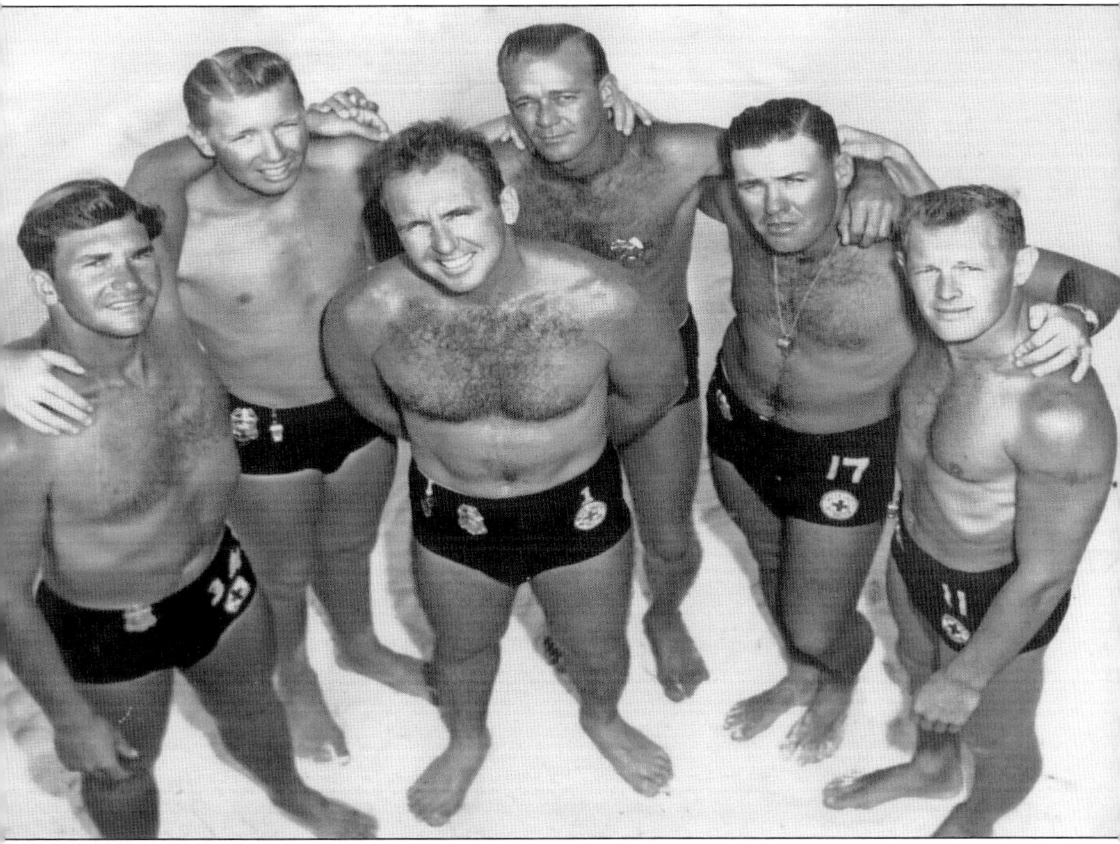

In 1953, the *Daytona Beach Morning Journal* reported that a total of 10,345,231 people had visited "the World's Most Famous Beach" the previous year. Eighteen Daytona Beach lifeguards manned six towers in the winter, but the corps had grown to more than 40 guards on the beach during the summer season. Making up the 1953 corps were, from left to right, Sam Crawford, Tom Dimmers, Don Kirkwood (captain), William Jebert, Guy Chase, and Charles "Billy" Willits. (Courtesy of Jim Willits.)

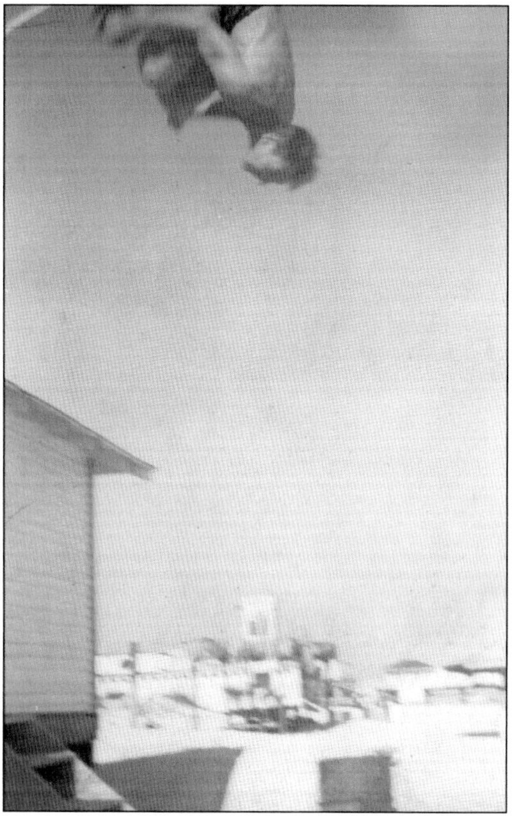

Don Kirkwood, one-time National Lifesaving Champion, is regarded as the greatest hero of the Daytona Beach Life Saving Corps. Stories of his physical feats are legion, including doing flips from the top of the lifeguard station (at left) and pressing 200 pounds (below). He was also known to set high standards for his guards, creating drills and exercises that separated the men from the boys.

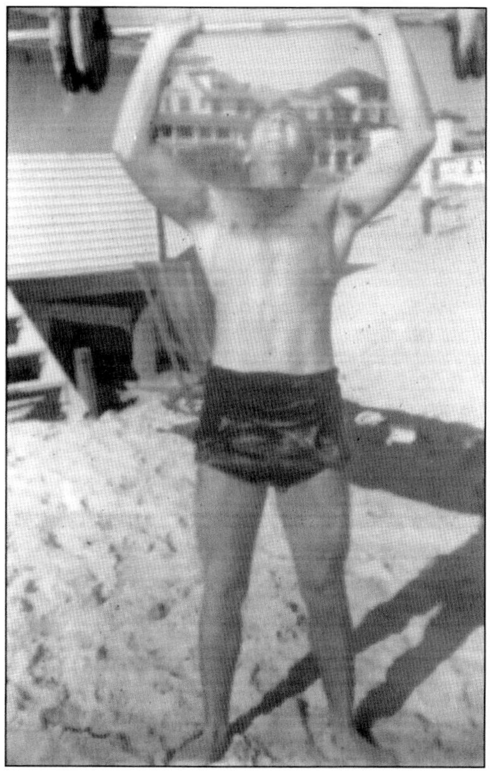

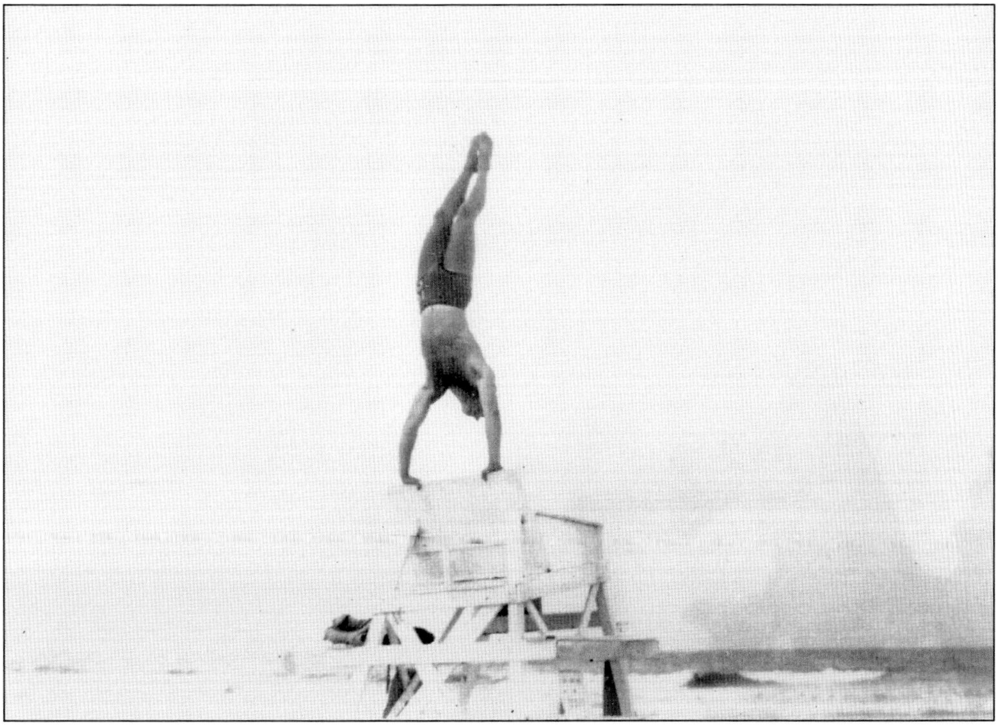

Along with his other acrobatics, Kirkwood would also regularly perform handstands on his lifeguard tower—and sometimes on the flagpole of the beach patrol station.

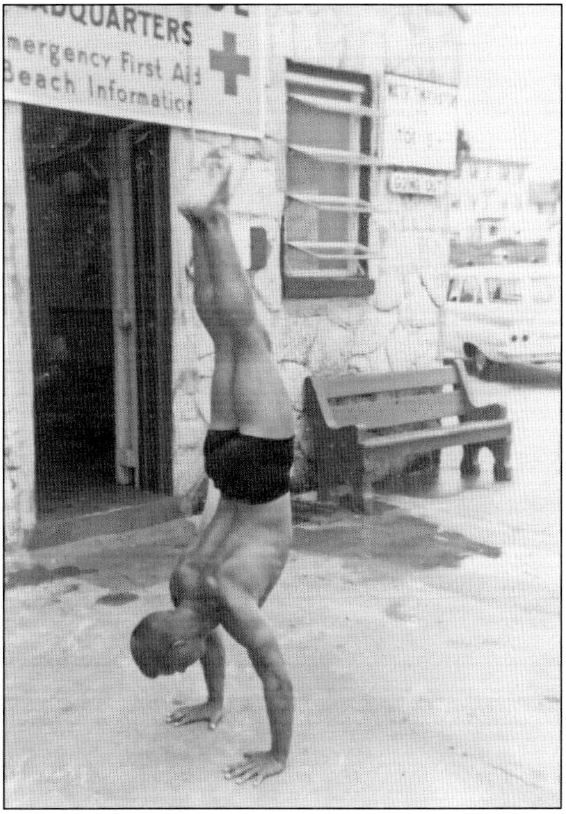

Not to be outdone, Jackie Asherle performs the handstand trick in front of the old band shell. Asherle later became chairman of the county council and Speaker of the Florida House of Representatives.

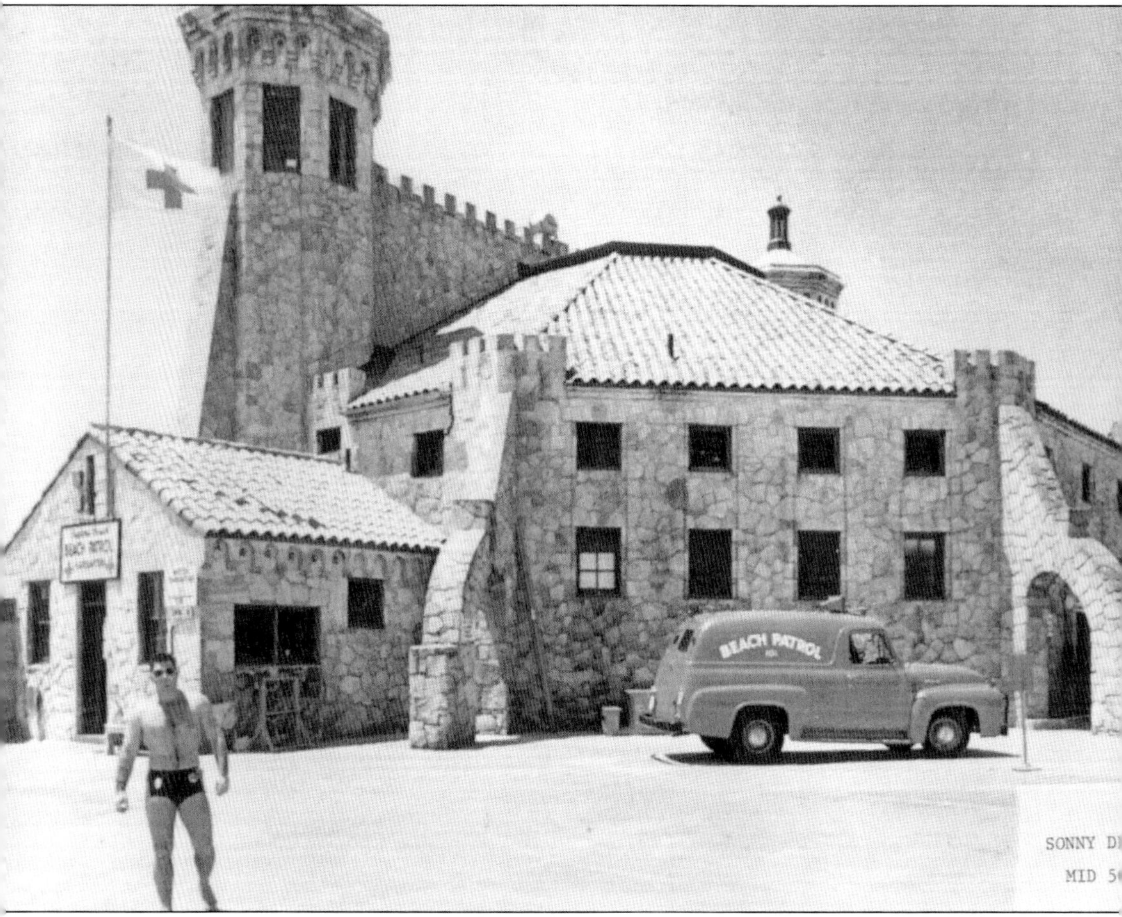

Sonny Dennis was captain of the Ormond Beach lifeguards when they joined to become part of the Volusia County Beach Patrol. Dennis remained with the corps. He is shown here in the mid-1950s in front of the Daytona Beach band shell.

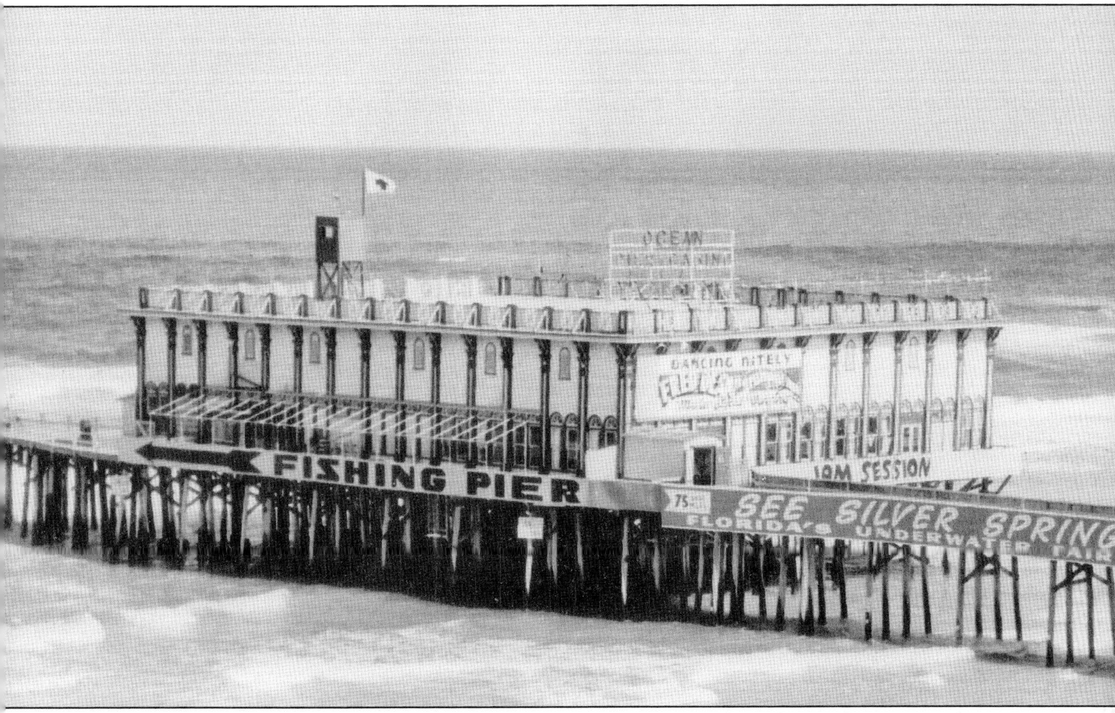

The central tower stood on the top of the Ocean Pier Casino, 80 feet above the sea. Eighteen towers, this control tower, the main station, and the beach patrol truck stayed in touch by public address, telephone, two-way radio, and light and flag signals. Whistles and body signals were used by guards on towers. In 1954, the *Orlando Sentinel* reported that 7,241,905 bathers had visited the 4.7 miles of protected swimming area in 1953, with the 61 members of the lifeguard force administering first aid to 7,395 people. There were 299 drowning rescues and 170 were assisted out of the surf with only one life lost in the 10 years previous.

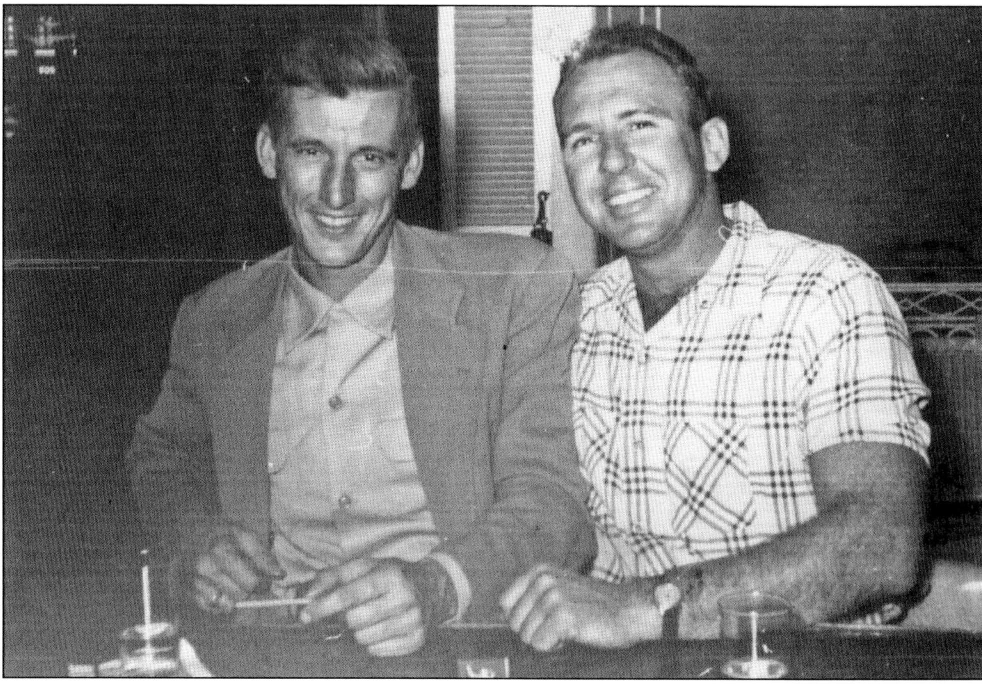

Two legends of lifeguarding, Bert Powell and Don Kirkwood, share a moment off duty in 1952.

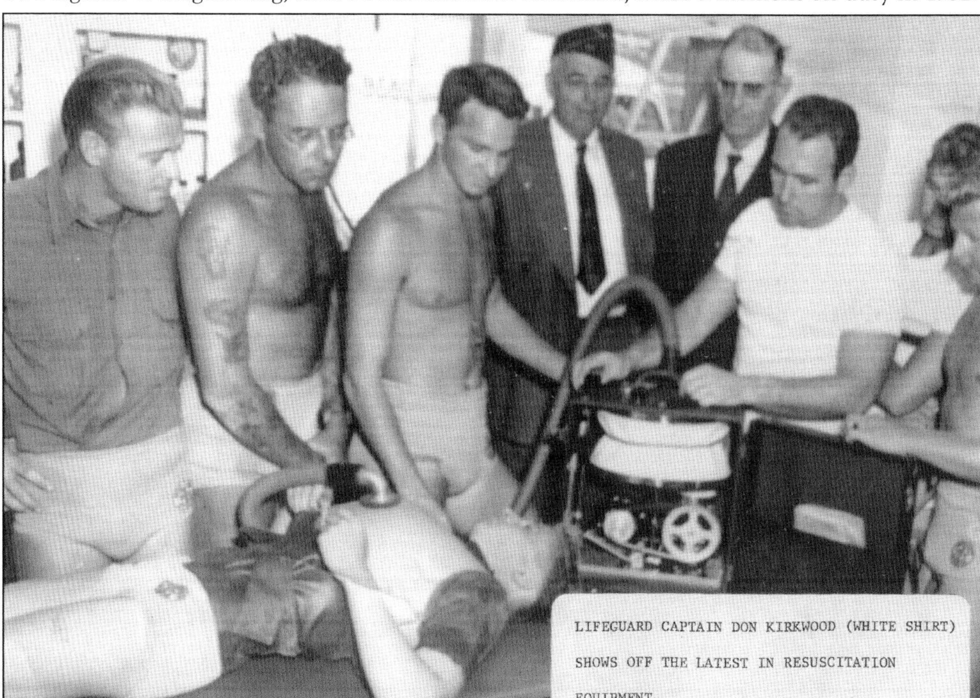

The caption on this early-1950s photograph reads, "Lifeguard captain Don Kirkwood (white shirt) shows off the latest in resuscitation equipment." Approximately $100,000 was spent annually on equipment and salaried civil service personnel to protect swimmers. Only one drowning occurred between 1944 and 1954.

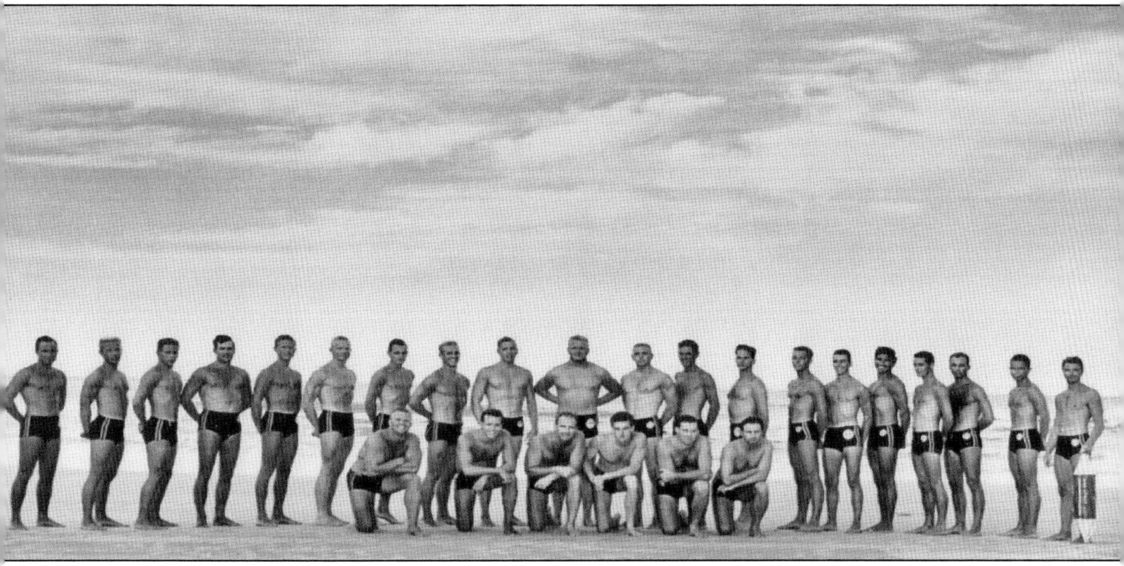

The 1955 Daytona Beach Life Saving Corps were, from left to right, as follows: (first row) Sam Haywood, Frank Warren, Don Kirkwood, Hubert Scott, Guy Chase, and Nick Triantefallu; (second row) Sonny Dennis, Lucian Rilay, Joe Morris, Bill Woods, Ernie Wiggins, Phil Back, Charlie Parrott, Rick Ames, Don Lewis, Bill Wenz, Dick Yelvington, Hank Wenz, Ronnie Hasselman, Sam Crawford, Harry Williams, Dick Stabell, Eugene "Chief" Lutke, Tubby Bradley, John Cherry, Gil Worth, and Les Croft. (Courtesy of Bob Wheeler.)

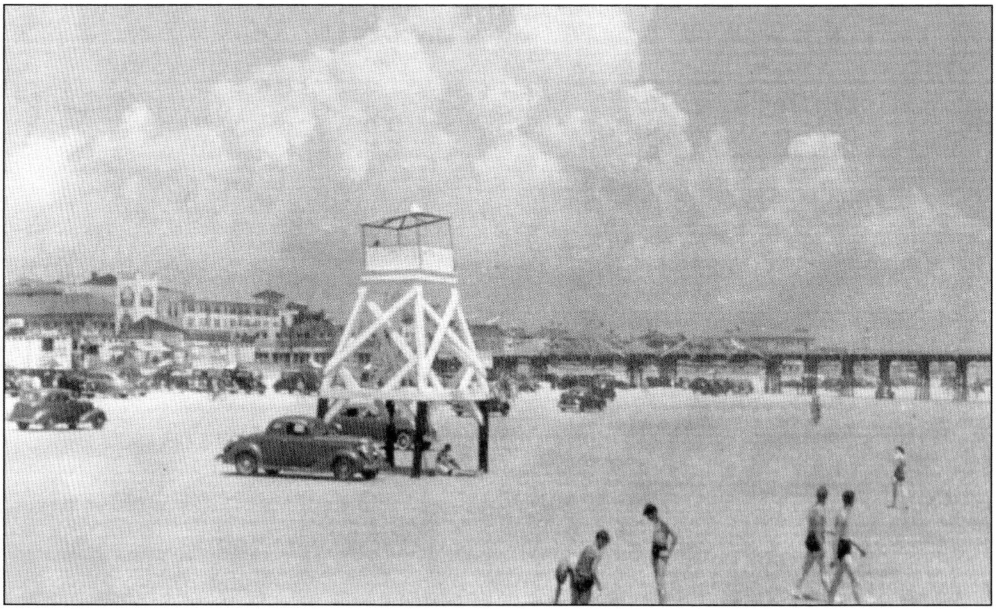

Just south of the Main Street Pier stands a Daytona Beach lifeguard tower at low tide, when the open sands can span 500 feet. Originally towers belonging to the city were painted white, while the county towers were red. After the Volusia County beaches unified, the towers were all painted red and white for visibility. The beaches here are welcoming year-round, with an average summer temperature of 81 degrees and a winter average of 61.5 degrees.

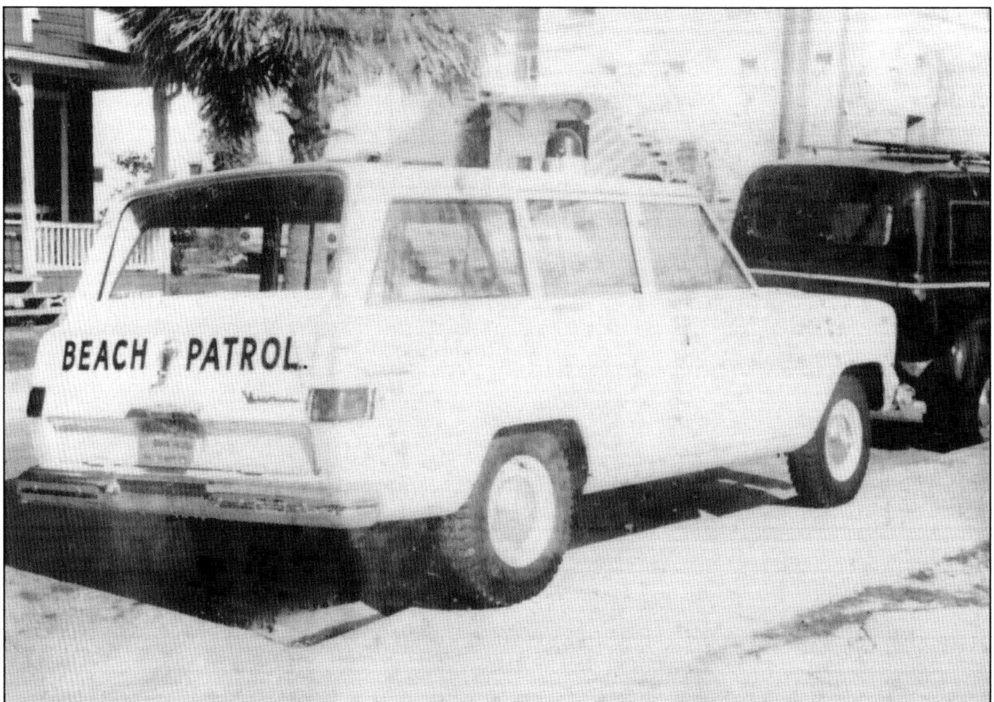

In the 1950s and 1960s, the beach patrol frequently bought used station wagons or Jeeps from the army surplus. Then the lifeguards would stencil or hand paint the emblems onto the sides.

Capt. Robert Lee "Bob" Wheeler operates the switchboard, which was located in the station at the band shell. The switchboard was connected to phone boxes at the lifeguard towers and at the boardwalk. Wheeler took over as captain in 1958. He was 23 years old, and he had 30 lifeguards working under him.

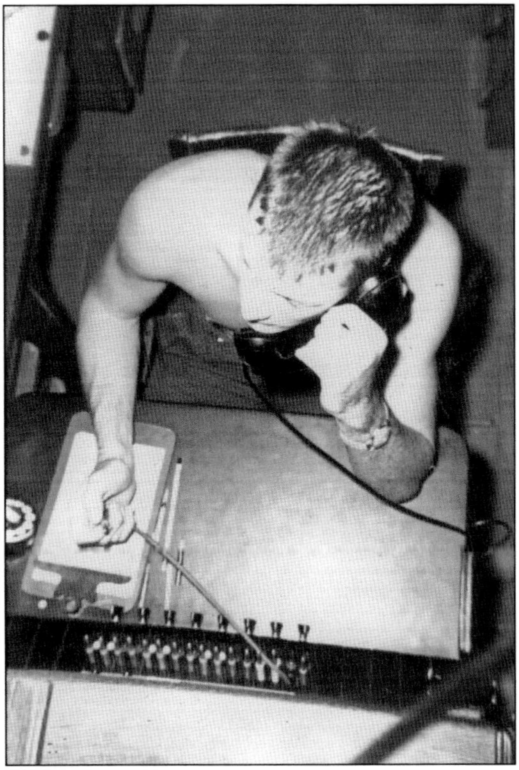

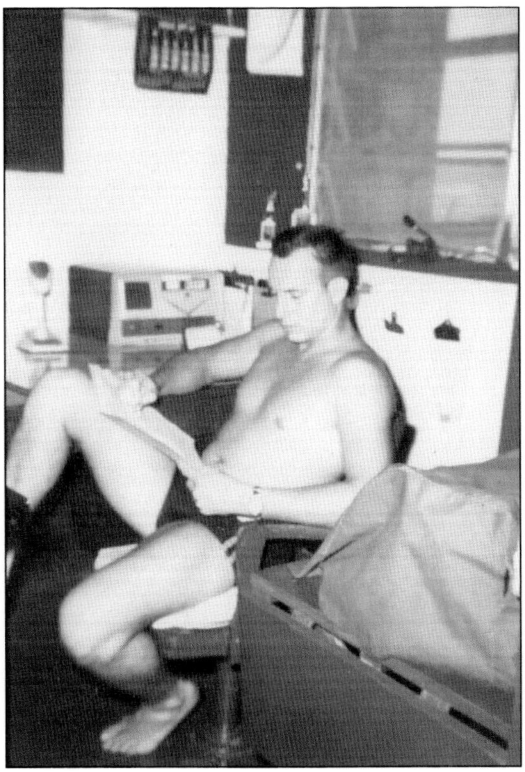

The radio and telephone operators' contribution to the rescue process was vital. In many cases, this was the link that made the difference between life and death. Operators would coordinate the rescue, alerting all necessary personnel and calling additional medical and police backup. This July 1960 photograph shows Fred Osterman catching up on reports while monitoring the switchboard.

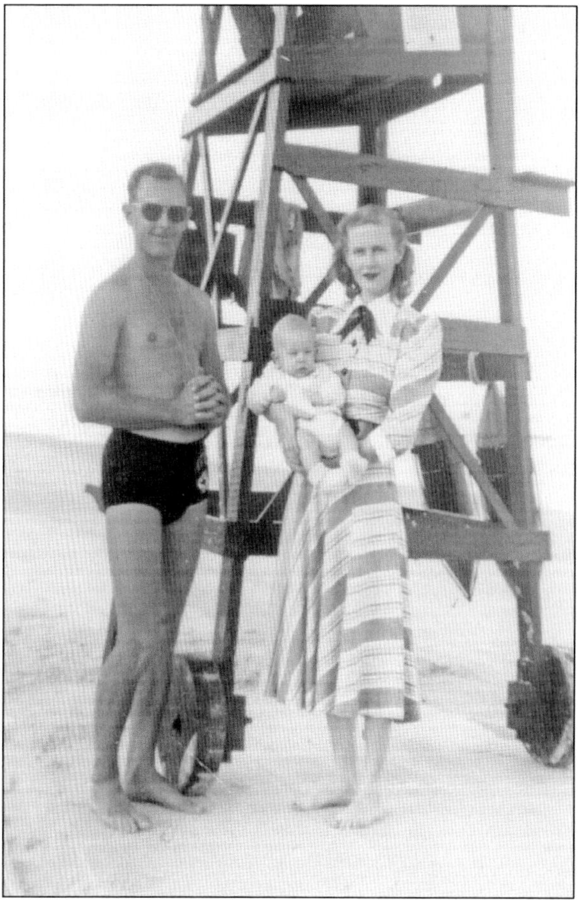

Charles "Billy" Willits and family stand in front of his tower. Willits became a lifeguard in 1945. In 1948, he left to join the navy, where he taught lifesaving and swimming at the Oakland, California, naval base. He returned to the corps in 1952, leaving in 1953 to become a Daytona Beach police officer. Over the next 35 years, he worked his way through the ranks, becoming chief of police in 1978. His affiliation with lifesaving and the American Red Cross remained dear to his heart, and he continued serving as a board member and a blood donor until his death in 2002. In this 1953 photograph, Peggy Willits holds their son Jim, who became a Daytona Beach lifeguard in the 1960s. (Courtesy of Jim Willits.)

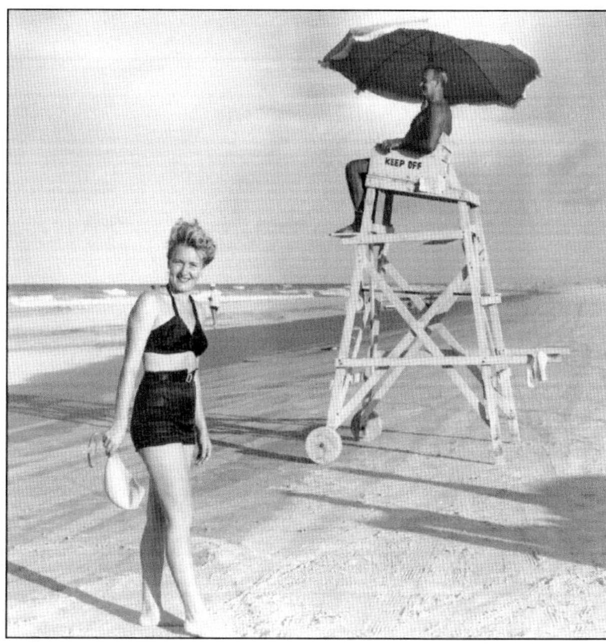

Although Mike Hensler's father was never an official lifeguard, he did volunteer and often sat in the tower in front of his business, the Surf Cottages at 2001 South Atlantic Avenue. In this photograph, taken in the late 1940s, his wife looks on as he "guards" the beach. Large hotels had yet to infiltrate the area, and rental cottages were prevalent. By 1967, Hensler was manning his own tower, and he remains a career guard as of this writing. His numerous contributions to the force include the invention of Beachwheels, wheelchairs designed for travel in sand. Available free of charge, they ensure beach access to persons with disabilities.

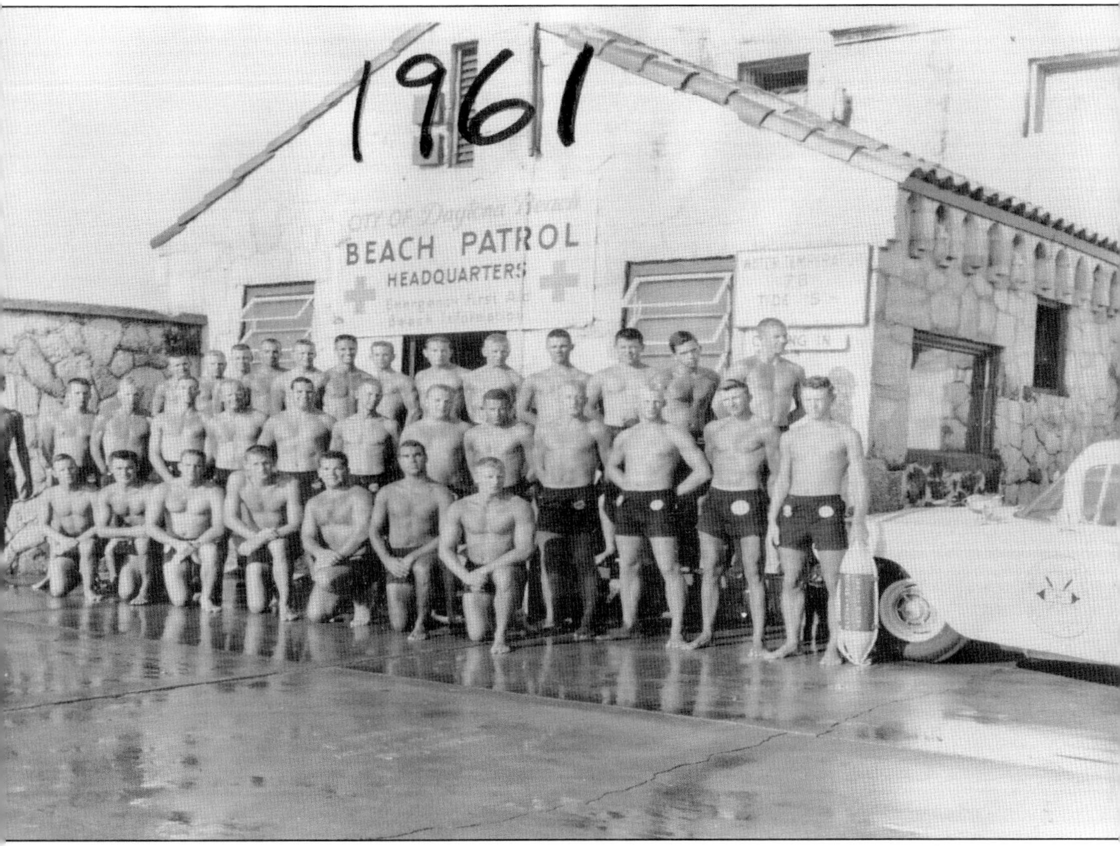

In 1962, the Daytona Beach Red Cross Life Saving Corps merged with the county to become Volusia County Beach Patrol. This 1961 group shot, taken in front of the beach patrol headquarters, may be the last photograph taken of the Daytona Beach corps before the merger. Guards that year were, from left to right, (first row) John Dauphinne, James Montgomery, Fred Osterman, Bob Wheeler (captain), Irvin Inney, Howard Roey, and George Meyer; (second row) Jon Greaves, William Hixon, Joe Gallagher, William Perry, Phillip Walser, Bob Veach, Mick Dugger, Paul Jacobs, Robert Sherrell, John Ashcraft, Robert Pressor, Jerome Serwas, and Floyd Graham; (third row) David Hofmeister, Ross Bailey, John Barnett, Dannel Green, Joe White, Sidney Smith, James Nelson, Wayne Frutchey, James Wirgman, James Hart, Robert Hillman, Joseph Dobbs, and Ray Wright. (Courtesy of Bob Wheeler.)

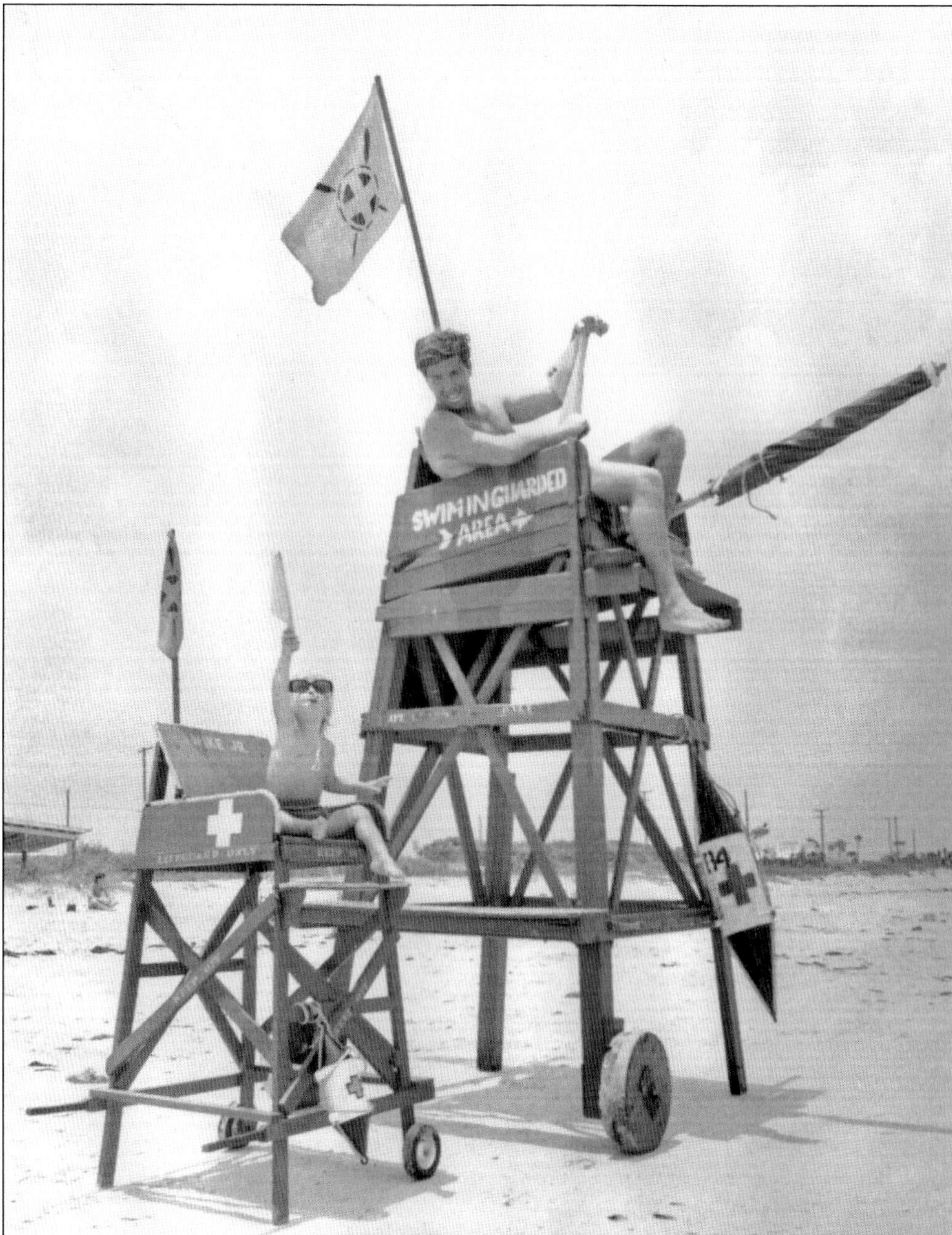

Little boys want to do what their dads do—so Mike Hensler, now a deputy chief with VCBP, built a scaled-down tower so his son could lifeguard with him. This publicity photograph was taken in 1969 at the North County station. (Courtesy of Mike Hensler.)

Three

World War II and WAACs

Daytona Beach became a training site for the Women's Army Auxiliary Corps (WAACs) during World War II, largely through the efforts of Mary McLeod Bethune, who lobbied Pres. Franklin Roosevelt in an effort to boost the city's economy. Here the recruits gained skills needed to "assist their male counterparts and make a major contribution to the World War II effort." The first WAACs arrived in October 1942, initially residing in "Tent City," a cluster of army canvas tents along the east bank of the Intracoastal Waterway. They were soon moved into beachside motels, including the Clarendon (now the Plaza Resort and Spa at 600 North Atlantic Avenue), the Princess Issena Hotel on Seabreeze Boulevard (where the Disneys stayed while scouting potential sites for Disneyland and which burned in the early 1980s before becoming the current site of Wachovia Bank), and the Streamline Hotel, which still stands at 140 South Atlantic Avenue. Eventually the military leased and built additional housing for the recruits, 20,000 of whom received training here. The presence of the base provided much-needed revenue for the city, generating a reported $5 million monthly. But in early 1944, the training center was closed when the organization, now fully part of the army and redesignated as the Women's Army Corps (WAC), moved to a larger facility at Fort Oglethorpe, Georgia.

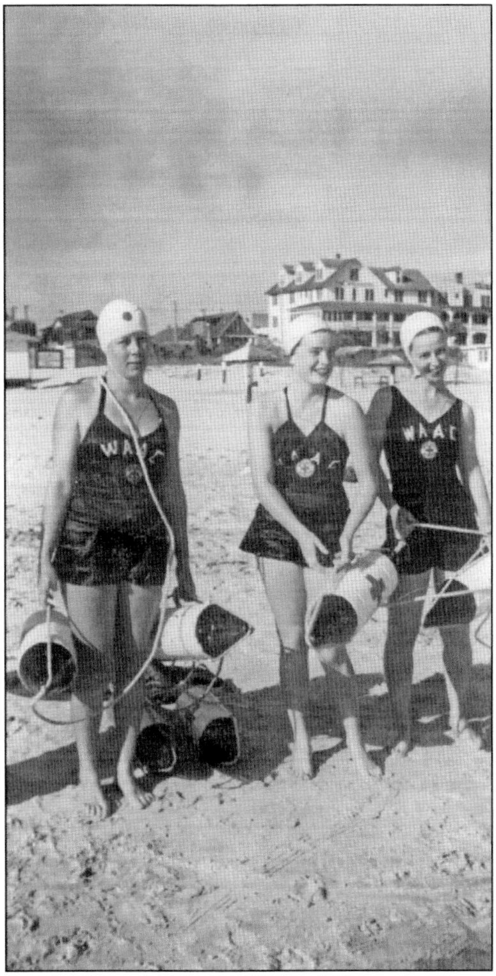

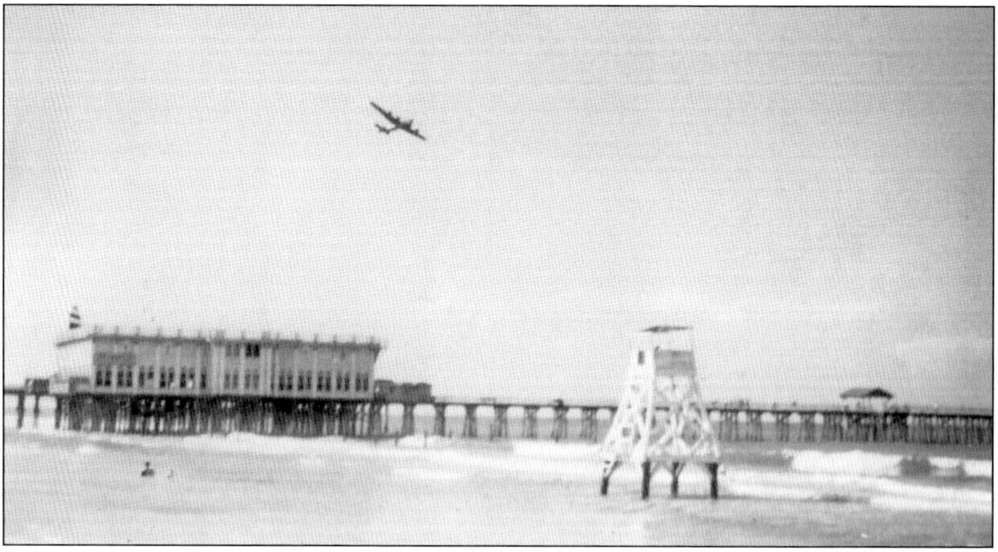

With its flat terrain and year-round flying weather, Florida proved the ideal location for military training of pilots. Consequently, in 1942, Florida produced more pilots than any other state, many in Volusia County. These 1940s photographs show military aircraft over the beach. Above, a B-24 flies over the Main Street Pier. Below, bathers watch as a B-26 flies along the Daytona Beach coastline.

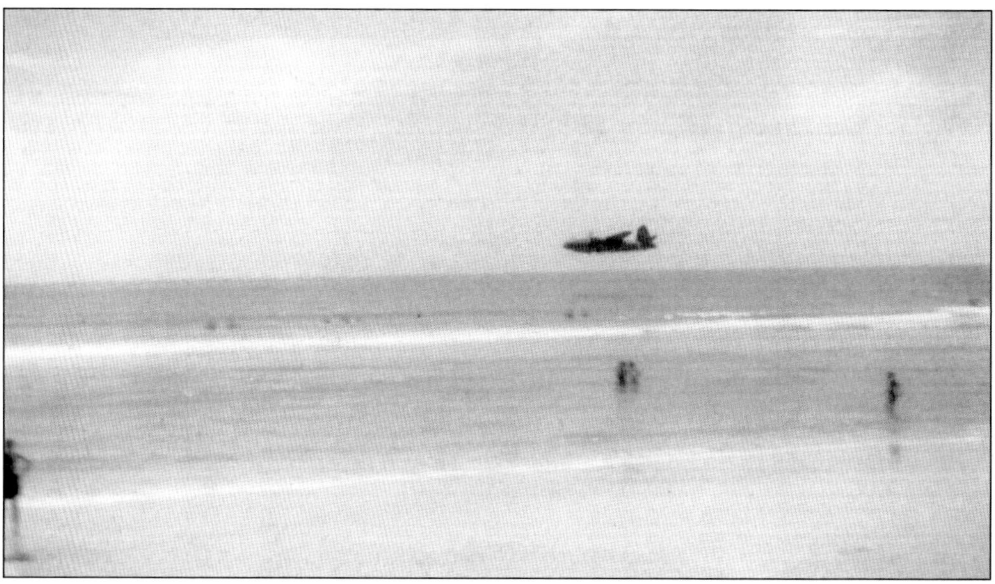

Many Daytona Beach lifeguards died in World War II, including Robert Moore, pictured here. Among the others who died in battle were Francis X. Deeley, Martin Roth, Robert Mannix, Thomas Willis, Thomas Henley, and Vernon Casto. In an area of the city near Clyde Morris Boulevard, the streets bear the names of young men who gave their lives serving their country, and Moore Street is one of them.

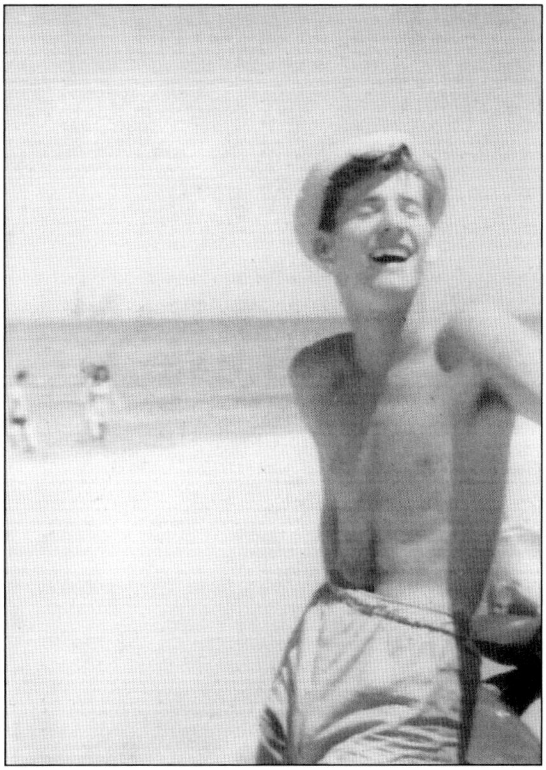

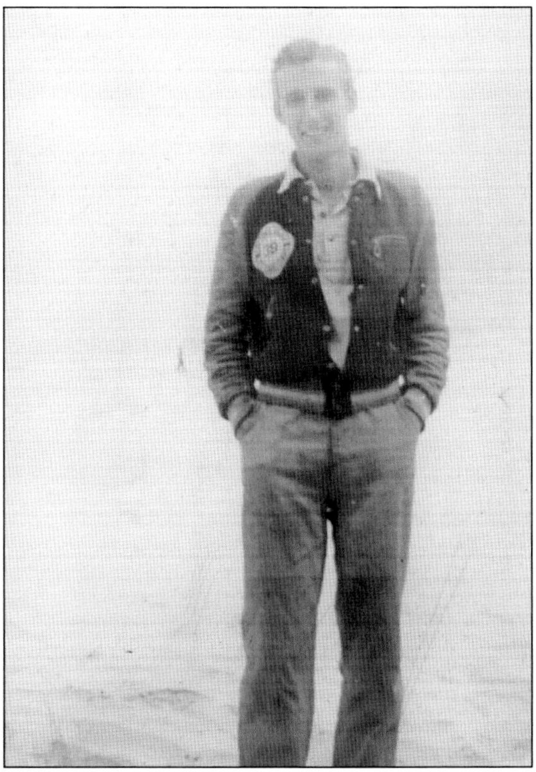

Bert Powell, lifeguard captain, remained on the force and trained the WAACs until he went into the military himself. He was shot down over Germany in 1941 and taken prisoner, spending over two years as a POW. After returning to Daytona Beach, he resumed his career as a guard.

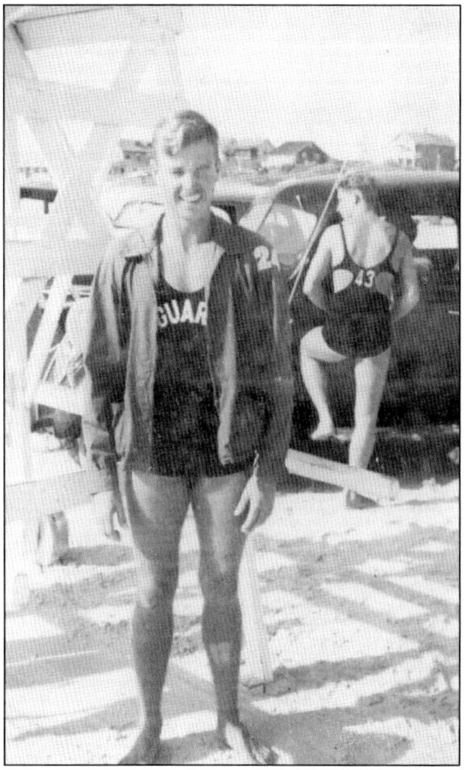

This 1930s photograph shows Bud Smith in his lifeguard uniform. The caption reads, "Just a J.O."

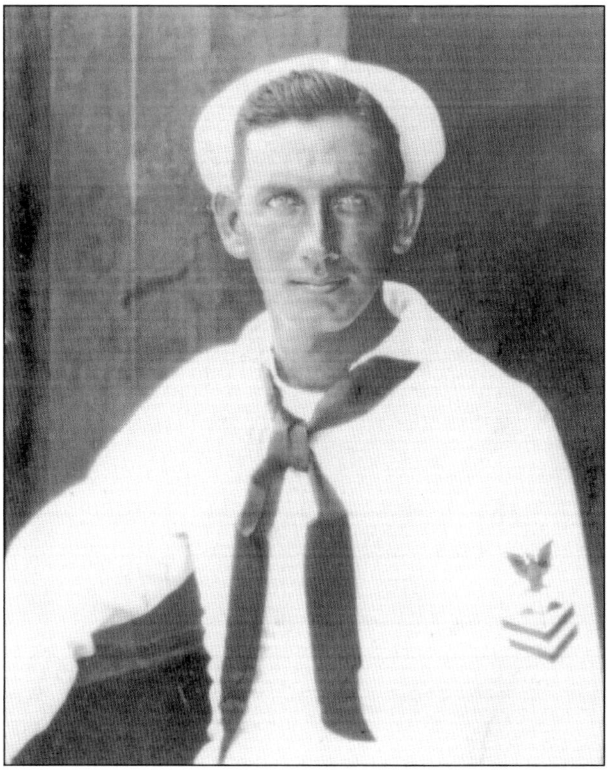

In July 1945, local newspapers reported that 90 members of the Daytona Beach Red Cross Life Saving Corps were serving in the armed forces: 47 in the U.S. Army, 37 in the U.S. Navy, 2 in the Royal Canadian Air Force, 2 in the U.S. Marine Corps, and 2 in the U.S. Merchant Marines. These included Bud Smith, pictured here in his military uniform. Smith later returned and married Phyllis Keating, whose brother was also a lifeguard and whose family built the Main Street Pier.

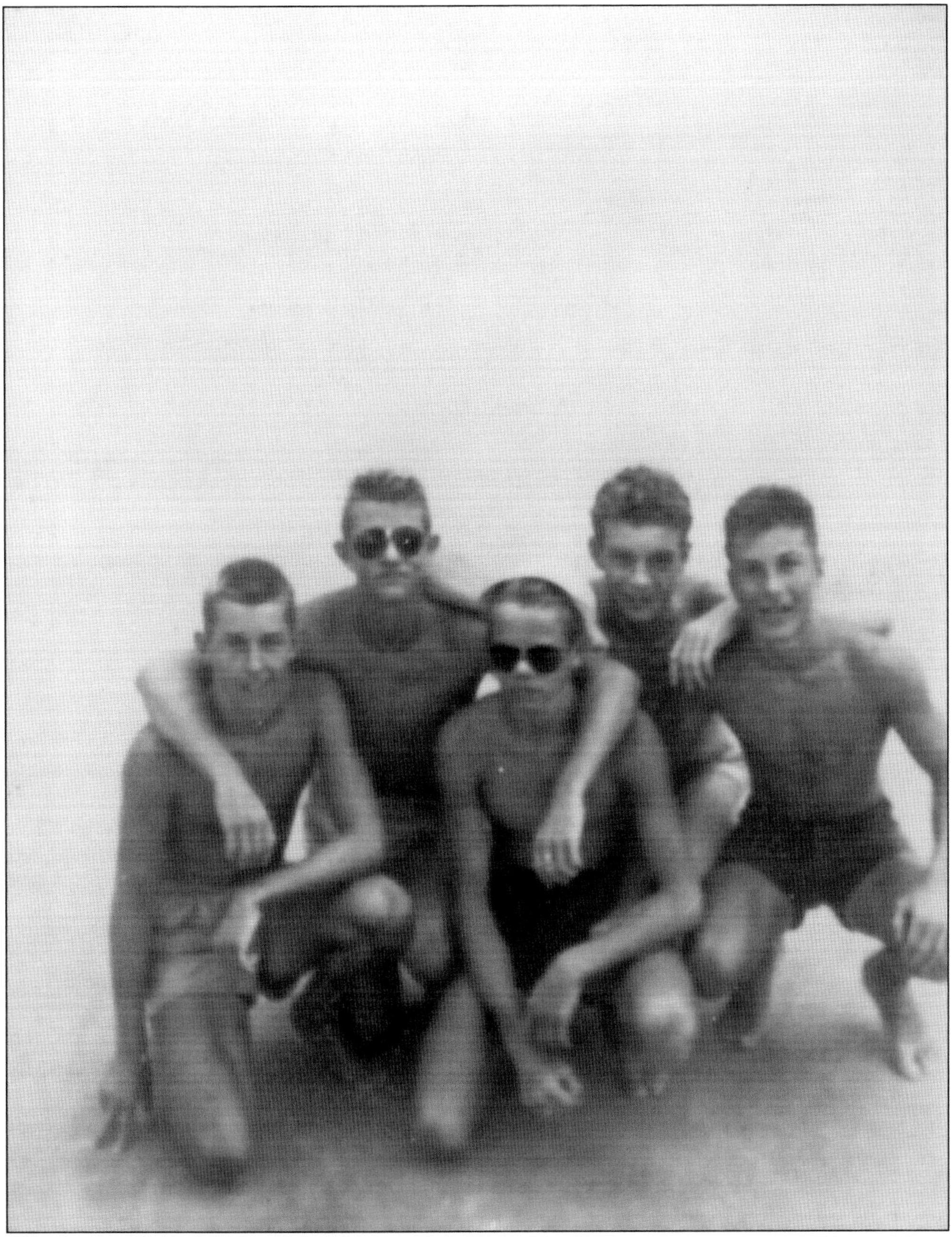

Lifeguard recruits filled in while so many of the regular force were away at war. Pictured here are, from left to right, George "Poodie" Linton, Harrison "Brutie" Thompson, Ralson Wells, Bill Thomas, and Sam Savas.

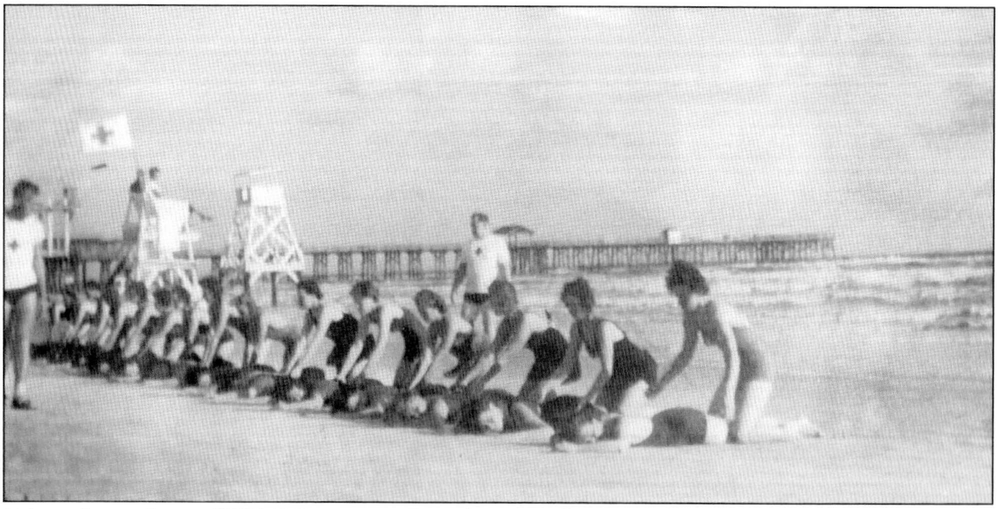

Selected members of WAAC personnel at the second training center in Daytona Beach were appointed to take over lifeguard duties on beach areas allotted for use by the recruits during off-duty hours. Here they practice artificial respiration during a Red Cross lifesaving course directed by Ben C. Stanton and his assistant, Harry Kenning.

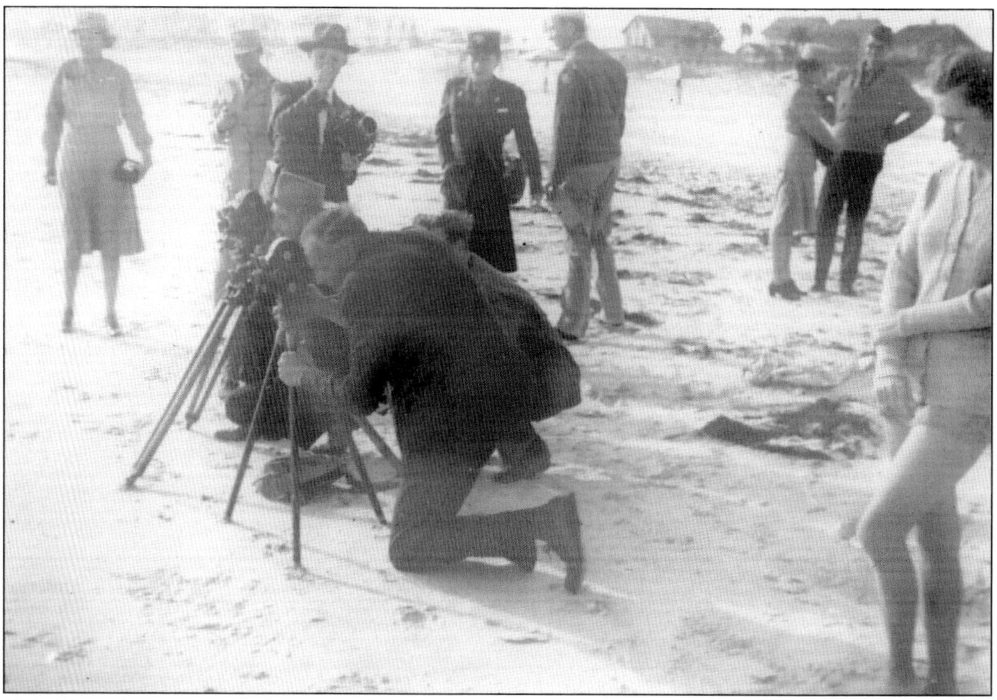

WAACs in Daytona Beach attracted the attention of civilians and servicemen in the town as well as on a national level. Here Paramount, Fox Movietone, and MGM news cameramen photograph the recruits while training. Often people gathered as they paraded down the boardwalk, and others would stop on the beach to watch them perform their drills and lifesaving exercises.

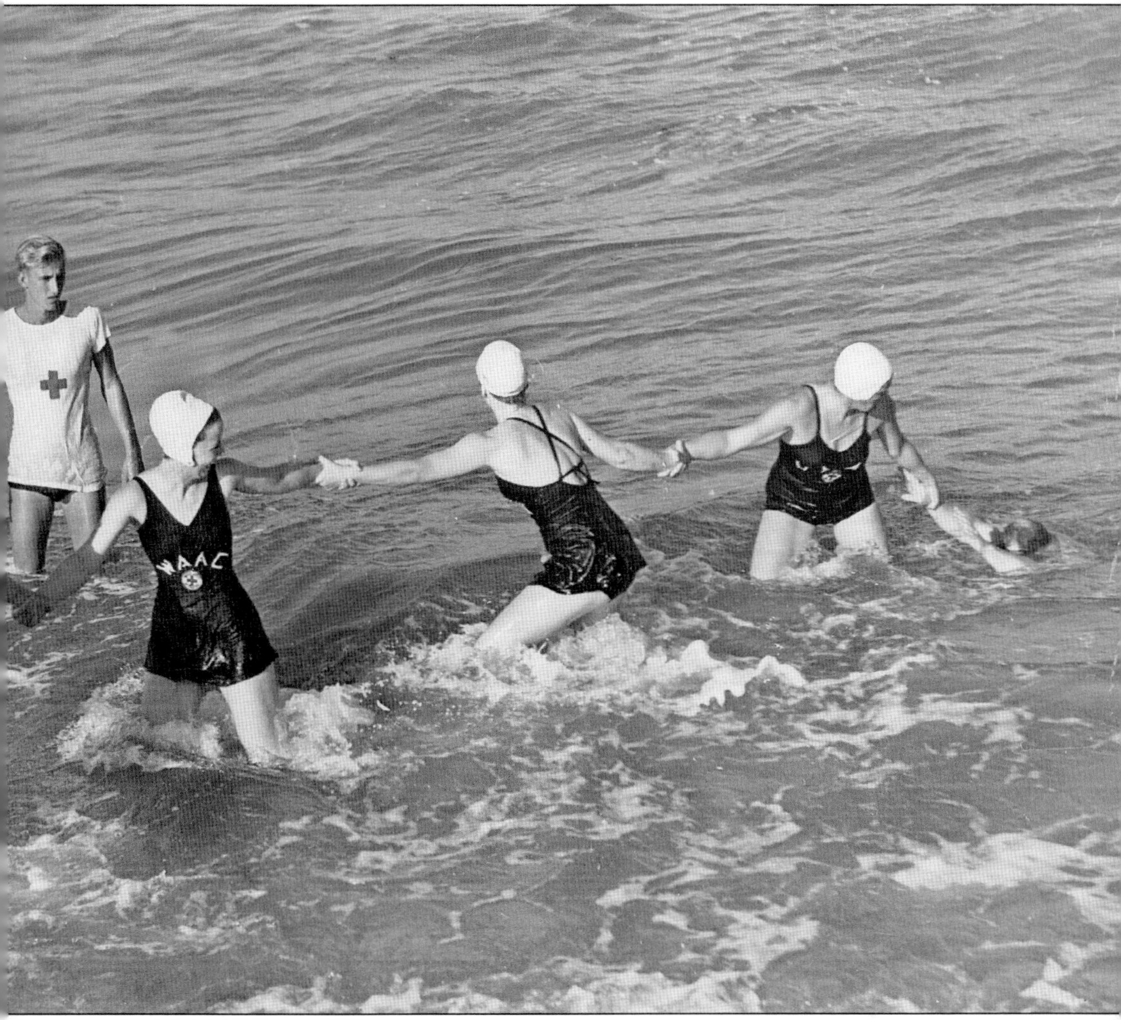

Although all the corps members were expert swimmers and Red Cross lifeguards, they were given refresher courses with special emphasis on surf and lifeboat work, as many had never worked in surf lifesaving. Here Bert Powell, captain of the Daytona Beach Red Cross Life Saving Corps, oversees training as Ben C. Stanton, Red Cross field representative, is rescued from the surf using the human-chain technique.

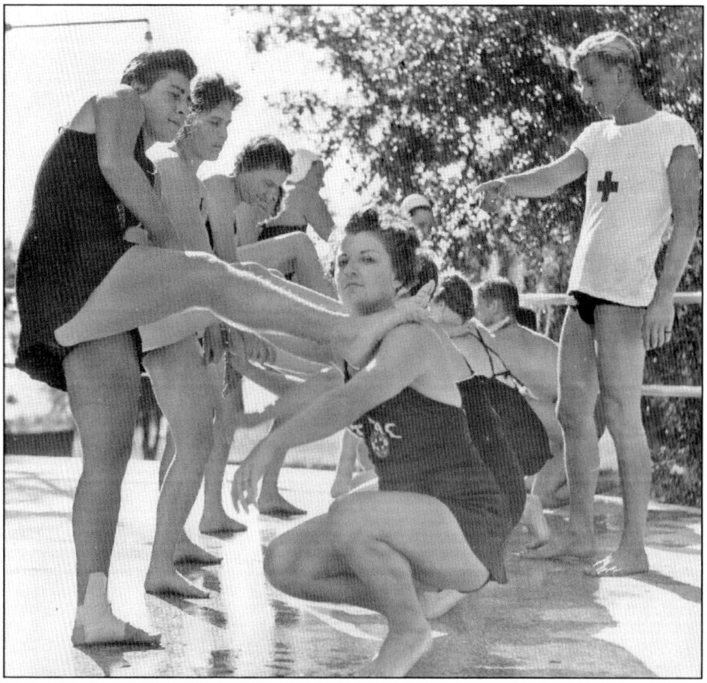

Along with drills and practices on the beach and in the surf, the recruits received additional training at the Bath and Tennis Club pool, learning advanced swimming maneuvers and practicing the commando technique of swimming fully clothed. Thirty-one WAAC third officers and 14 auxiliaries took the 10-day course. Left, Bert Powell makes a correction as the team practices the proper way to break a double-grip-on-one-wrist hold. Below, Powell watches the corps practice a technique for pulling a victim to safety.

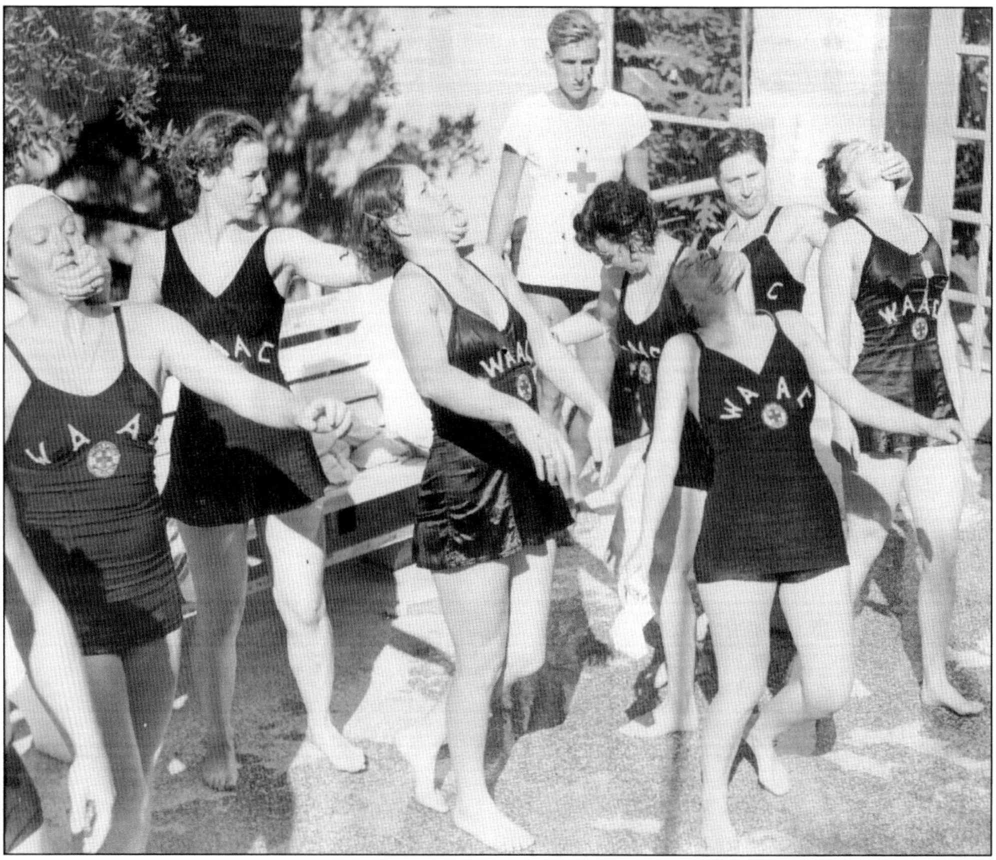

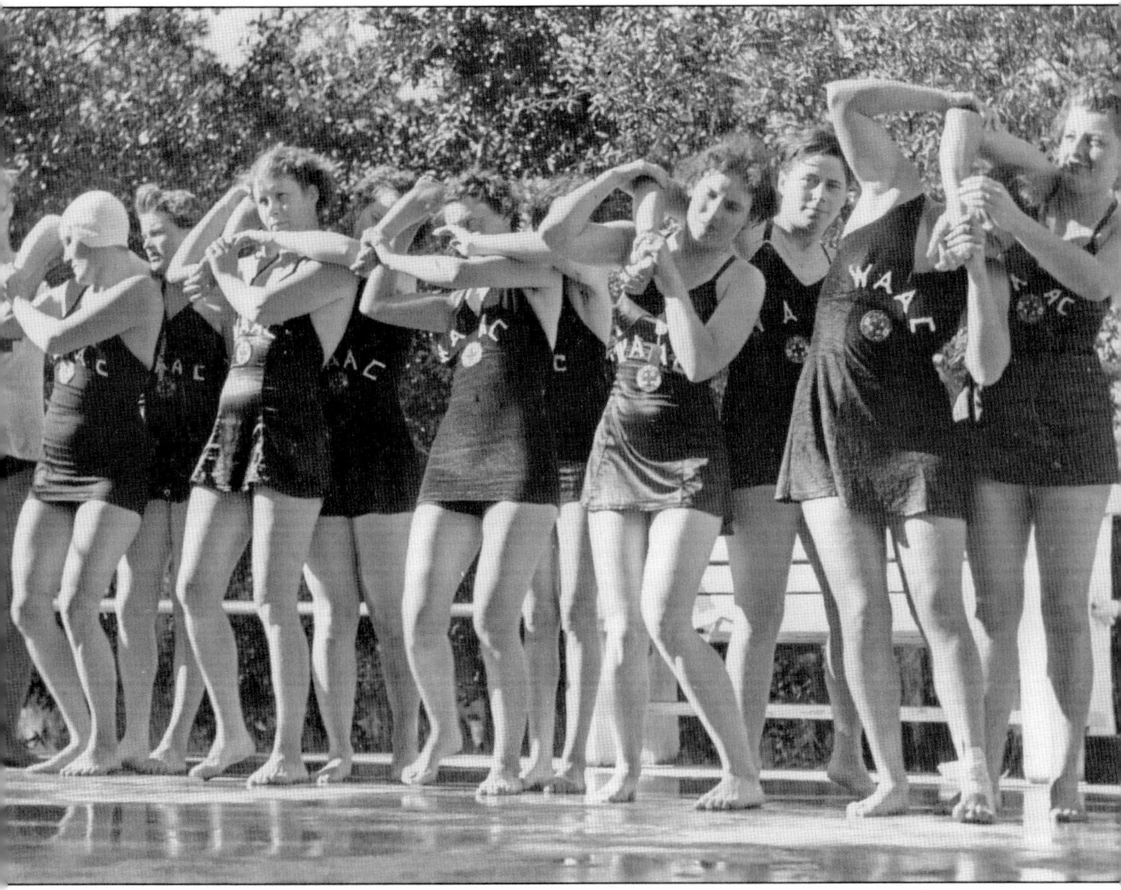

In the event a drowning victim grabs the lifesaver from behind in a panic to stay afloat, it is necessary to be familiar with a means of breaking free. Here Powell instructs the recruits in effective methods of breaking the hold.

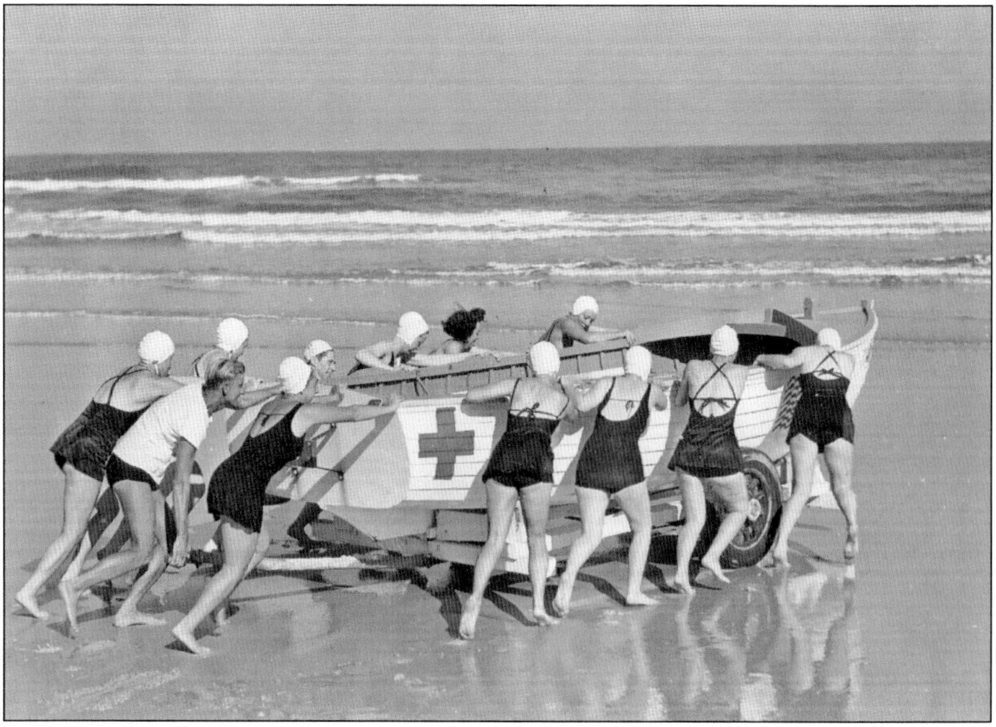

Along with refresher courses in lifesaving and water safety, the members of the WAAC lifeguard corps were given extra practice in surf rescue, as some had done no work in the ocean or with lifeboats, which were used only in cases of plane or ship emergencies offshore. Above, members of the corps rush a lifeboat into the water on this practice run, as Bert Powell guides the carrier. Below, after the practice pull out to sea, the team makes the run in to shore. This time the surf is beneficial.

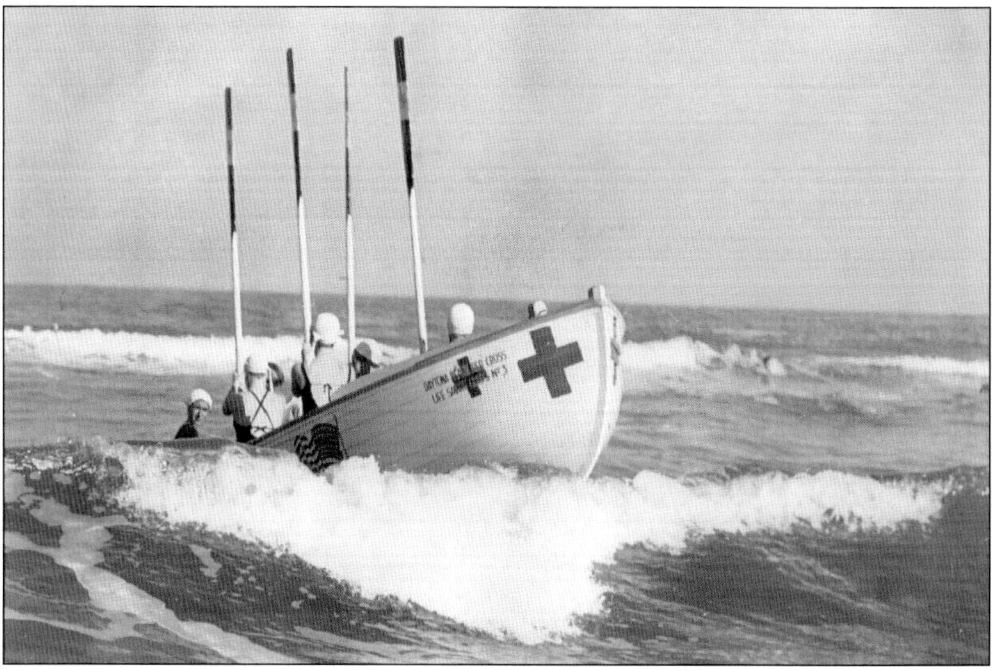

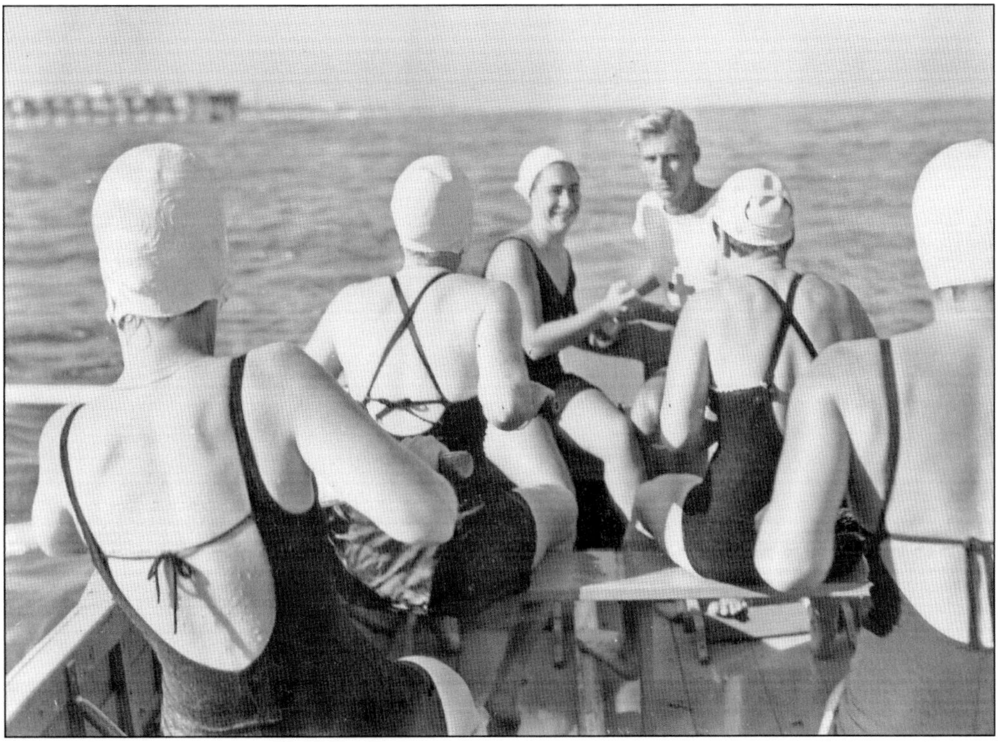

The five-woman team has launched the boat and climbed aboard. Here Powell directs them as the crew prepares to lower their oars into the surf and "Give Way To-Gether," the chant that synchronizes their efforts as they make the strenuous pull out to sea.

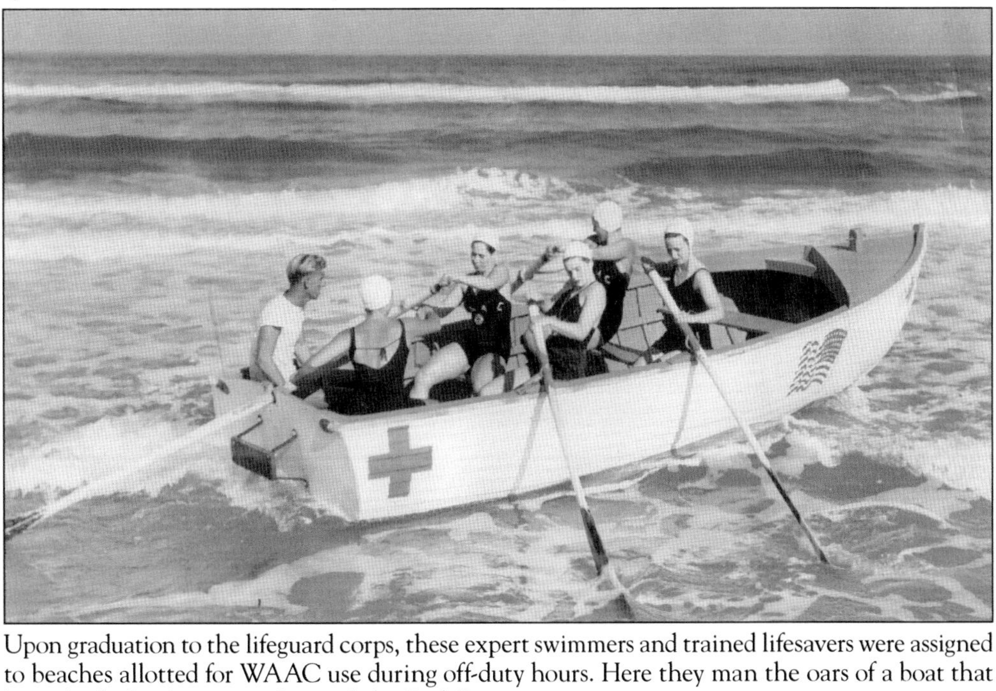

Upon graduation to the lifeguard corps, these expert swimmers and trained lifesavers were assigned to beaches allotted for WAAC use during off-duty hours. Here they man the oars of a boat that bears both the American flag and the Red Cross insignia.

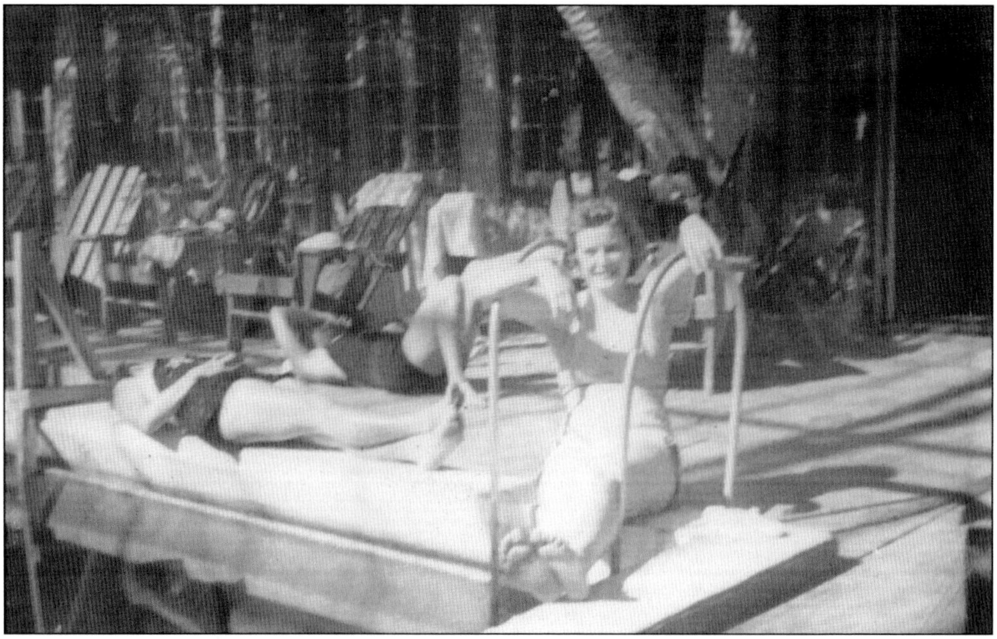

WAAC trainee Janet Durell catches her breath—and the attention of the photographer—during a break in the intense training.

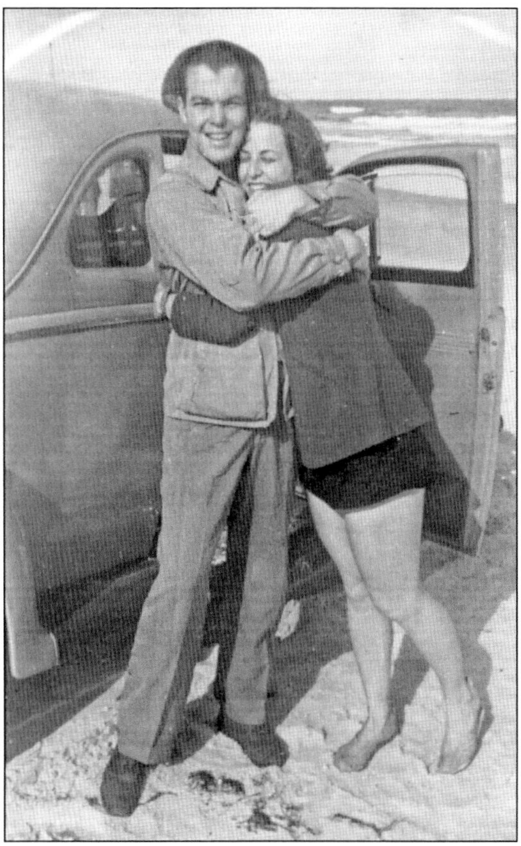

While it was not all fun and games, training in Daytona Beach did have its advantages, as lifeguards and WAAC trainees managed to enjoy the beach in their off-duty hours. Here Walter Lally and Pat Campeon share a hug and a laugh.

Four

Ormond Beach, New Smyrna Beach, and Volusia County Lifeguards

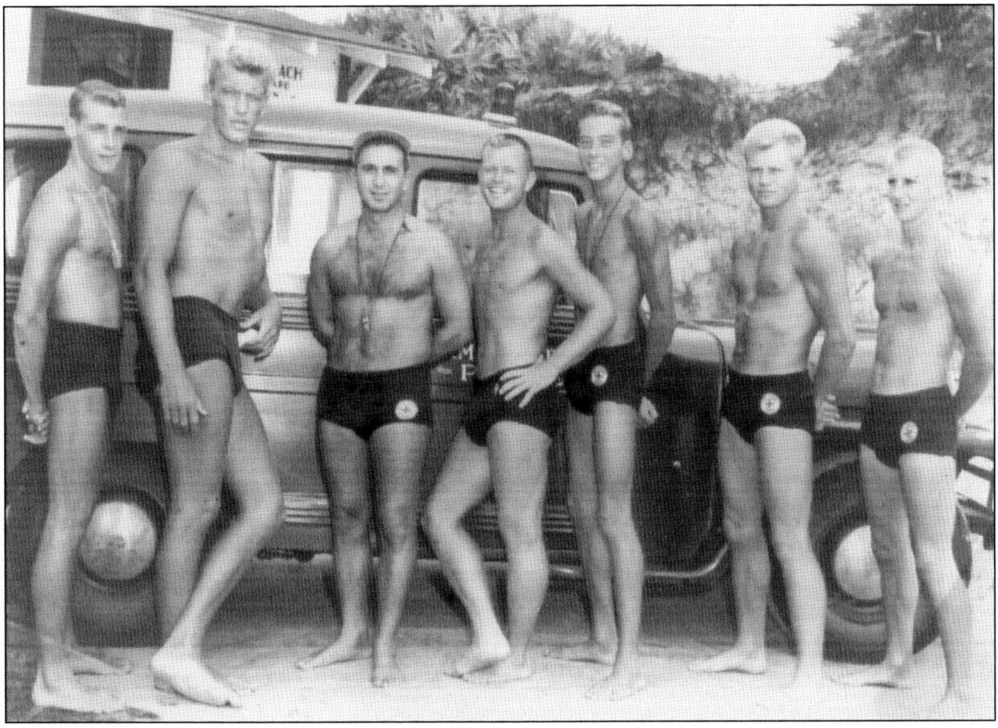

The Ormond Beach Life Saving Corps was formed in 1949, when the concessionaires were required to provide lifeguards in order to obtain permits to operate on the beach. Three lifeguards, plus one supplied by the city, manned the beaches within the city limits. In 1952, the organization became official, and this group photograph of the 1952 corps shows, from left to right, original guards Maurice Hendricks, Ted Cassidy, Andy Romano (captain), Bobby "Honeypath" Hawthorne, William Gunn, Richard Schonamaker, and Jerry Naugle. (Courtesy of Andy Romano.)

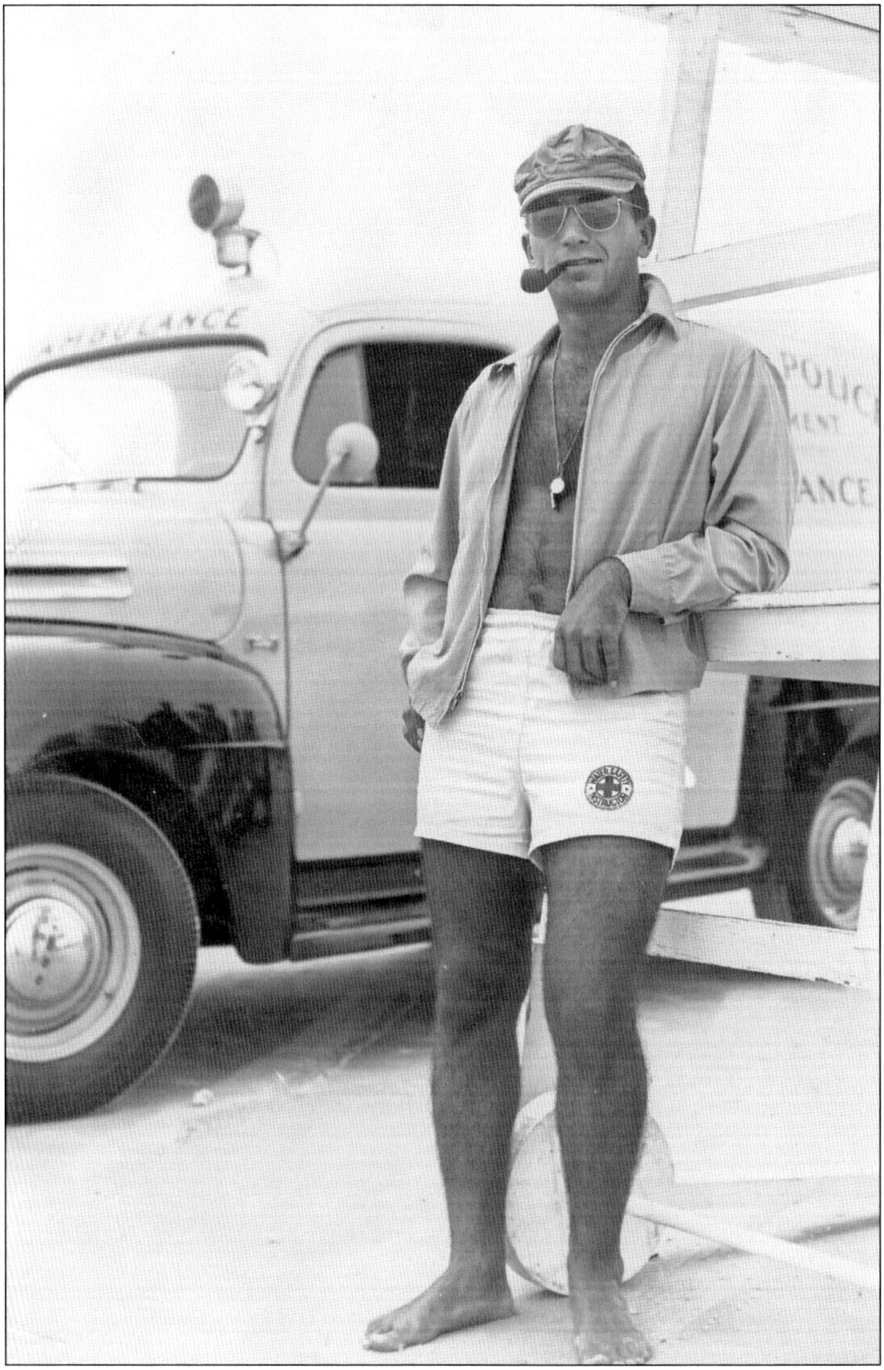

An original member of the Ormond Beach Life Saving Corps, Andy Romano (pictured above in 1952) entered the military in August 1950 and, after being discharged in the fall of 1951, returned to serve as the first captain. In 1957, he left the force to become a teacher at Ormond Elementary School and then took the position of principal at Ormond Beach Junior High. Romano was replaced as captain by Sam Crawford, who held the position until the corps merged with the county in 1961, when he was made assistant to captain Ray Hutton. (Courtesy of Andy Romano.)

Ted Cassidy always stood out in the crowd, due to his unusual size. After leaving Ormond Beach, he went on to achieve fame as Lurch on the popular television show *The Adams Family*. In this 1952 photograph, two tourists requested a picture with Cassidy (third from left) and Andy Romano (far right). (Courtesy of Andy Romano.)

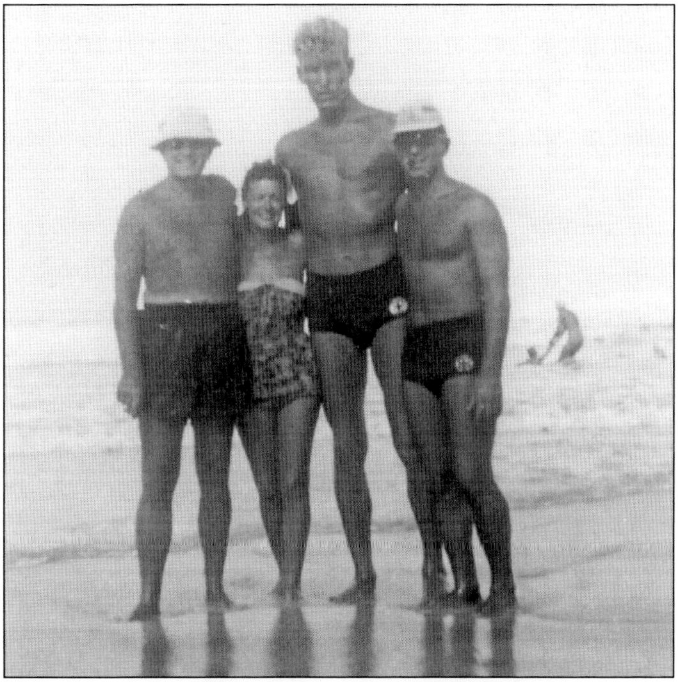

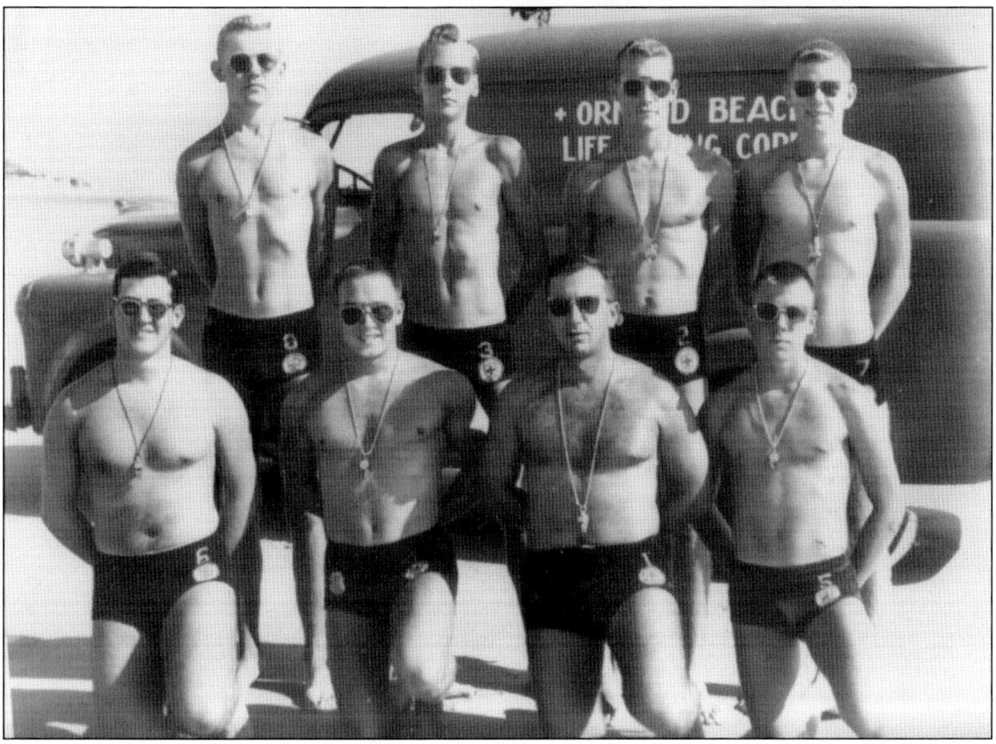

Gathered in front of the Ormond Beach Life Saving Corps truck, the 1953 guards were, from left to right, as follows: (first row) Phil Capo, Chuck Holachuck, Andy Romano (captain), and Tommy Lauderbach; (second row) Bill Grau, William "Timmy" Gunn, Maurice Hendrick, and Larry Webb. (Courtesy of Andy Romano.)

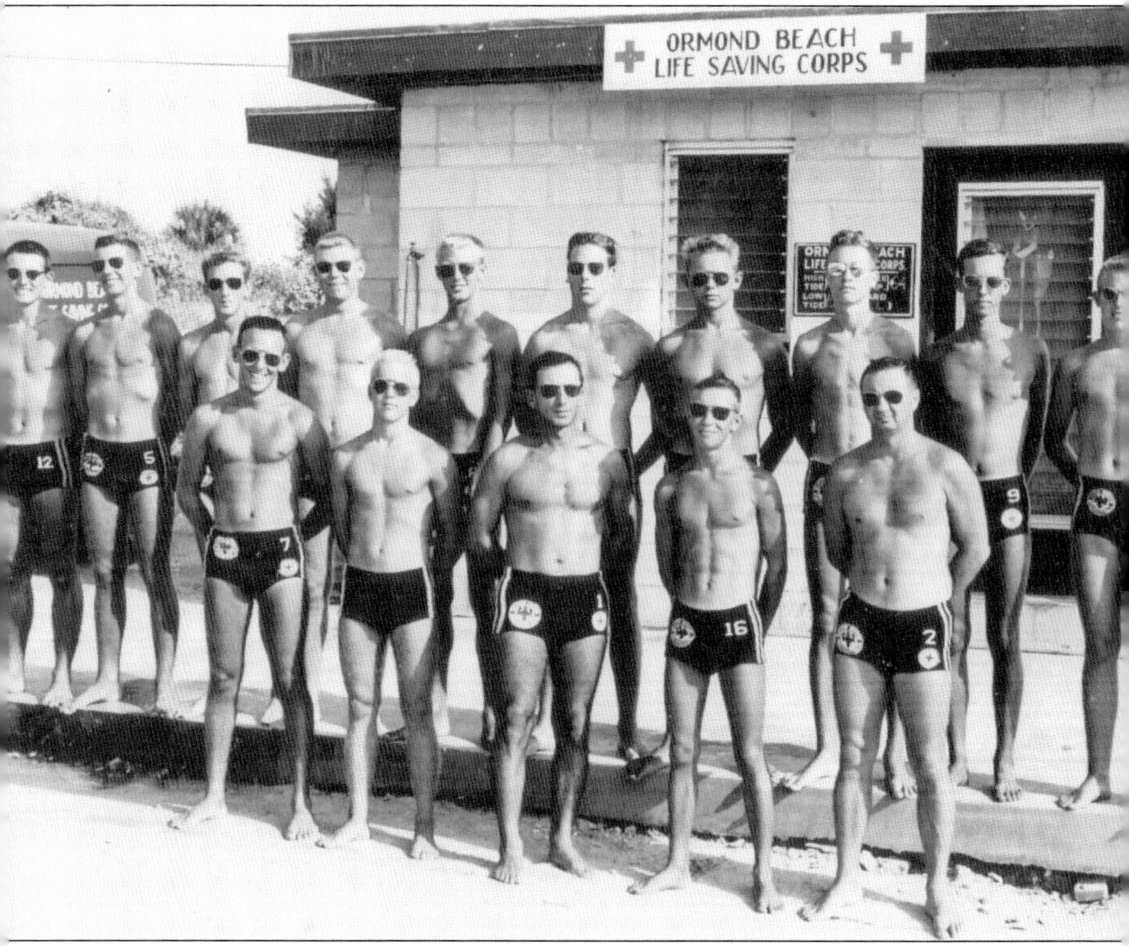

The first official Ormond Beach station was built by the lifeguards themselves. It and the subsequent station were washed out by storms; the third station built stands today at the Cardinal Avenue approach. The group photograph of the 1955 corps includes, from left to right, (first row) Pete Lasker, Jim Ickner, Andy Romano (captain), Leo Spangler, and Nick Triantefallu; (second row) Sisco Deen, Tommy Henderson, Bill Coulter, Larry Webb, James "Jim" Mintner, Buddy Nay, Bill Gray, Don Maxwell, unidentified, and Hank Cartwright. (Courtesy of Andy Romano.)

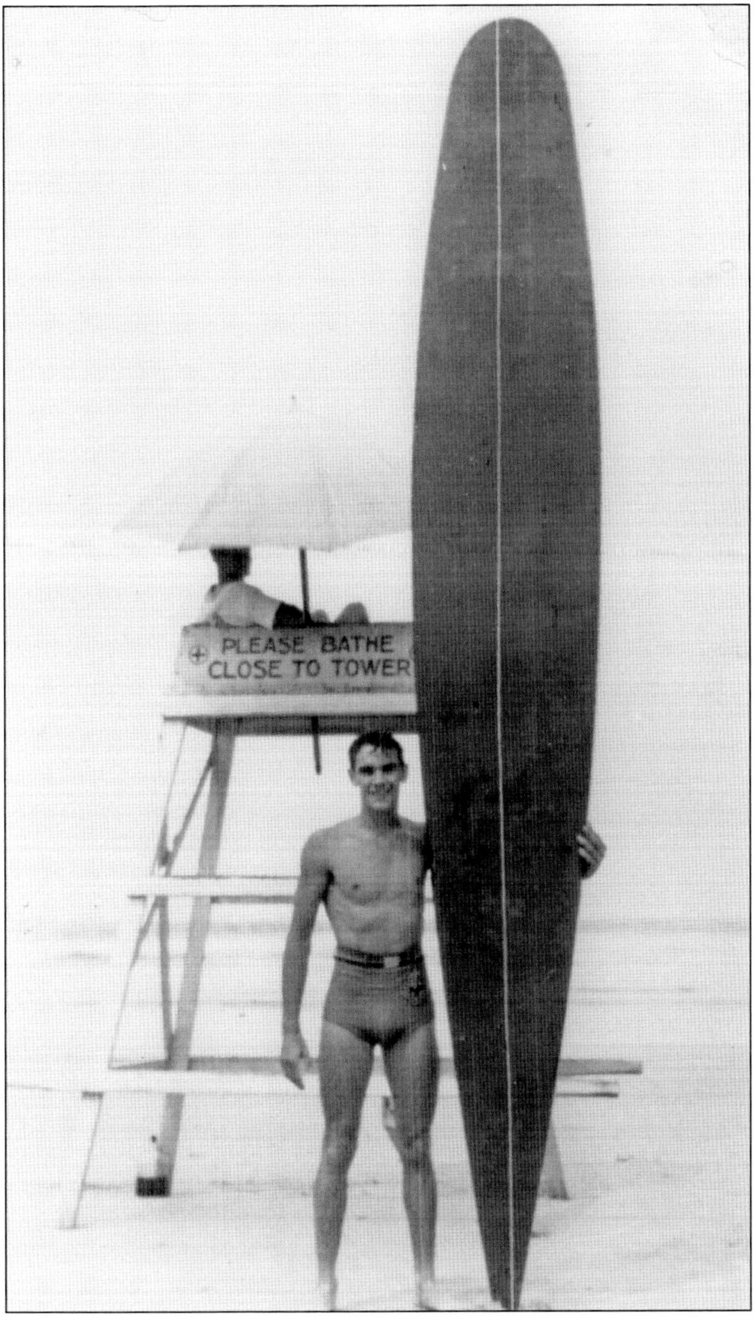

In 1936, Edward J. Tarver and Richard "Dick" Paxton started the Coronado Lifeguard Service on a volunteer basis. During the first two years of its existence, the Coronado Beach guards provided swimming instruction to approximately 300 of the community's youngsters. The Red Cross Life Saving Corps served the city of Coronado, which became part of New Smyrna Beach in the 1940s. Paxton, who graduated from New Smyrna Beach High School in 1937, was captain of the corps for three years and served as instructor for first aid courses sponsored by the local chapter of the American Red Cross. Shown here in the late 1930s, Paxton stands in front of an early tower with the paddleboard used for rescues. (Courtesy of Charlie Baldwin.)

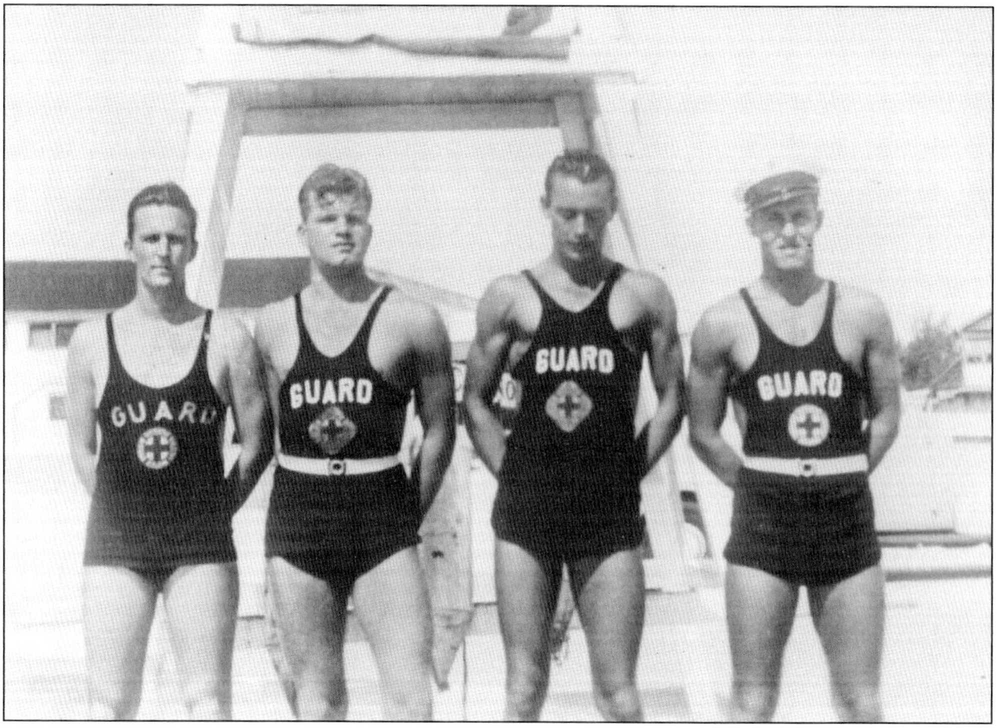

When this picture of the Coronado Lifeguard Service guards was taken on July 4, 1939, the pay was 25¢ an hour. Since there were no city funds available, the lifeguards held dances to fund equipment, including a dory built by Albert Moeller, whose father operated the ferry between Coronado and New Smyrna Beach. Guards pictured are, from left to right, Bob McCarthy (captain), Herbert Copeland, Richard Paxton, and Charles "Fuzz" Benet. (Courtesy of Gary Luther, Luther Printing.)

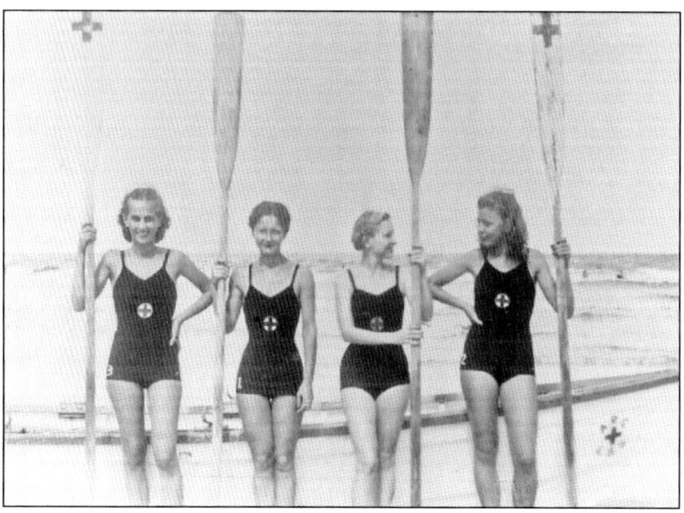

With the men off to war, the women of Coronado Beach stepped up to the plate and onto the sand. Taken in 1940, this photograph shows, from left to right, Dorothy Roero Burgess, Harriett Burgess, Lavonne Lambert Paxton (wife of Hayward Paxton), and Marion "Babe" Tyron Paxton, who were Volusia County's first female lifeguards. (Courtesy of Charlie Baldwin.)

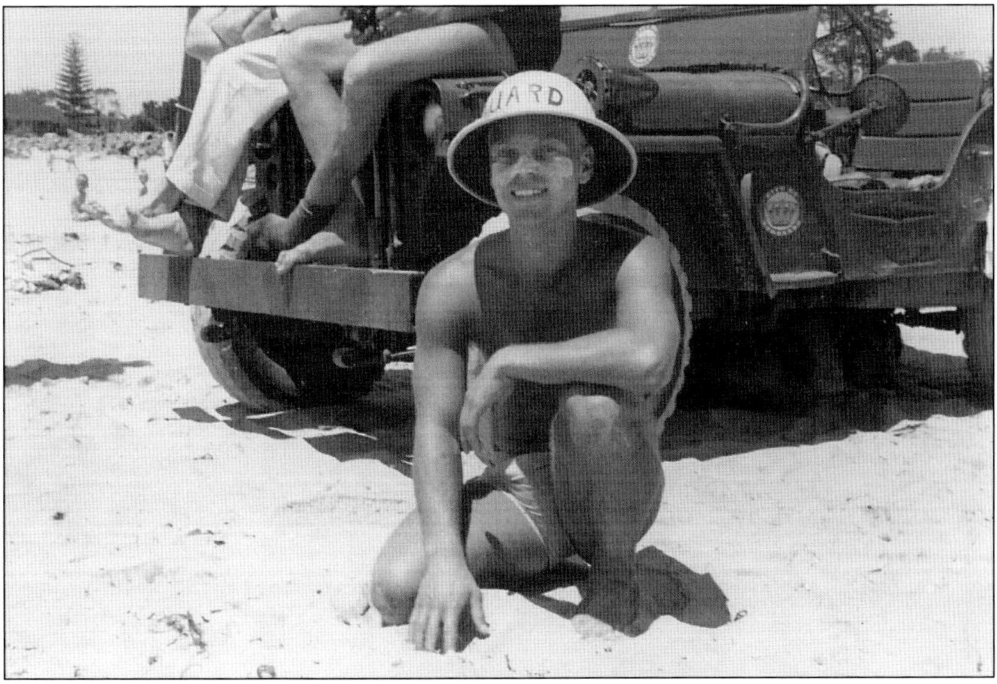

In the late 1930s, local papers reported that the guards stressed safety first in an effort to make Coronado Beach the "World's Safest Beach." Volusia County has since become known as the shark bite capital of the world, and the old taboos such as riding on running boards pale in comparison to present-day concerns. Here an unidentified lifeguard keeps an eye on the bathers. The Jeep bears the seal of the City of Coronado. (Courtesy of New Smyrna Museum of History.)

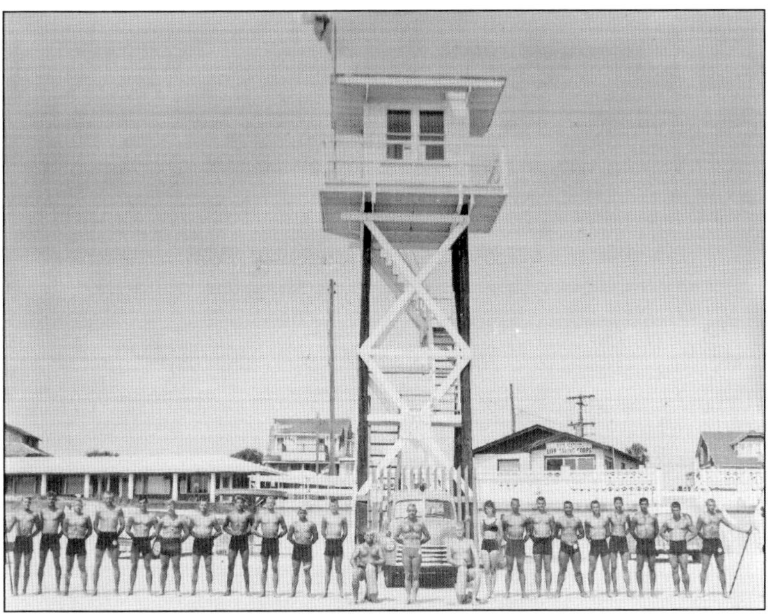

The first lifeguard tower on Buenos Aires Street was originally a coastal observation tower used to watch for enemy submarines in World War II. Destroyed by hurricanes in the early 1960s, it was replaced by the tower shown here. (Courtesy of Toni and Joe's Cocktail Lounge.)

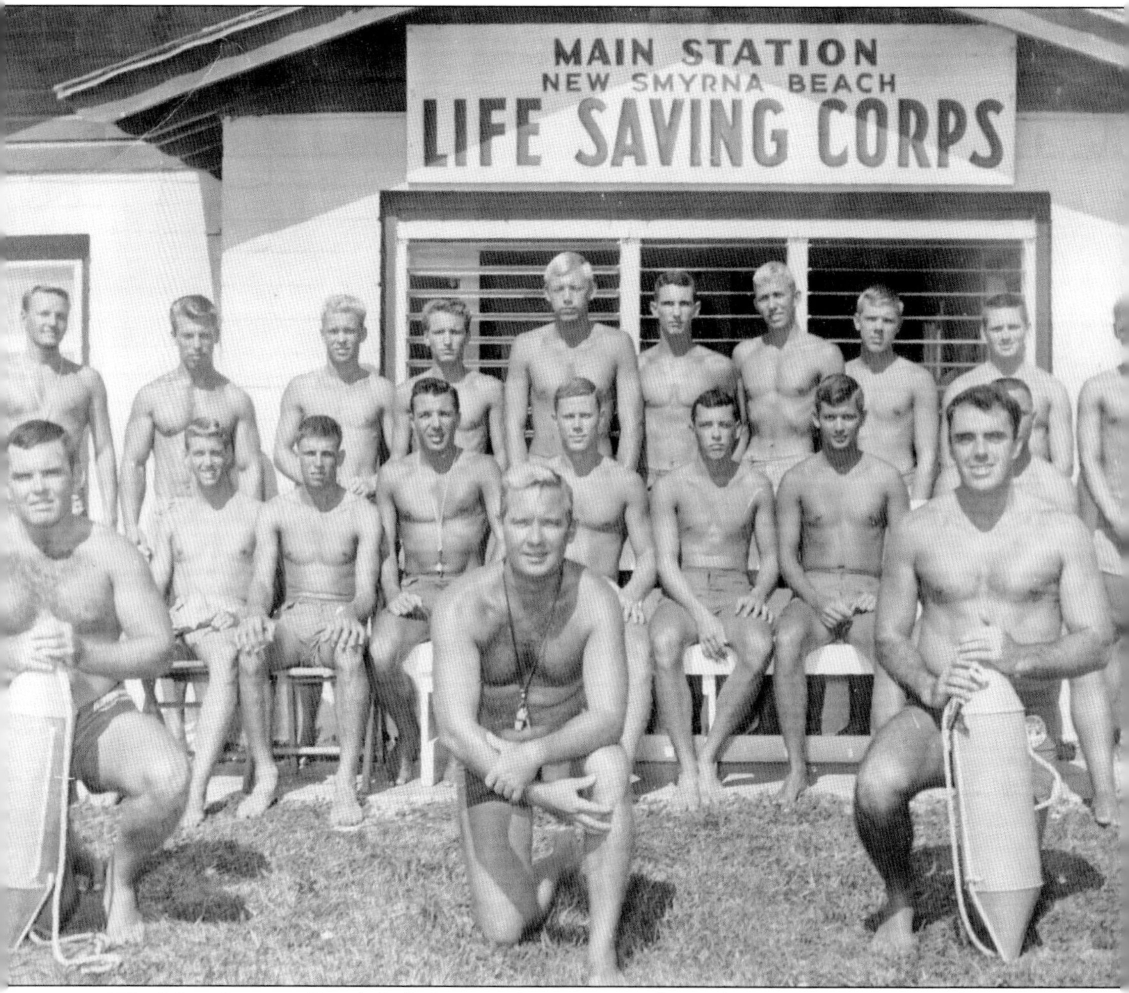

The New Smyrna Beach Life Saving Corps was independent until merging with the Volusia County Beach Patrol in 1972. The 1964 guards were, from left to right, (first row) Mickey Bowles (cocaptain), Milton Drewry (captain), and Dick Heberle (cocaptain); (second row) Clyde "Buddy" Wright, Donnie Hill, Larry Williams, Mike Laswell, Tom Bowles, unidentified, and John Deal; (third row) Mickey Boucher, Billy Hall, Skipper Eppelin, Tom Kimp, Arthur "Skipper" Wallberg, Jim Shinholser, John Biddle, unidentified, Frank Farmer, and George Kilkna. (Courtesy of Buddy Wright.)

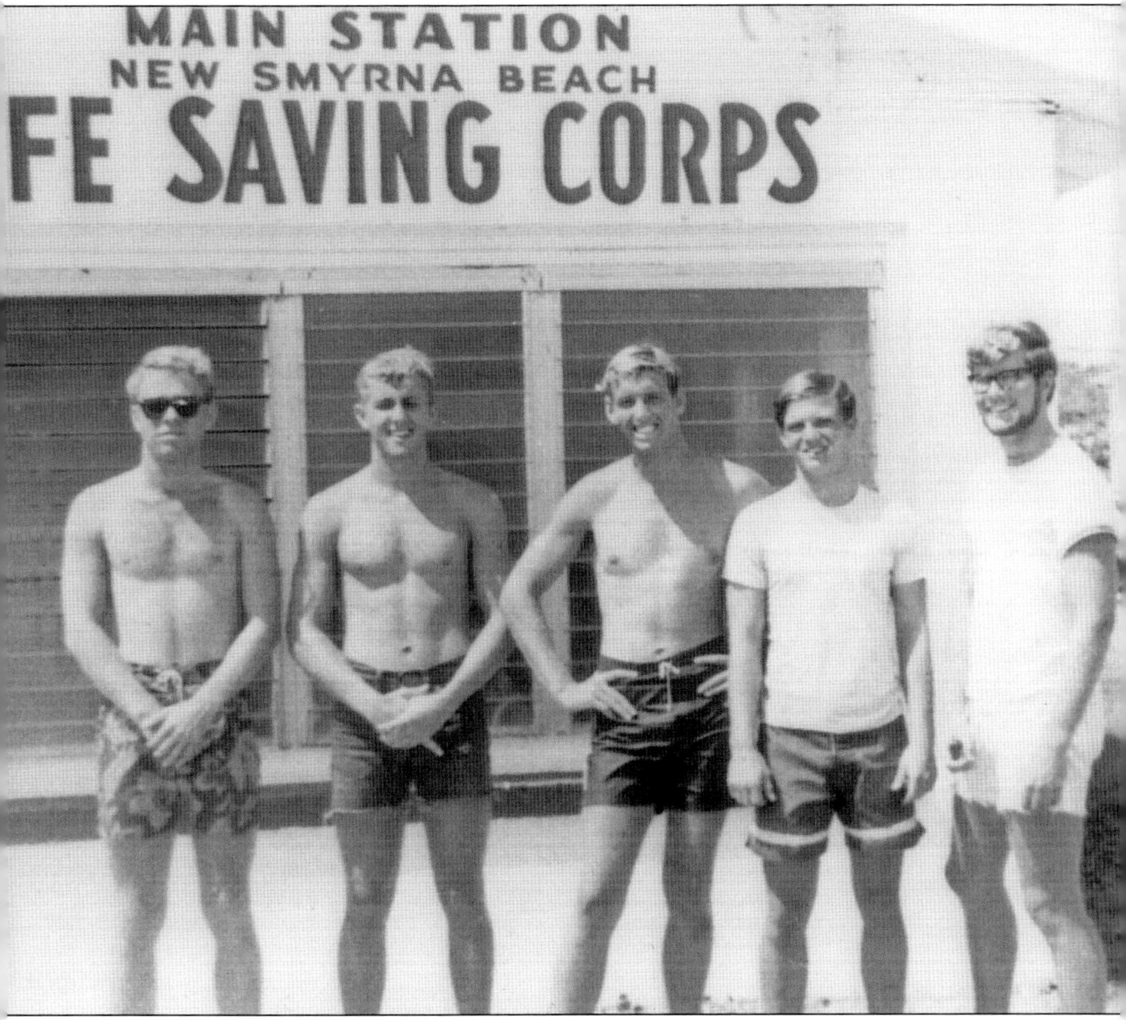

In the 1960s, surfing was in full swing in New Smyrna Beach. As seasoned watermen, these lifeguards were the area's pioneers of the sport. Pictured after a session of surfing on Easter 1967 are, from left to right, Skipper Eppelin, James "Jim" Smith, Clyde "Buddy" Wright, John Oliver, and Charles Lyons. (Courtesy of Buddy Wright.)

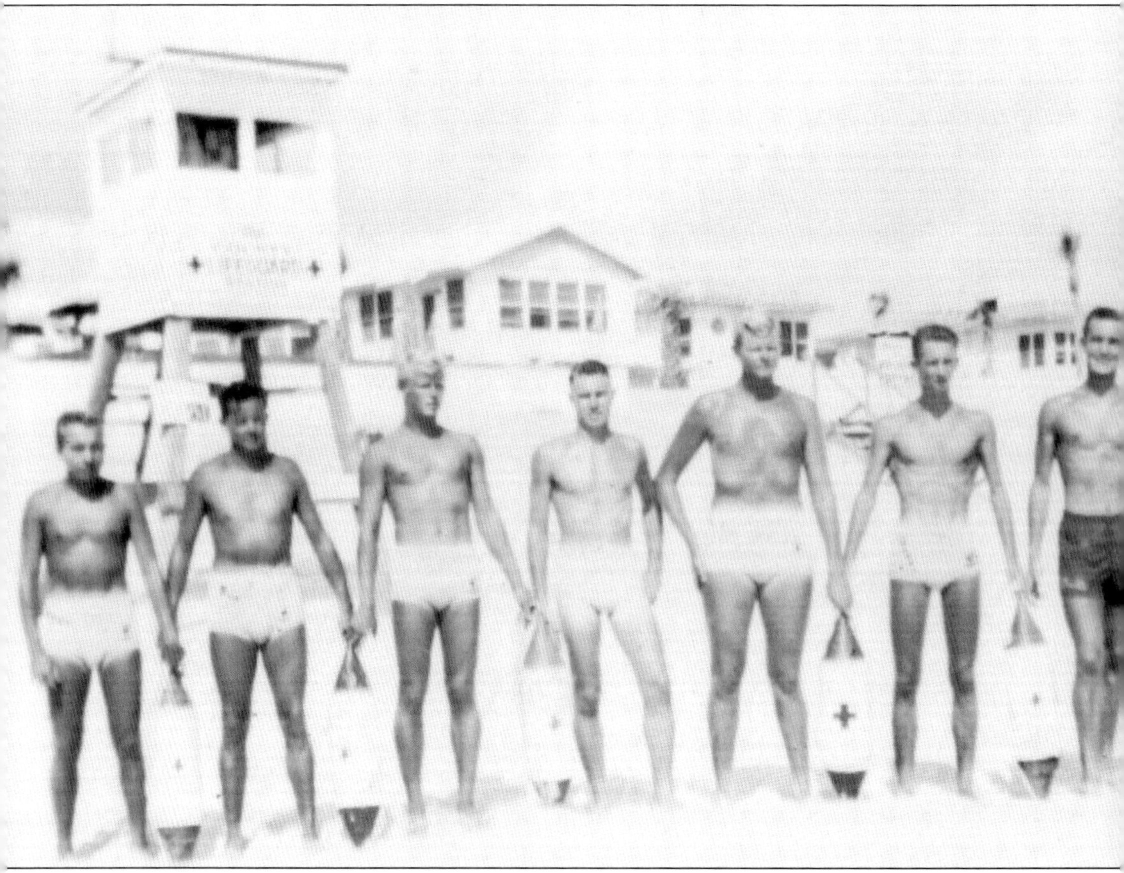

In 1946, Ray Hutton was appointed chief of the newly formed Volusia Beach Patrol, which monitored all areas of the beach not guarded by Ormond Beach, Daytona Beach, or New Smyrna Beach lifeguards. By 1948, there were seven Volusia County lifeguards, as shown in this group photograph. They are, from left to right, Charlie Carlin, "Pete" Lawrence Decker, Ray Hutton (captain), Ernest Widmer, Charlie Gay, Bernie Far, and unidentified. (Courtesy of Ray Hutton.)

This is another early tower originally built by the government for the purpose of looking out for submarines. After the war, it became the North County lifeguard station. Here Don Maxwell and an unidentified guard stand in front of the tower, which was destroyed by hurricanes in 1955. Maxwell was a lifeguard captain and later went into law enforcement for the state of Florida.

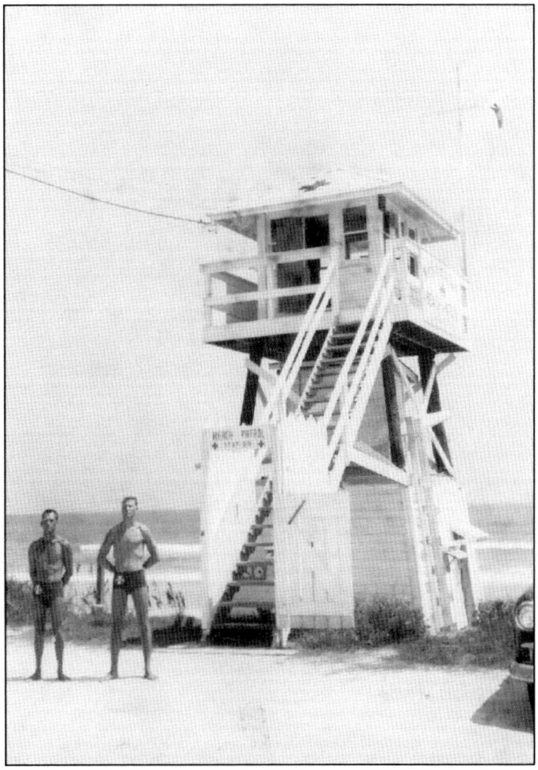

Standing in front of their official Volusia County Beach Patrol vehicle are the 1956 lifeguards of District 4. Running north of Granada Avenue to Flagler County, this district was also known as North County. The guards pictured here are, from left to right, unidentified, Gordon Foote, unidentified, Gordon Reynolds, and Kenny Edwards. Due to limited funding, the vehicles were generally purchased at auction and frequently posed problems. The need to push a vehicle to jump-start the battery was common, and one battery even fell out of a vehicle altogether.

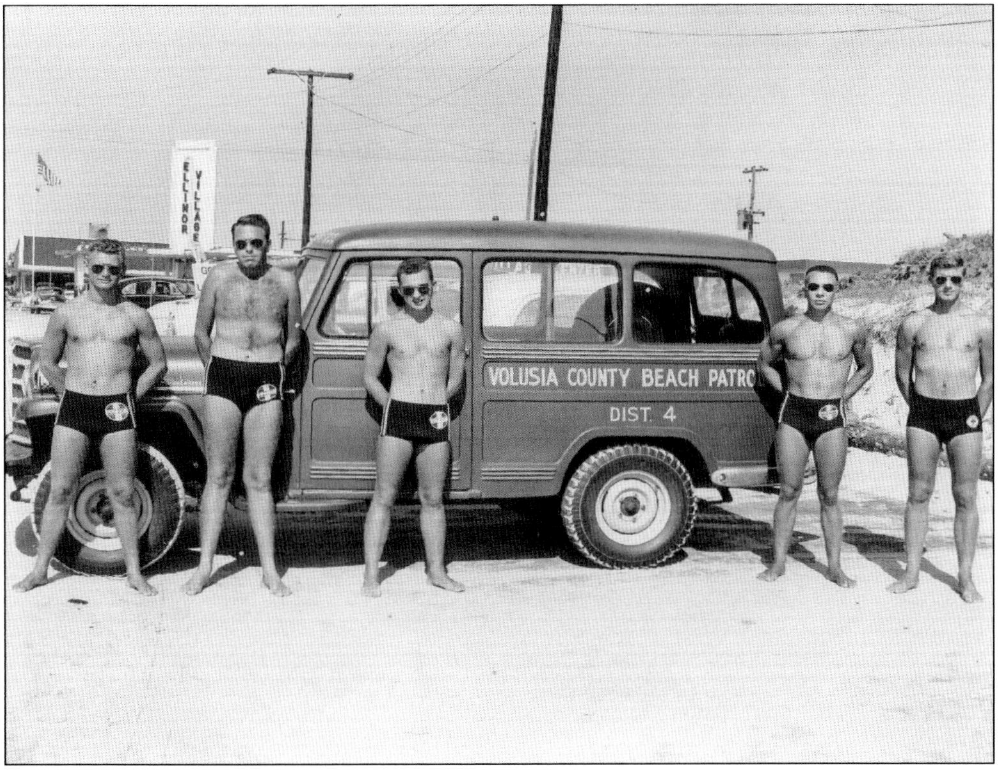

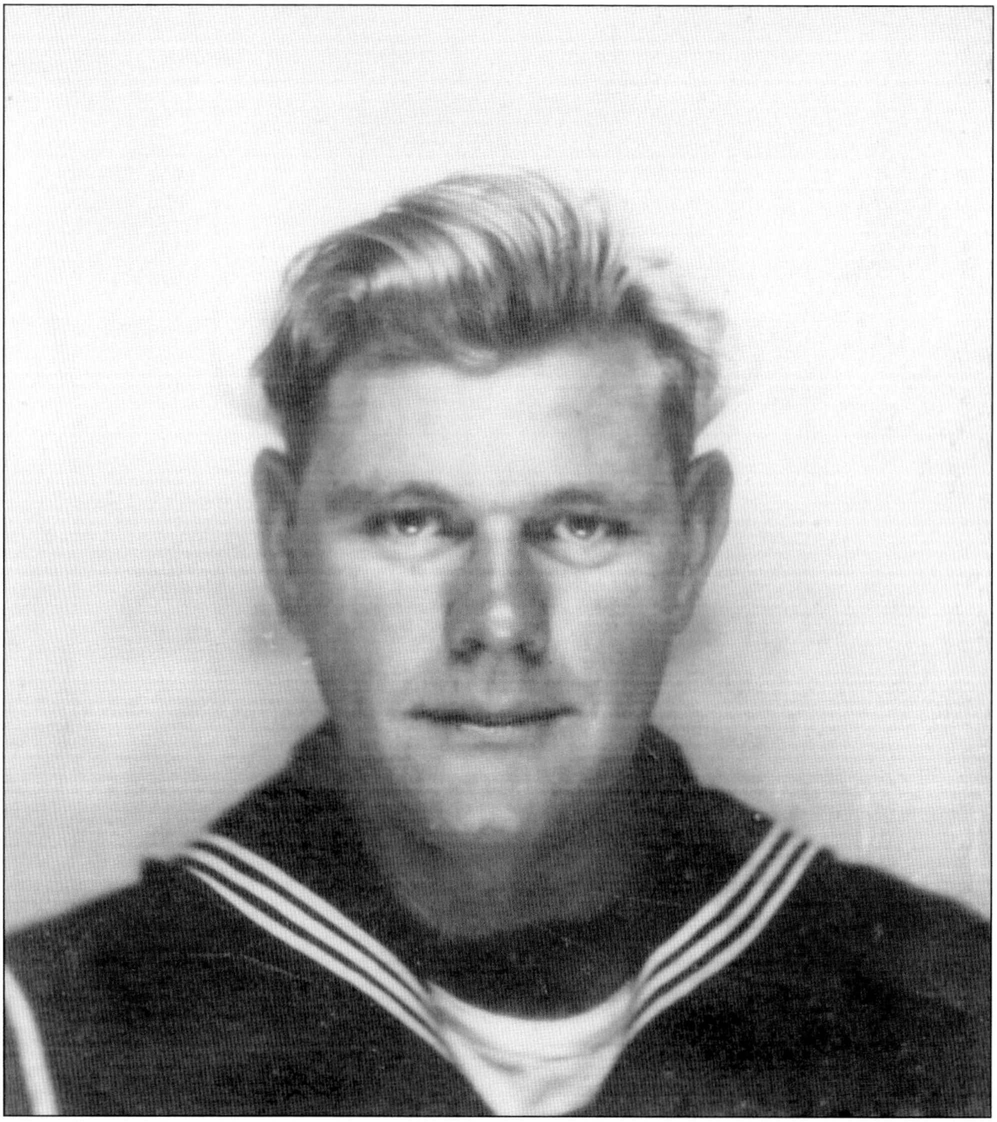

This photograph of Ray Hutton was taken when he joined the navy in 1942. He returned to Daytona Beach after a four-year stint in the Caribbean. When he read about the county's plans to organize a beach patrol, he realized his naval training made him a natural. Hutton was hired and made chief, a position he maintained through the merger with the other beach patrols of the area. In 1965, the National Lifeguard Foundation granted a charter to the state of Florida, and Hutton was named as one of the three original officers. Among the procedures and designs initiated by Hutton are the symbols of a black buoy with crossed oars on an orange flag, used to this day to signify that a lifeguard is on duty. The direction of the lifeguard tower is another indication—if the tower faces west (away from the ocean) the lifeguard is away; an east-facing tower is manned. (Courtesy of Ray Hutton.)

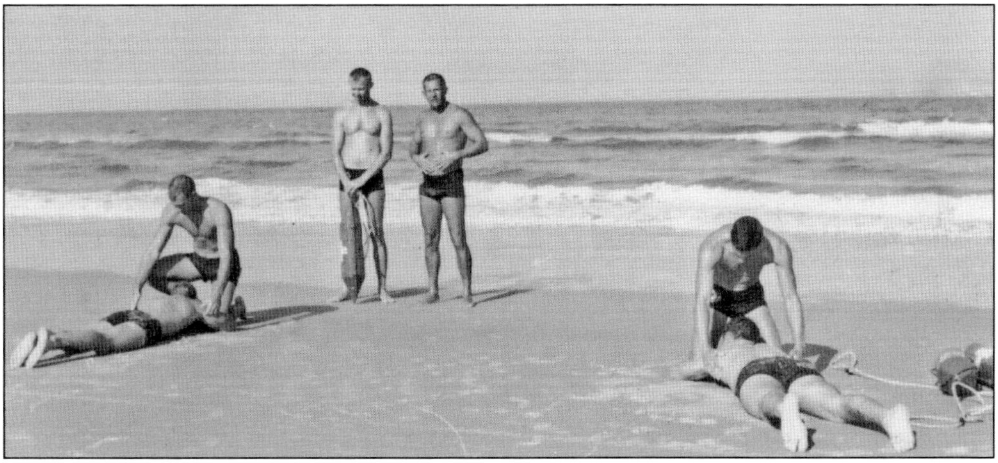

Lifeguard chief Ray Hutton was once named the dean of lifesaving by the Red Cross. He was a member of the Red Cross aquatic school faculty for years, teaching surf rescue to personnel at Patrick Air Force Base. Two of his guards, David Peckham and ? Cass, are shown here conducting training exercises for the county in 1961.

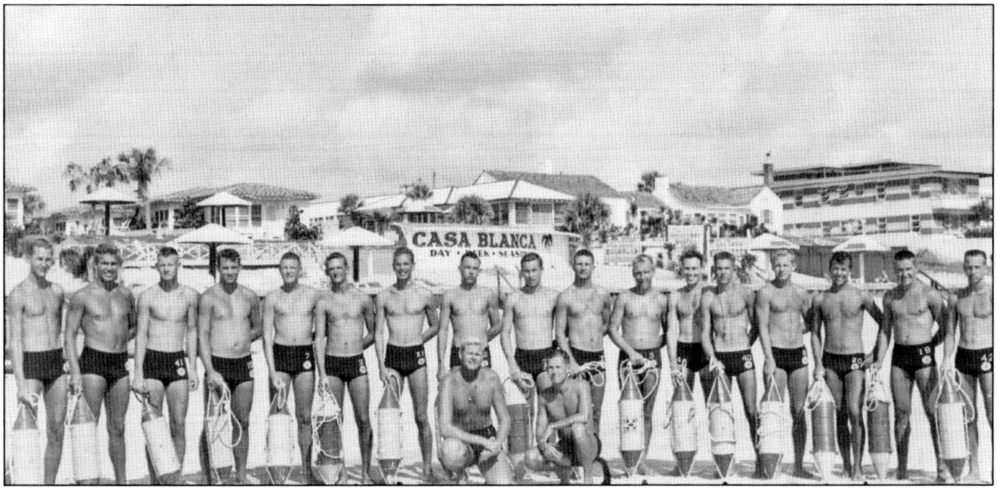

Taken in the late 1950s, this photograph shows the Volusia County Beach Patrol members. They are, from left to right, (first row) Ray Hutton (captain) and ? Cass; (second row) Ed Wurzback, Dick Heberle, ? Talton, Ronny King, Atwood Taylor, Jay Adams, Pete Decker, two unidentified men, Dick Benner, Bobby Smith, Ernest Widmer, Pete Seeman, Dave Kemp, Dick Griswold, Dick Dunkle, and Freddie Osterman.

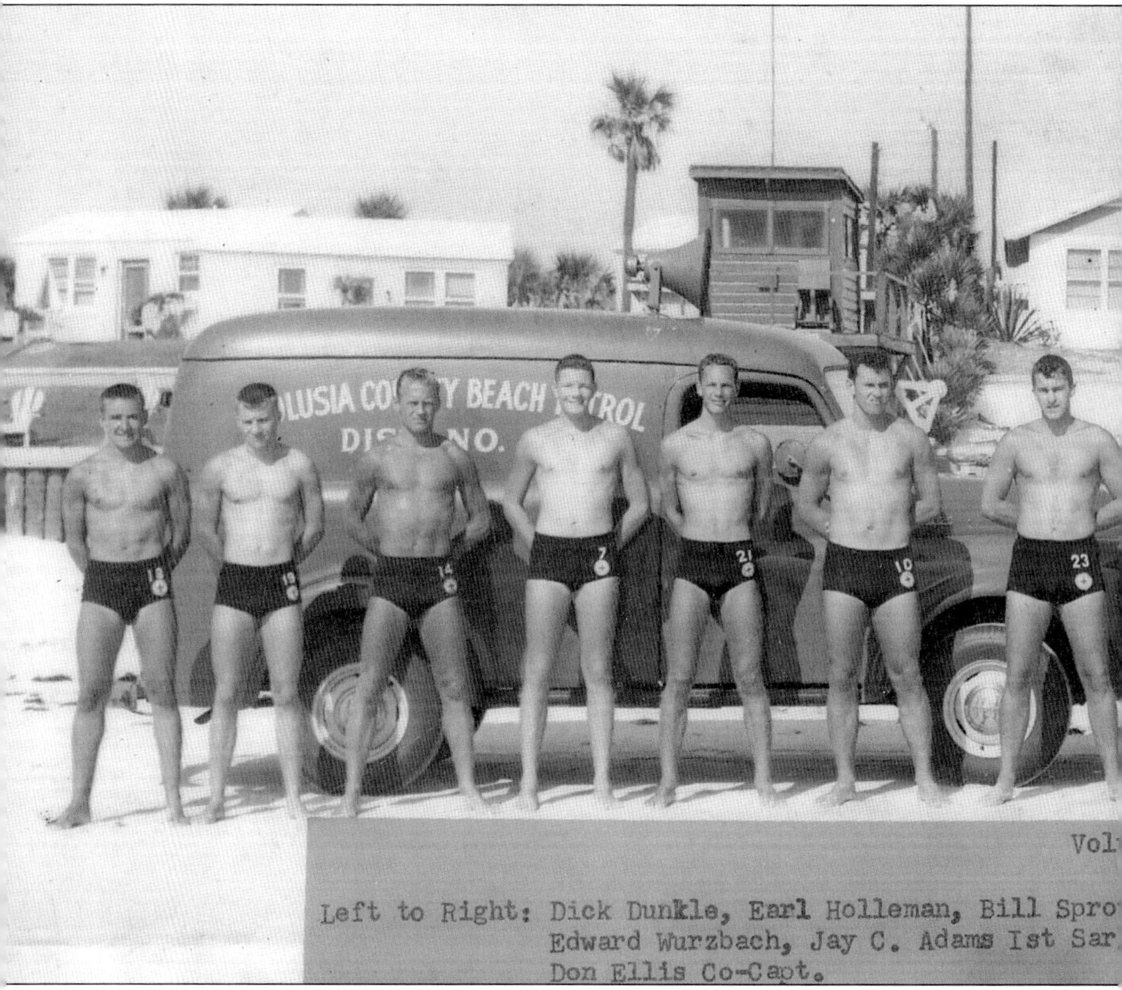

This group shot of the 1955 Volusia County Life Saving Corps shows the members standing in front of their rescue vehicles. Pictured are, from left to right, Dick Dunkle, Earl Hollaman, Bill Sproul,

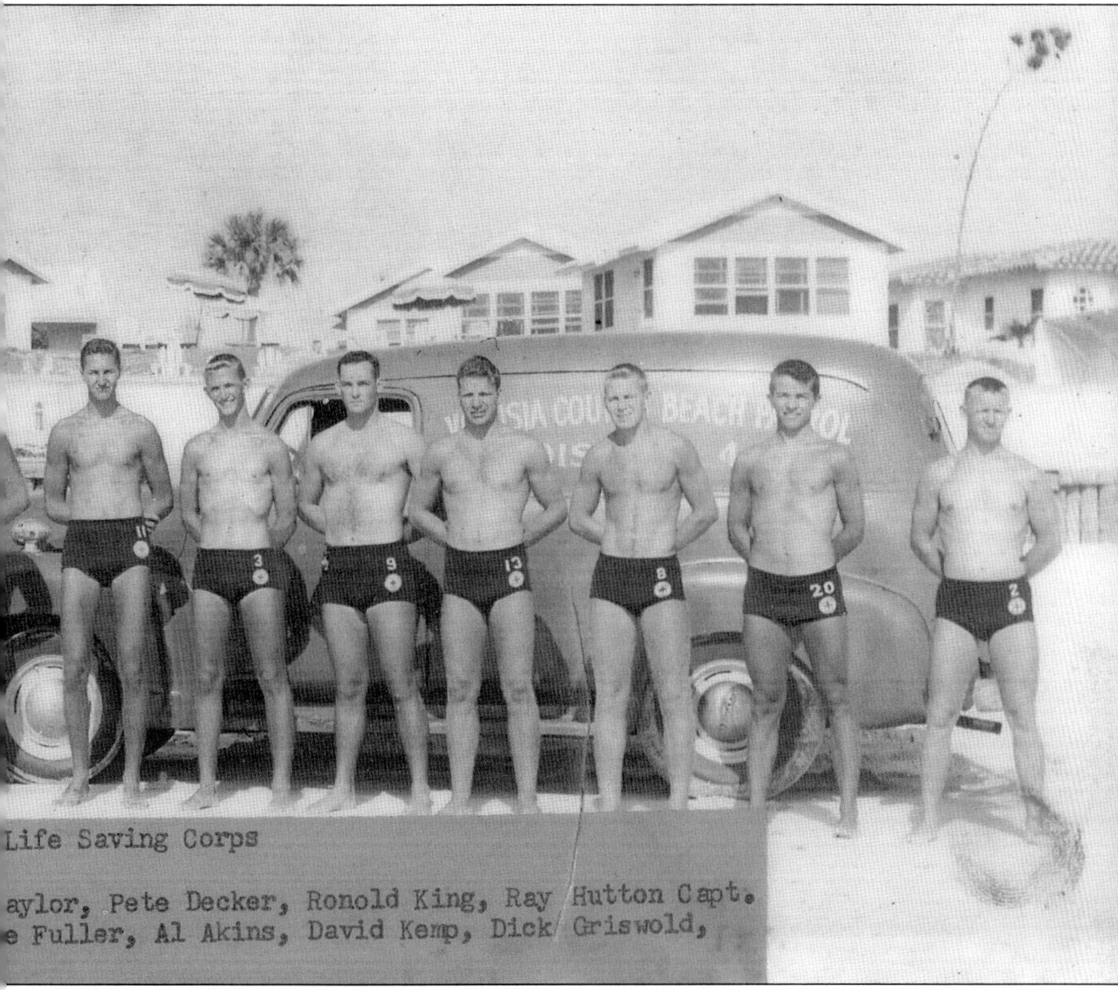

Atwood Taylor, Pete Decker, Ronald King, Ray Hutton (captain), Edward Wurzbach, Jay C. Adams (first sergeant), Rutlege Fuller, Al Akins, David Kemp, Dick Griswold, and Don Ellis (cocaptain).

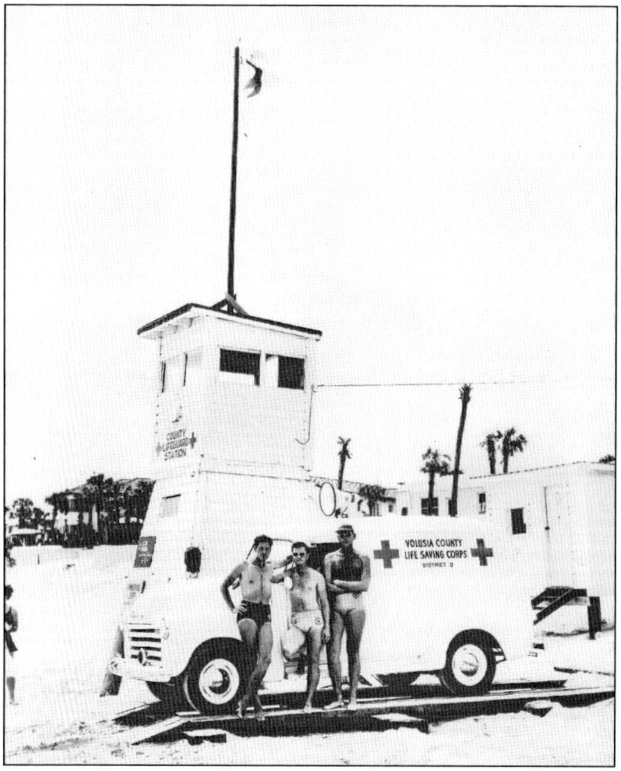

Built just after World War II, this station was located at 2100 South Atlantic Avenue, near Perry's Ocean Edge Motel. Featuring a building for storage in back, it was rebuilt in 1948 and again in 1955 after being washed away by hurricanes. Here an unknown guard (left) stands with Gordon Pfeifer (center) and Ray Hutton (right). This photograph was taken after the final time the station was rebuilt. It has since been taken down permanently.

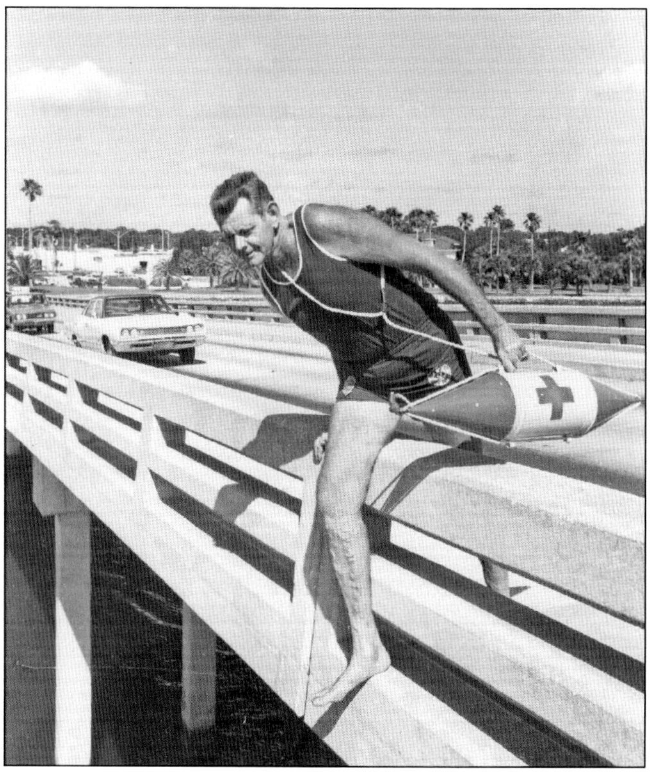

Lifeguards in Volusia County have always responded to any emergency, whether or not it occurred on the beach, as is demonstrated by Ray Hutton in this late-1950s reenactment for the local newspaper. As Hutton was heading across the Main Street Bridge one morning, he was flagged down by the bridge attendant, who explained that a man had jumped into the Halifax River. Hutton grabbed a buoy and dropped into the channel of the Halifax River, rescuing the man and thwarting a suicide attempt. Members of the beach patrol are not ones to say, "That's not my job."

Five

Volusia County Beach Patrol

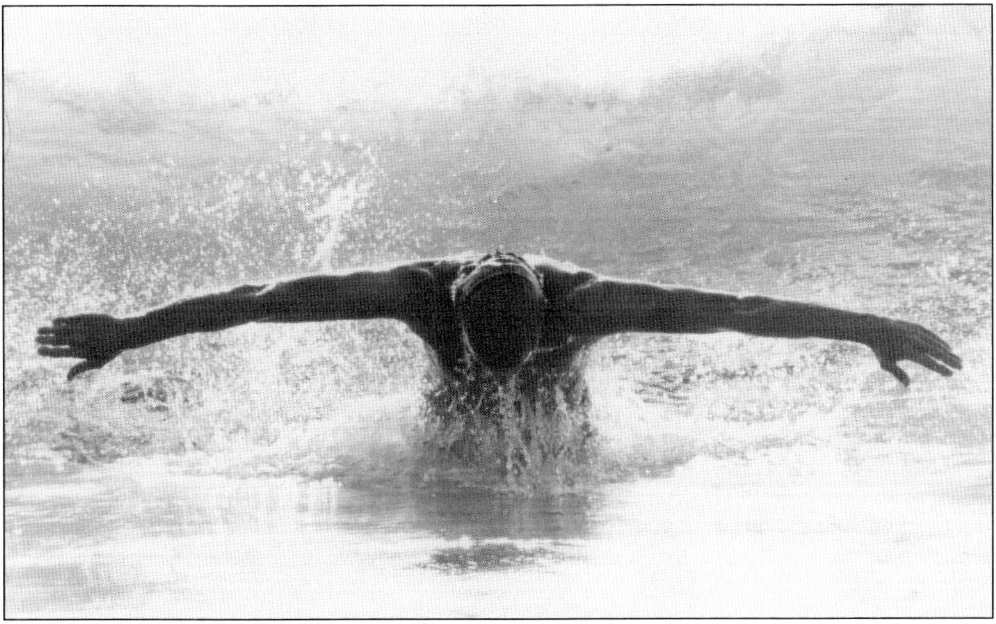

In 1962, the city of Daytona Beach merged its lifesaving force with that of the county. Volusia County Beach Patrol had 80 guards manning 42 towers on a stretch of beach from the Flagler County line to Ponce Inlet, excluding the city of Ormond Beach, which had yet to join. This consolidated corps was separated into three divisions. North County, under the direction of Donald Maxwell, ran from the Flagler County line to the Ormond Beach city limits. Central Division stretched ran from the north city limits of Daytona Beach to Lenox Avenue at Daytona Beach Shores. Bob Wheeler, former captain of the Daytona Beach guards, became chief of Central Division, and his former cocaptain Irving Jannety was made assistant chief. David Peckham, a six-year veteran, was made chief of the South County Division, which extended from the south limits of Daytona Beach to the Ponce Inlet. Ray Hutton, captain of the Volusia County Beach Patrol, was placed in charge of the entire operation and divided his time between the towers of the divisions. Each division received a patrol truck, and the county provided new equipment and a new radio system.

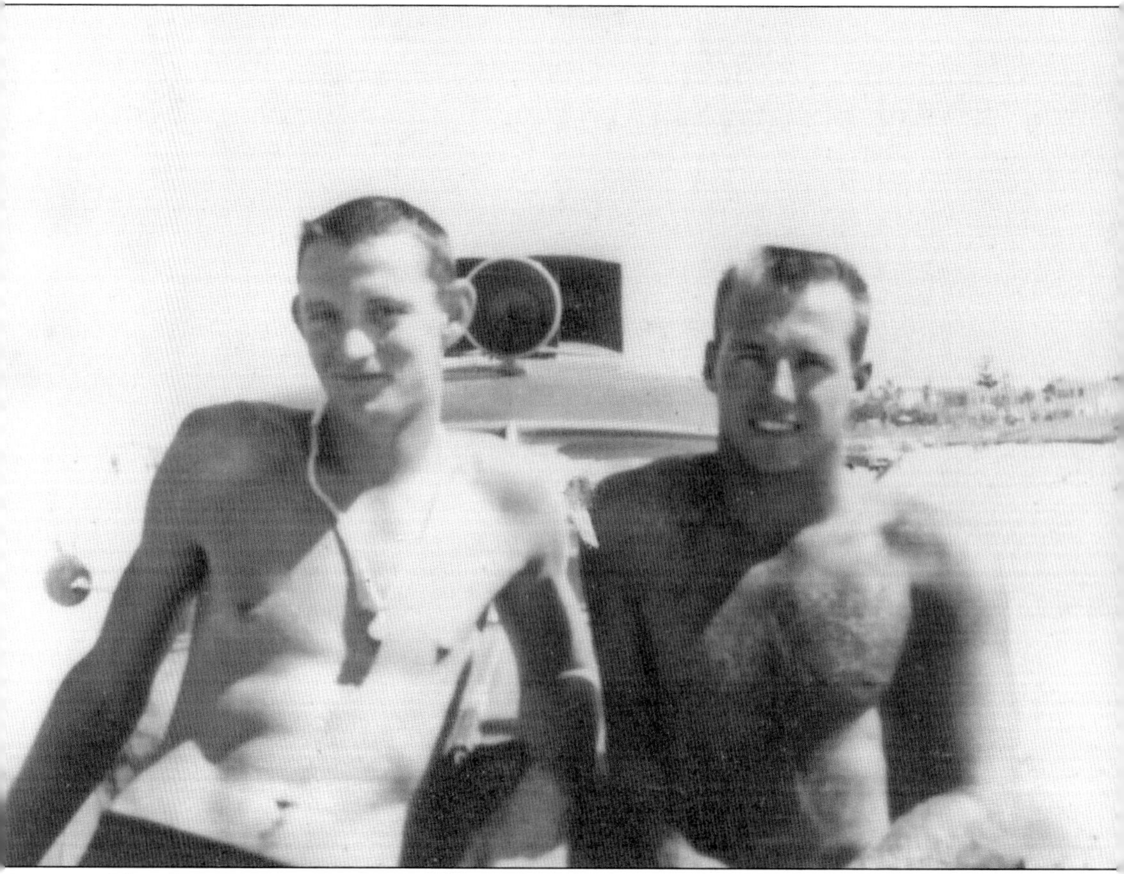

The phrase "11 is 10-8" meant chief Bob Wheeler was on duty and on the move. (Eleven was his number, and "10-8" meant he was officially working.) Upon hearing those words come over their radios, every guard along the 47-mile stretch of Volusia County coastline sprang to life. Equipment was checked, spines straightened, and the already watchful eyes of the guards became even sharper. Wheeler was known for running a tight ship, but he was also known for being a fair boss and an outstanding leader. And when the need arose, he was first in the trenches. Pictured are Wheeler (left) and an unidentified guard.

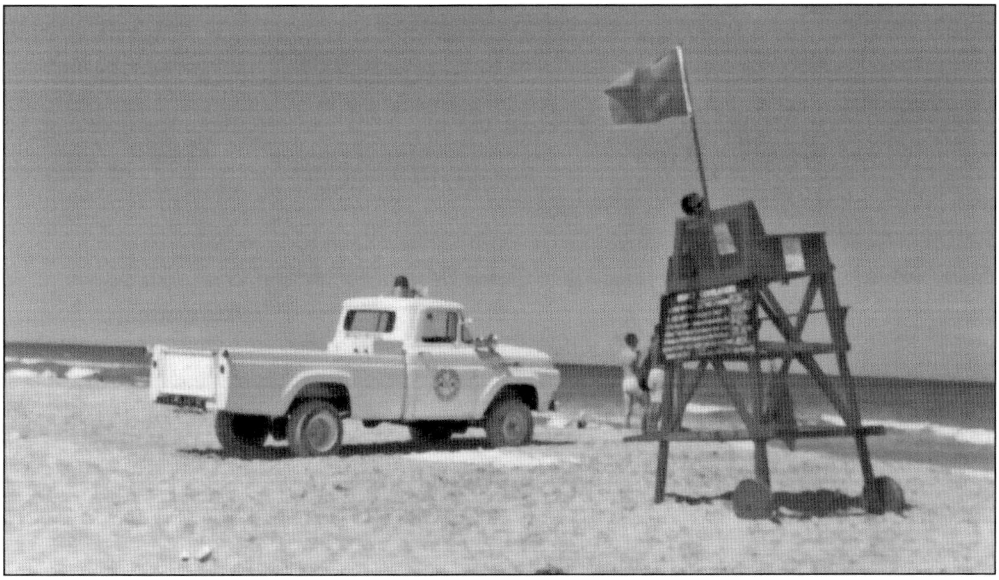

By the mid-1960s, towers of the Volusia County Beach Patrol were painted red, and the trucks bore county emblems.

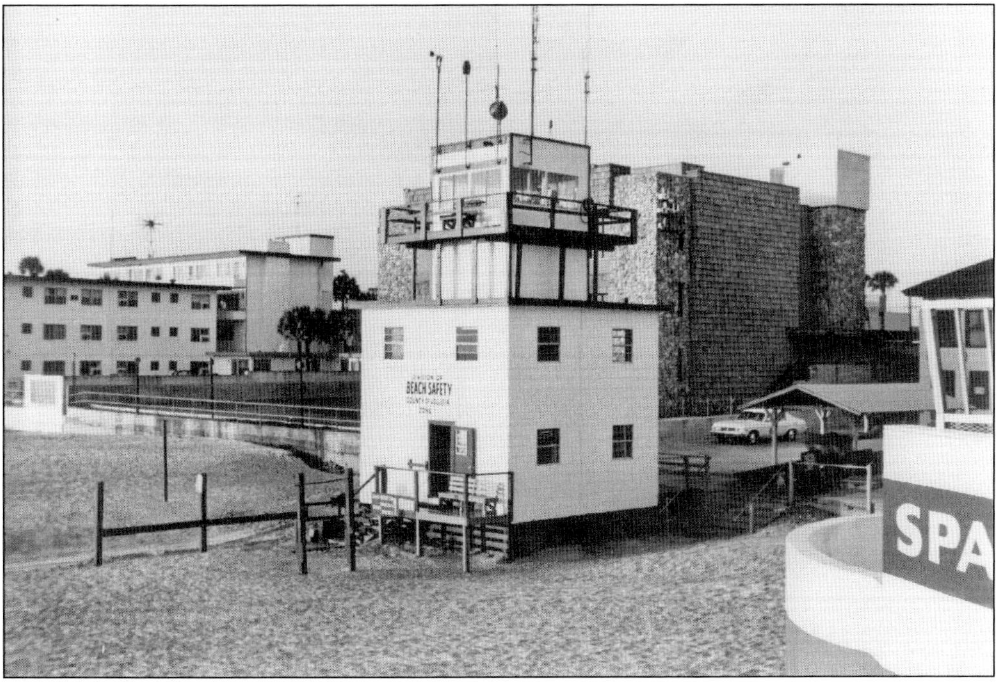

The lifeguard station at the band shell and the control tower on the ocean pier both moved to new headquarters. This structure just south of the Main Street Pier became home for the central division and featured a first aid room, a clerk's office, and a bathroom with a shower on the main floor. Upstairs provided office space for chief Ray Hutton and deputy chief Bob Wheeler, and the control tower was placed on the roof. The structure was built by county employees, and lifeguards helped with the completion. (Courtesy of Jim Willits.)

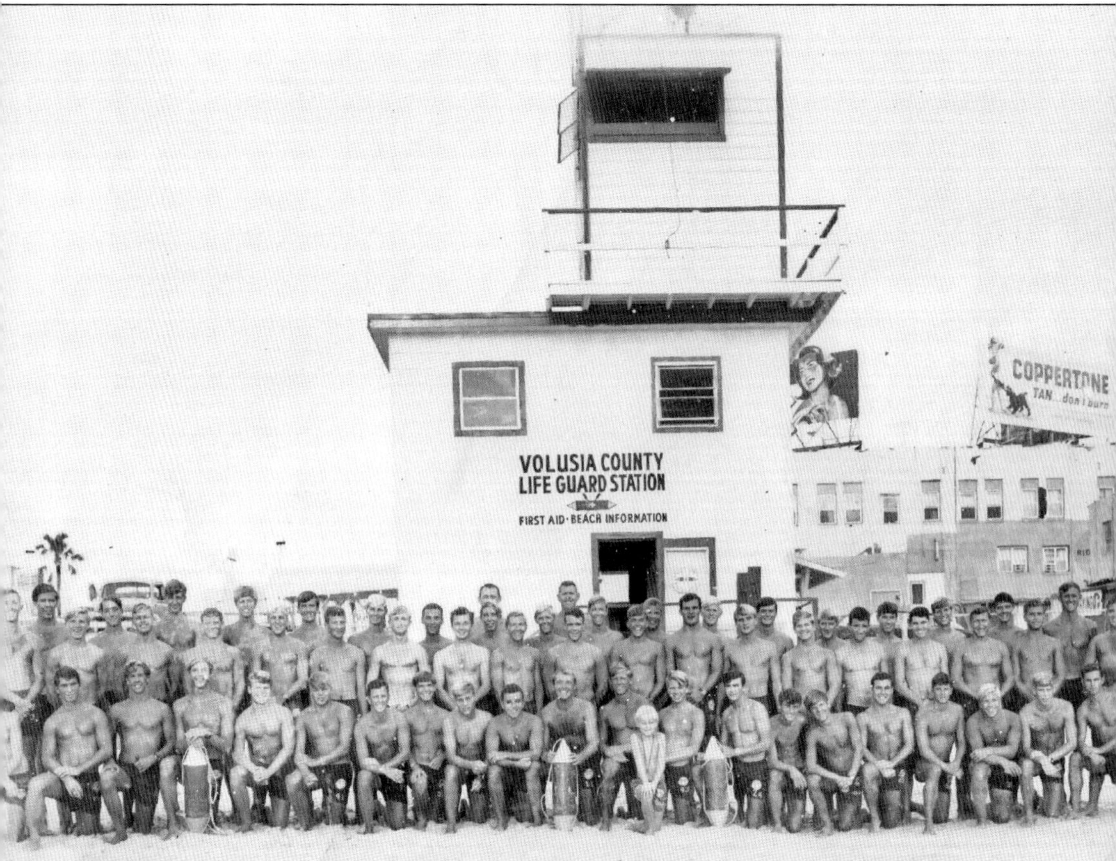

The Volusia County Beach Patrol, class of 1968, lines up in front of headquarters.

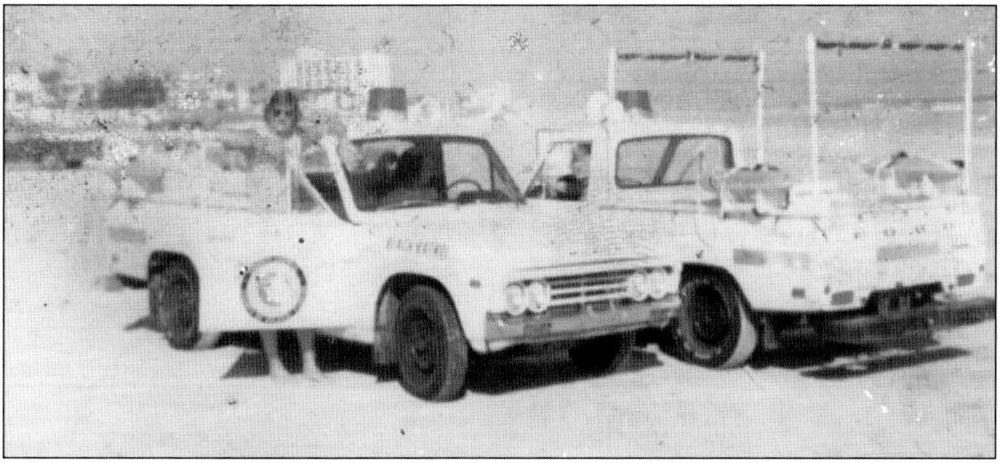

Bob Michaud talks with another lifeguard south of Main Street Pier. This 1971 photograph shows the county emblem on the truck. Funds were still low, and Hutton and Wheeler frequently purchased the fleet vehicles at auction, resulting in a variety of trucks and Jeeps on the beach.

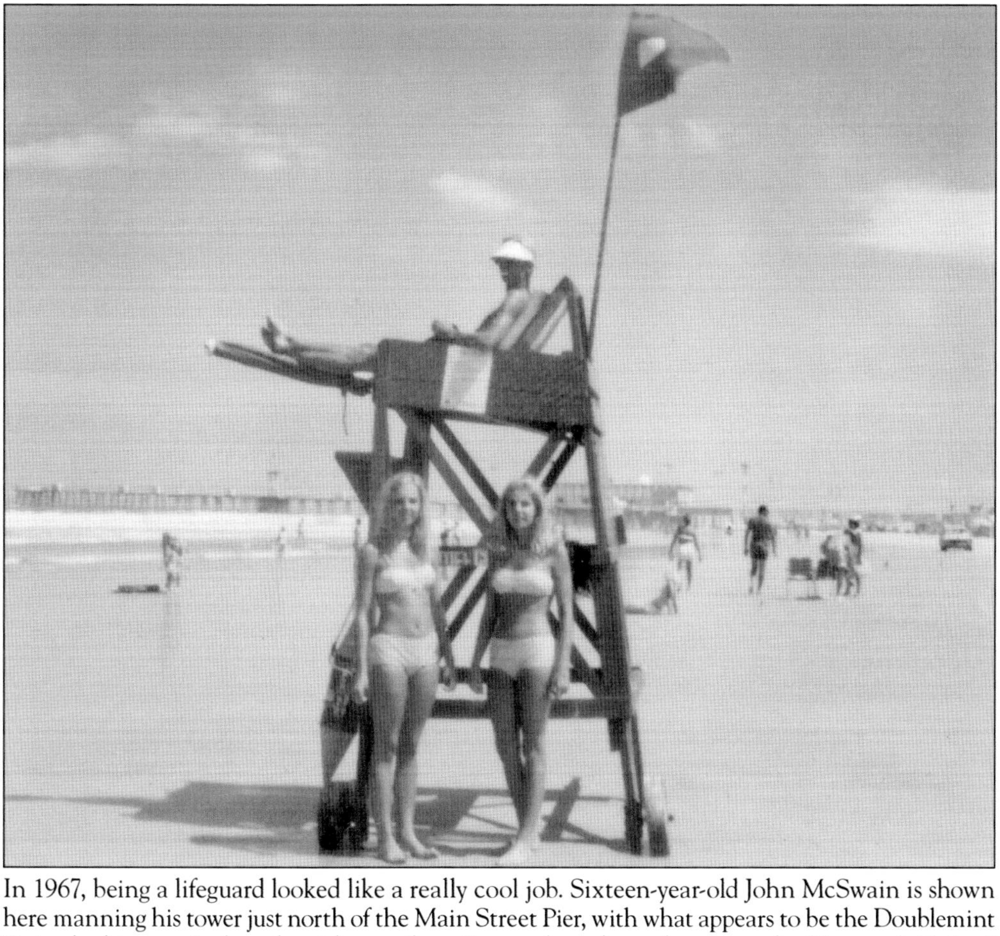

In 1967, being a lifeguard looked like a really cool job. Sixteen-year-old John McSwain is shown here manning his tower just north of the Main Street Pier, with what appears to be the Doublemint Twins looking on. In fact, the girls were from Pensacola and were known as the "Pensacola Twins." (Courtesy of John McSwain.)

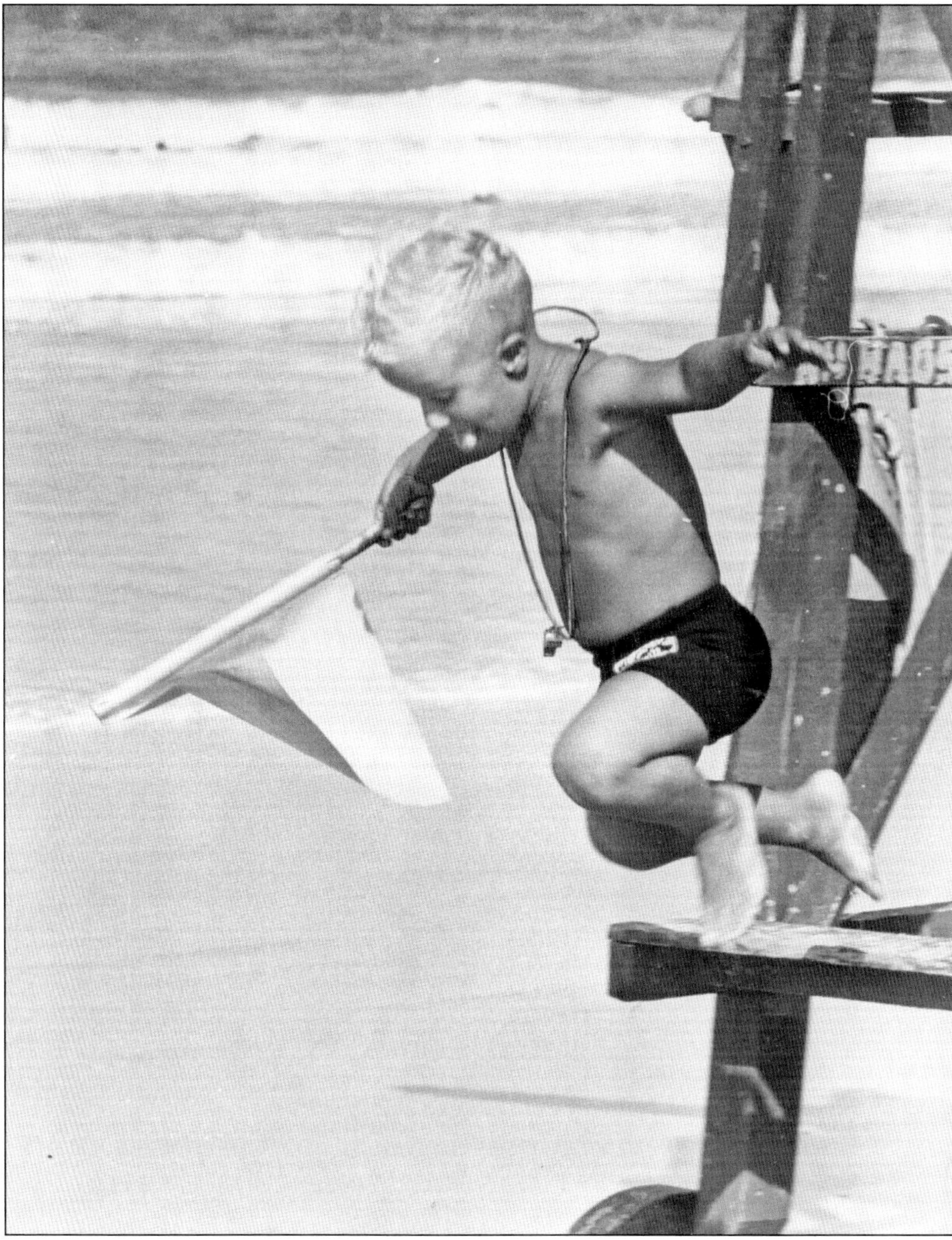

Jim Cook was an unofficial mascot for the beach patrol. He was given an honorary patch for his trunks, and he kept his whistle and flag close by in case of an emergency. Cook is a feature in the annual group photographs for several years, including 1968. (Courtesy of Bob Wheeler.)

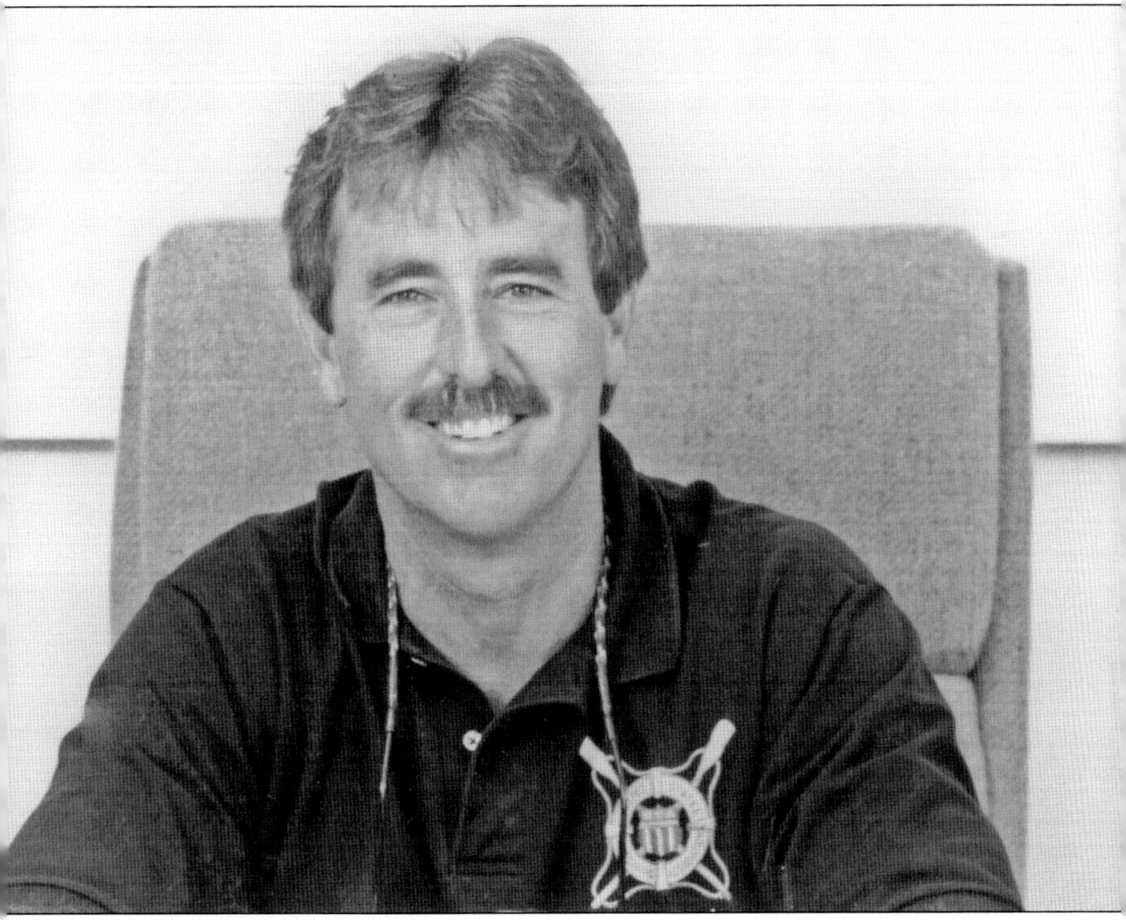

Called the foundation of the beach patrol as it stands today, Tom Renick is a legend of the VCBP. Renick moved to Daytona Beach from Fort Meade, Maryland, in 1963. He took a summer job with the beach patrol after graduating Mainland High School in 1969 and went on to become beach director in 1995, seeing his force through the 1996 reorganization, which required cross training for lifeguards to become law enforcement officers. A founding member of the U.S. Lifesaving Association and the South Atlantic regional president, Renick helped establish the nationwide standard, including training, minimum requirements, and exchange and certification programs. After his untimely death in 2001 at age 51, the Beach Policy Advisory Board unanimously recommended naming the Ormond-by-the-Sea beach park in his honor.

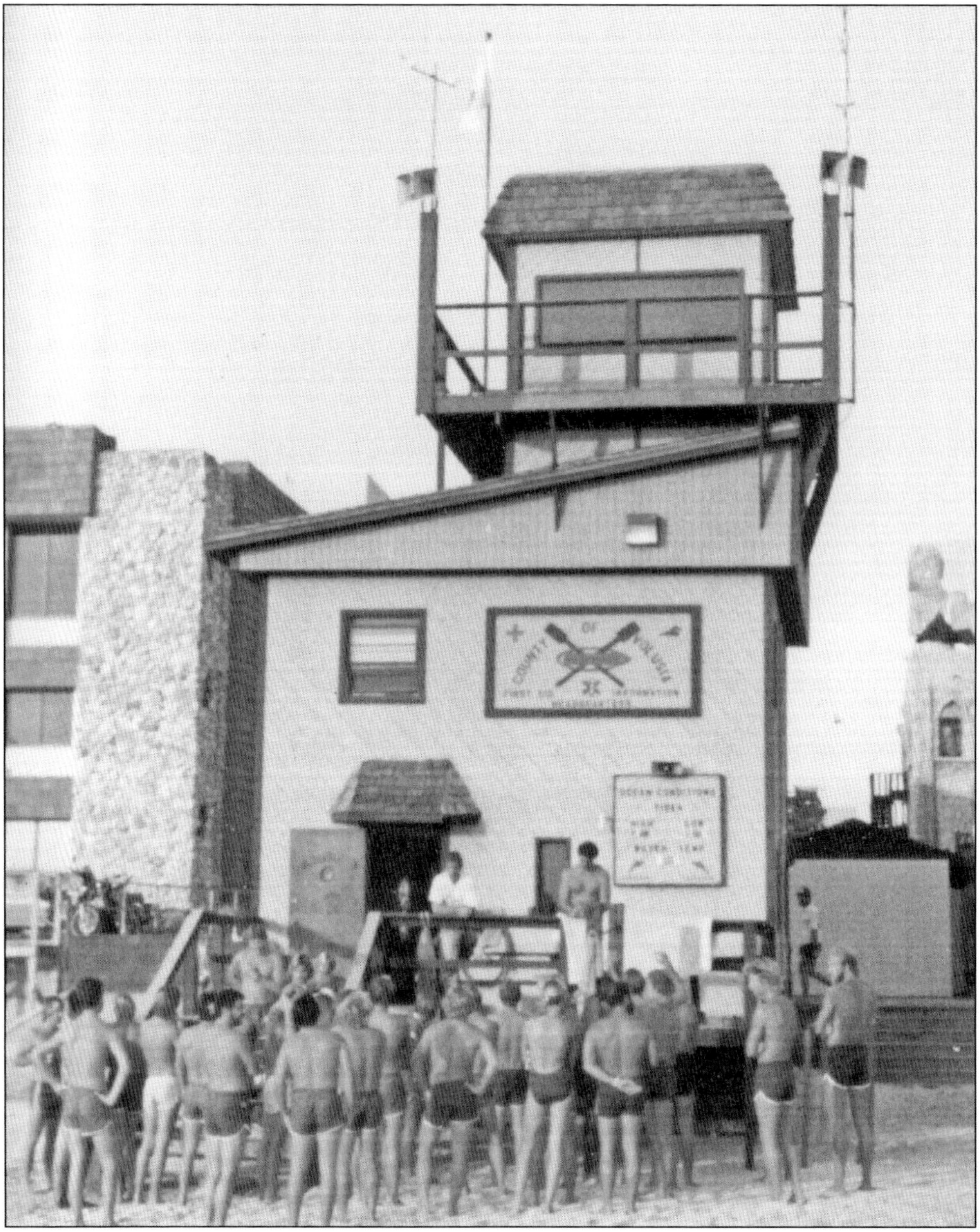

Prior to the 1980s, drill was held weekly, an information/social gathering session for updates on rules, policies, and schedules for the beach, followed by a half-mile swim and run. Near the end of the 1980s, the daily drill required all guards to show up and work out together before heading off to their designated towers. Pictured here conducting the weekly morning drill are, from left to right (on deck), Roger Barger, Tom Renick, and John Crisp.

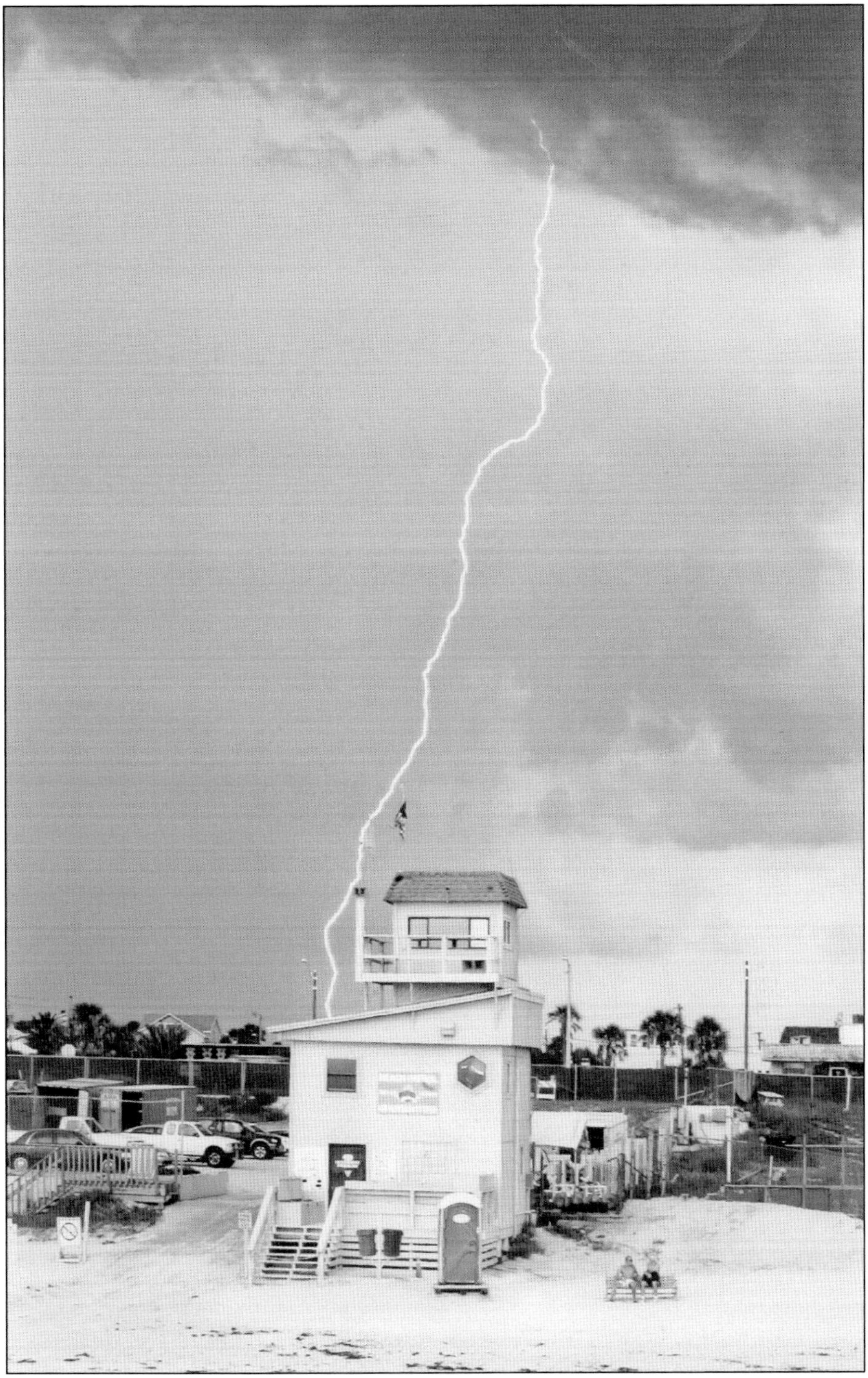

Along with normal concerns of rip currents and shark bites, lifeguards have to be aware of changing weather conditions—and storms can develop quickly. Here a lightning strike is captured by photographer Jim Tiller. Apparently the storm approached so rapidly that the two people sitting on the bench were unaware of the impending danger, as lightning can travel through wet sand.

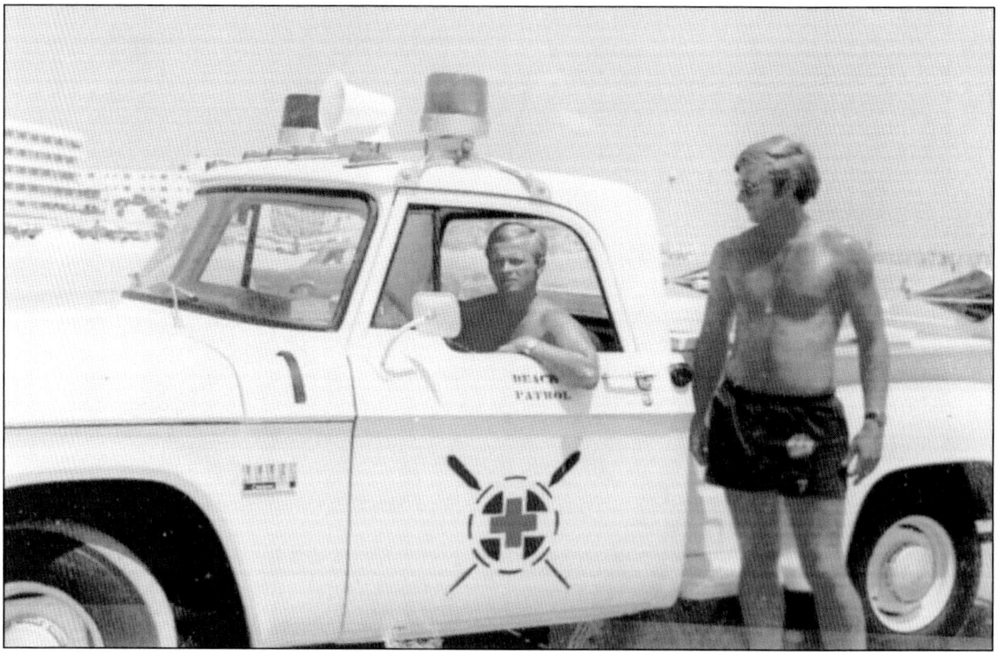

Capt. Dave Webster (left) talks with Capt. Ken Edwards in this photograph taken around 1969. The number one on the truck signifies zone one, Daytona Beach.

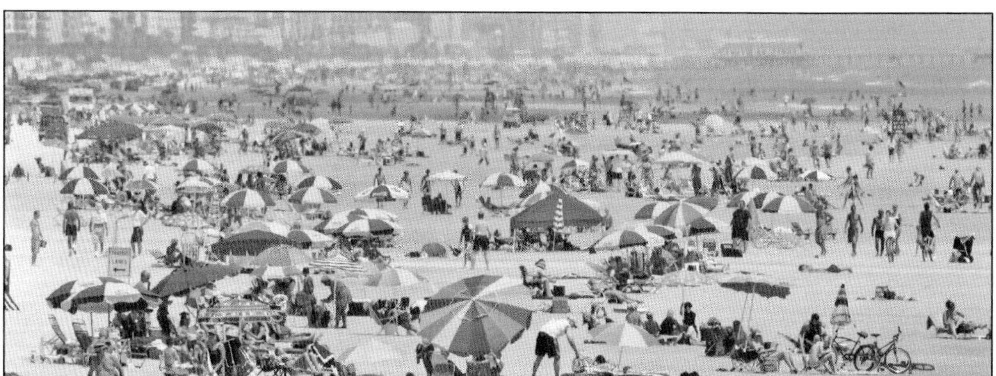

Daytona Beach proper is not the only stretch of Volusia County beaches that draws a crowd. This picture, taken from the Dunlawton Pier northward, shows the vast crowds of people, cars, and umbrellas on the miles of sand between it and the Main Street Pier.

Jim Willits, son of Charles "Billy" Willits (beach patrol member 1944–1949), began lifeguarding at age 17, working full-time until 1974, when he joined a branch of the county working in beach safety, including fire, EMS, medical examiner, emergency management, animal control, and corrections. In the 1990s, he was the fire department director. Willits is now a retired public protection director. Here he picks up man-of-war stingrays, which were then buried in an effort to clean up the beach and prevent stings. (Courtesy of Jim Willits.)

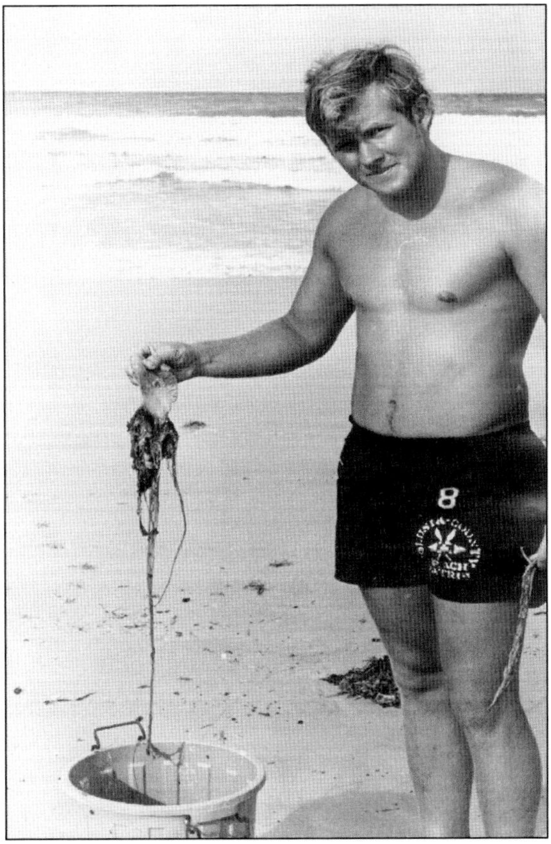

Jan Olson is living proof that being a lifeguard has its privileges. This 1974 picture shows the signs of the times—vans, tans, and surfboards.

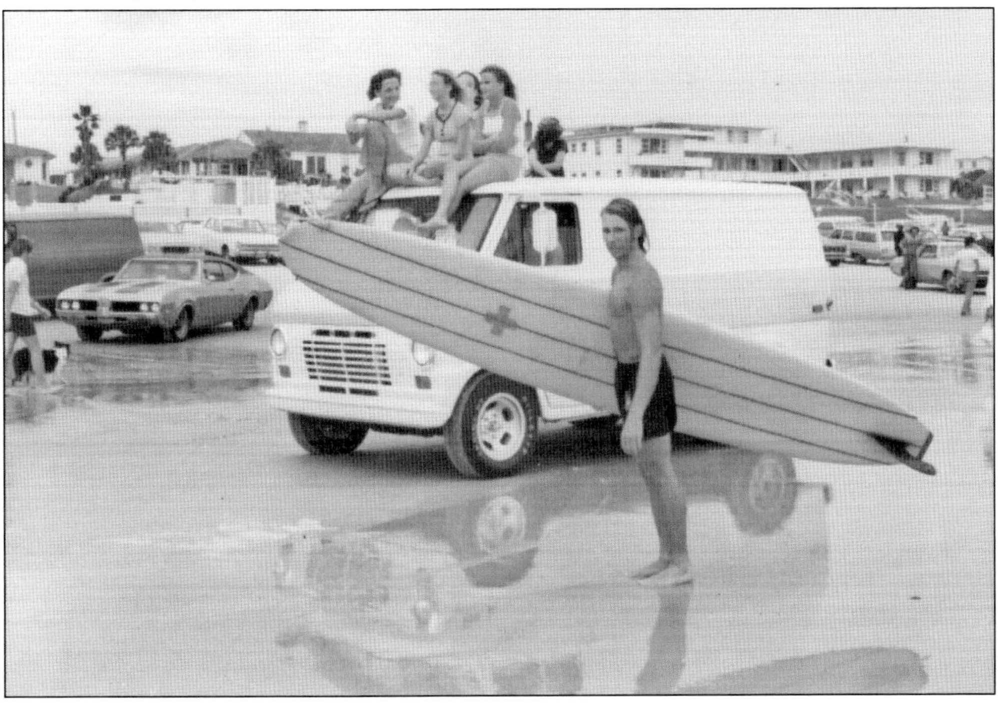

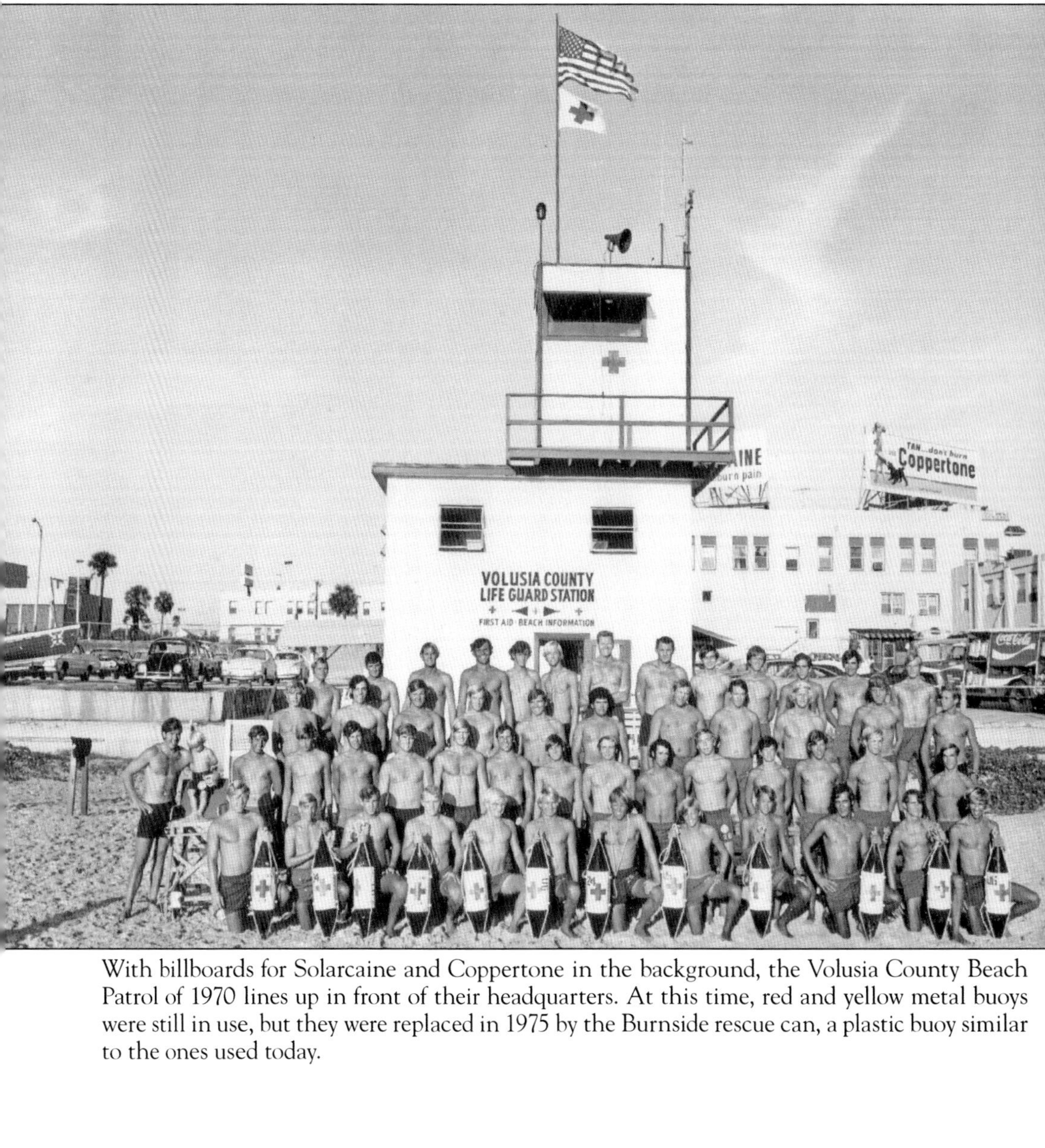

With billboards for Solarcaine and Coppertone in the background, the Volusia County Beach Patrol of 1970 lines up in front of their headquarters. At this time, red and yellow metal buoys were still in use, but they were replaced in 1975 by the Burnside rescue can, a plastic buoy similar to the ones used today.

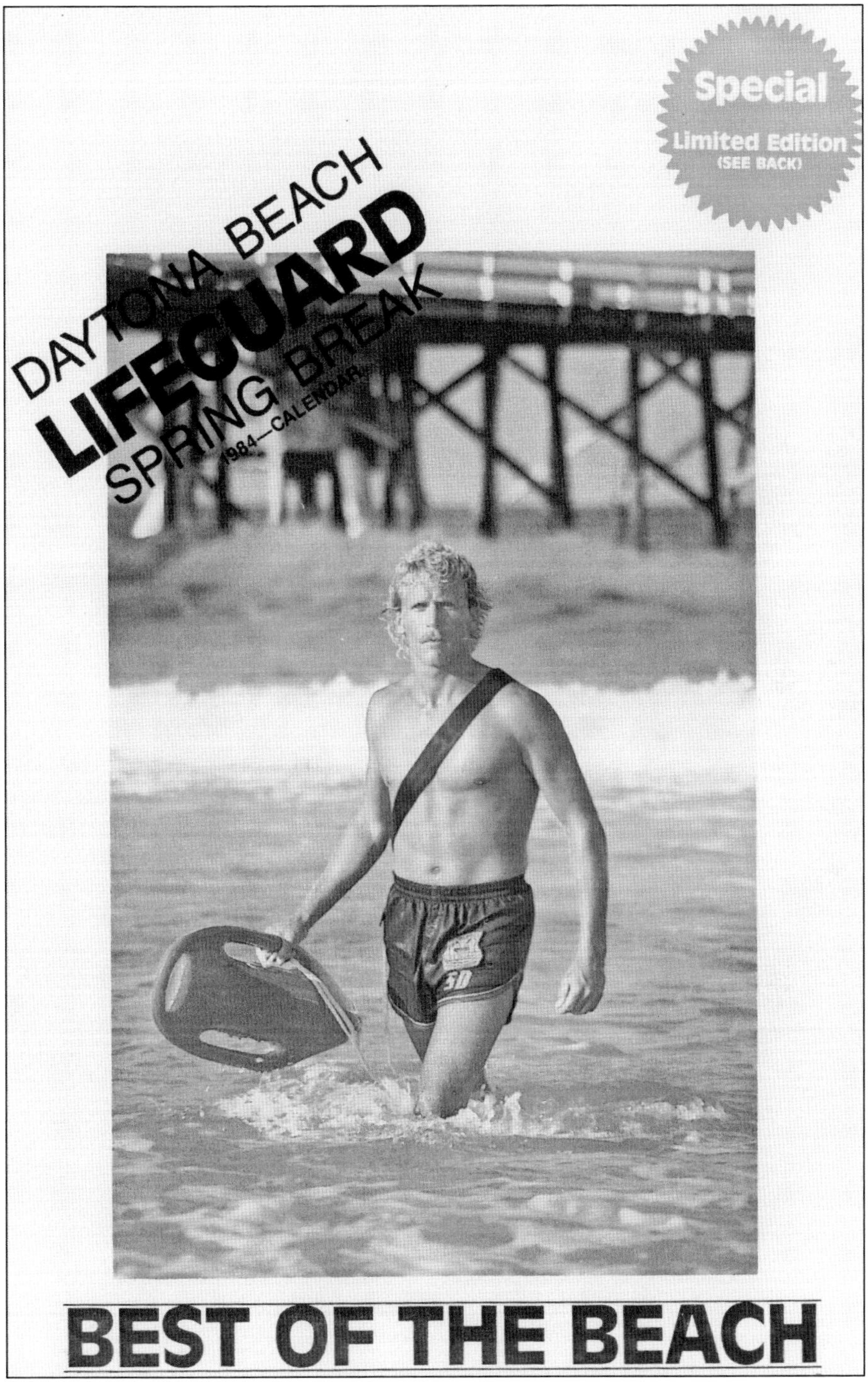

In 1984, a limited edition spring break calendar was produced featuring Daytona Beach lifeguards. With a portion of the proceeds benefiting the Volusia Surf Lifesaving Association, this was a seven-month sneak-peek calendar with plans for a 1985 release. That failed to materialize, but this collector's item featured seven of Daytona Beach's buffest of the day, including Jeffrey "J. T." Thorla, shown here in the cover shot.

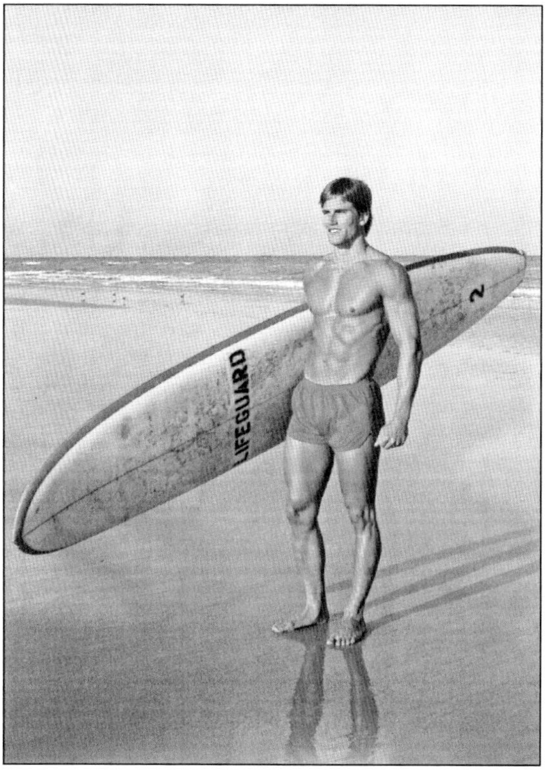

Now a professional in the field of bodybuilding and training, Lee Apperson went on to appear in countless fitness and bodybuilding magazines and placed in numerous bodybuilding competitions, including Mr. Universe and Mr. America.

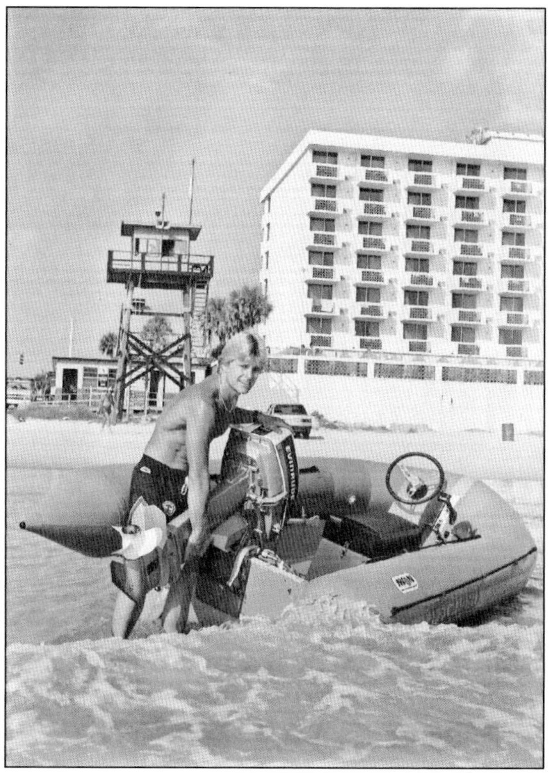

Joe Wooden enjoyed a long career with the beach patrol, representing Volusia County internationally as he studied surf lifesaving techniques and stations and developed relationships with other beach patrols.

A lieutenant with the lifeguards at the time of this photograph, Darl Bonnema had made approximately 750 rescues and participated regularly in triathlons.

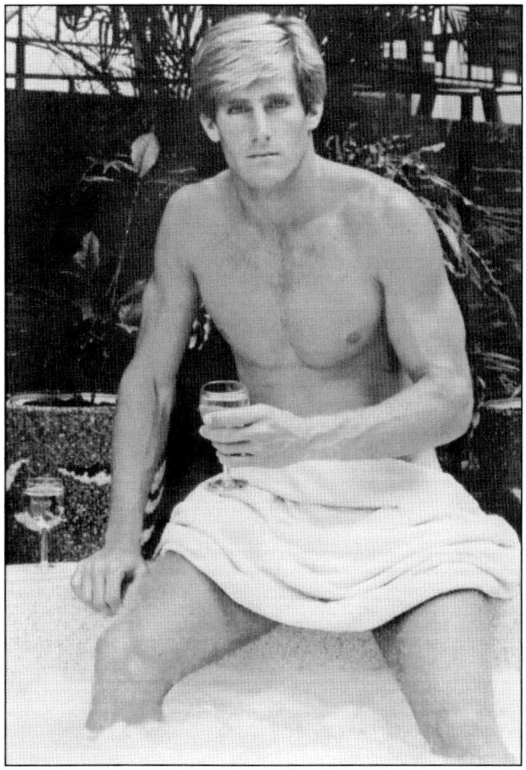

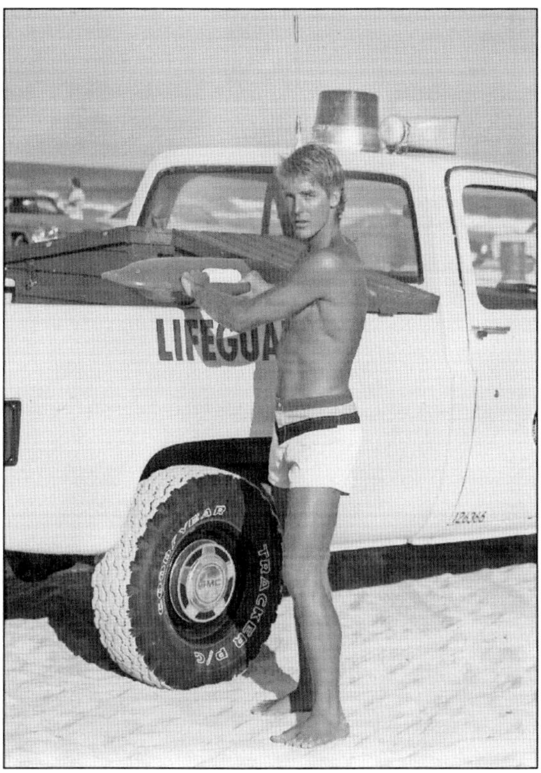

A champion surfer, Stephen "Beaver" Massfeller still resides in Daytona Beach, providing surfing instruction and camps and instilling his love and respect for the ocean in future generations.

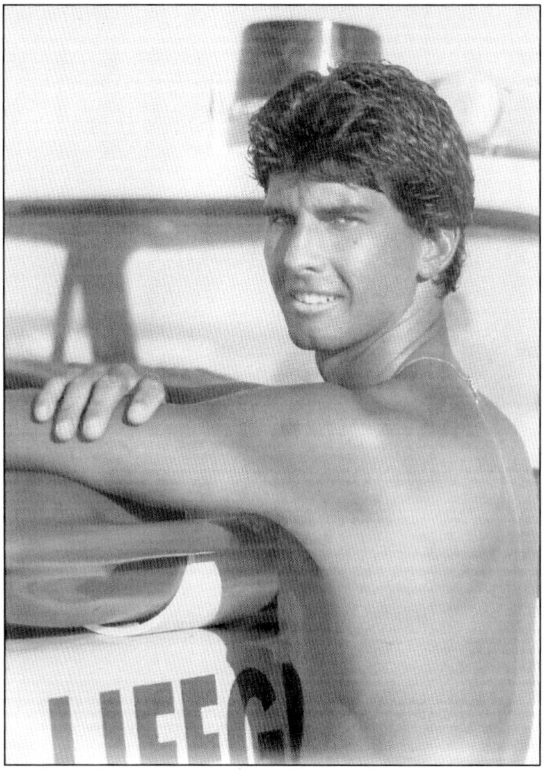

Lansing, Michigan, native Tom Fositz spent three years as a guard. He still resides in Ormond Beach, where he is a contractor.

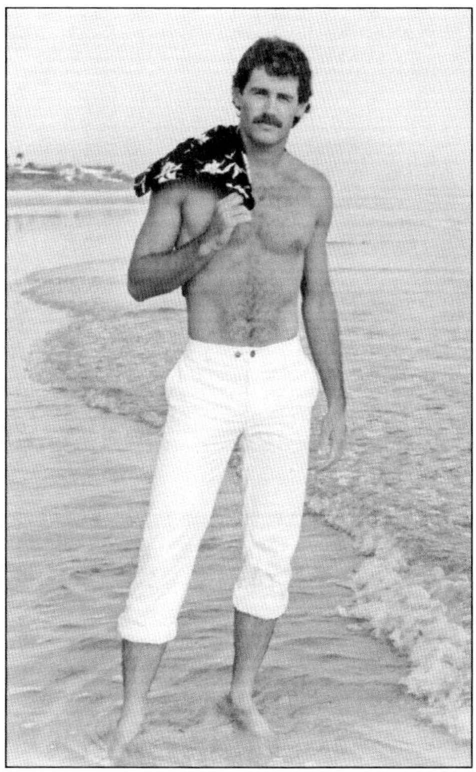

Mark Pyles had only been a guard for one year when the 1984 spring break calendar was issued, but he had already made 20 rescues. He currently works as a career firefigther in North Carolina.

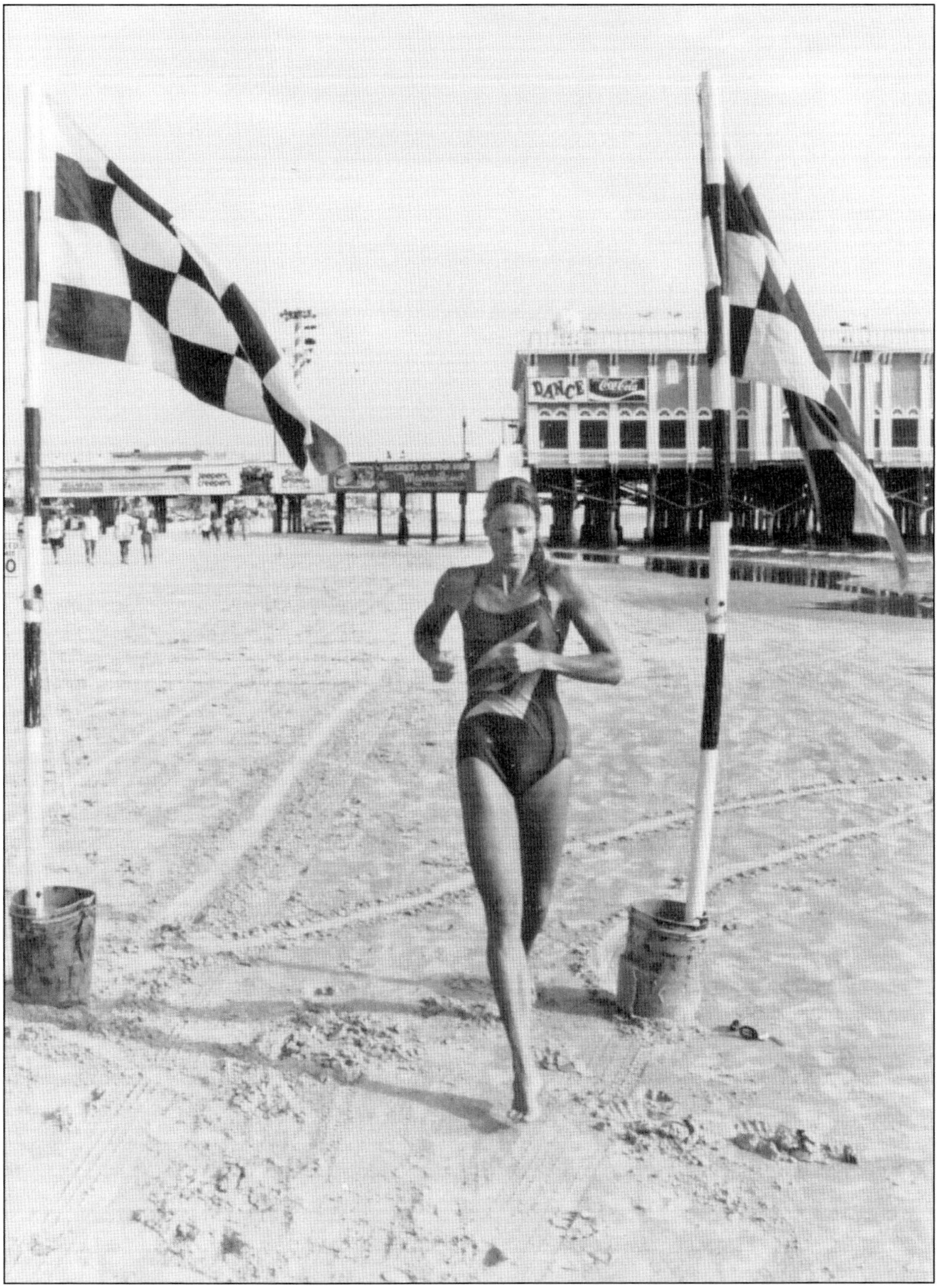

Although Laura Sherrill (photograph unavailable) was the first female lifeguard hired by the Volusia County Beach Patrol, Kathy Martin Shulzinsky was the first woman to become a career beach patrol officer. Shulzinsky joined the force in 1979, working every station from North County to New Smyrna Beach and filling every station crew position at some point in her career, including her current position at the beach patrol headquarters. Here she competes in a relay in the early 1990s.

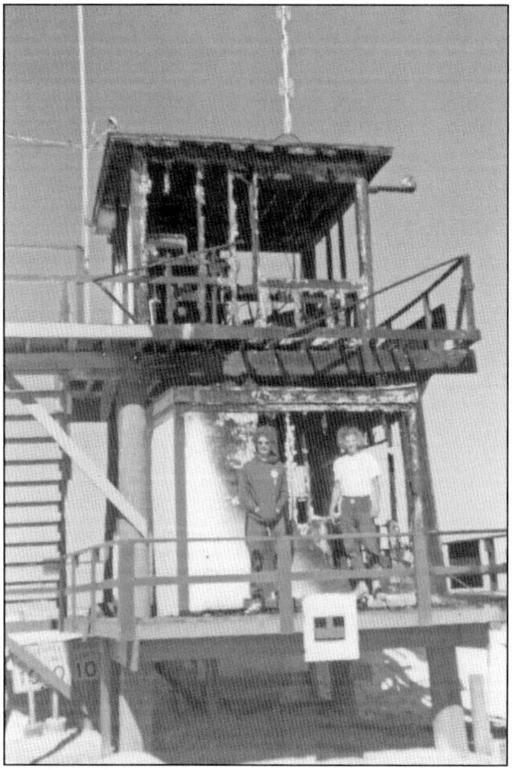

In the early 1980s, the Dunlawton Station burned down, probably due to an electrical problem. It was eventually rebuilt by the county, but in the meantime, the guards worked from a trailer placed between pilings. They also operated out of the Pirate's Cove Motel while the county rebuilt the station. Here lifeguards Bill Franklin and Paul Pivec assess the damages.

Parked in front of the headquarters just south of the Main Street Pier, this yellow truck is part of the evolution of the vehicles, equipment, and colors of the beach patrol. The truck is called 1-Bravo, taking its name from the zone (Daytona Beach was zone one); Alpha was the first in the two-truck fleet, Bravo the second. It was equipped with plastic buoys, oxygen, a backboard (or spine board), and a first aid kit. The first walkie-talkie on the beach was carried by Tim Cunningham in 1973.

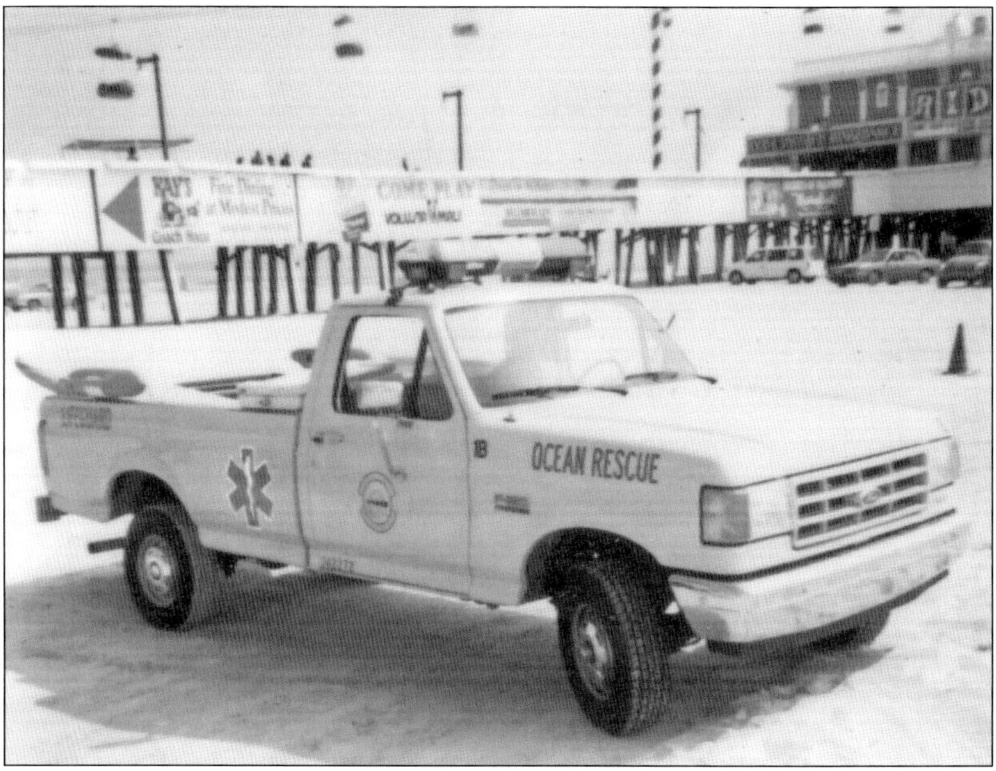

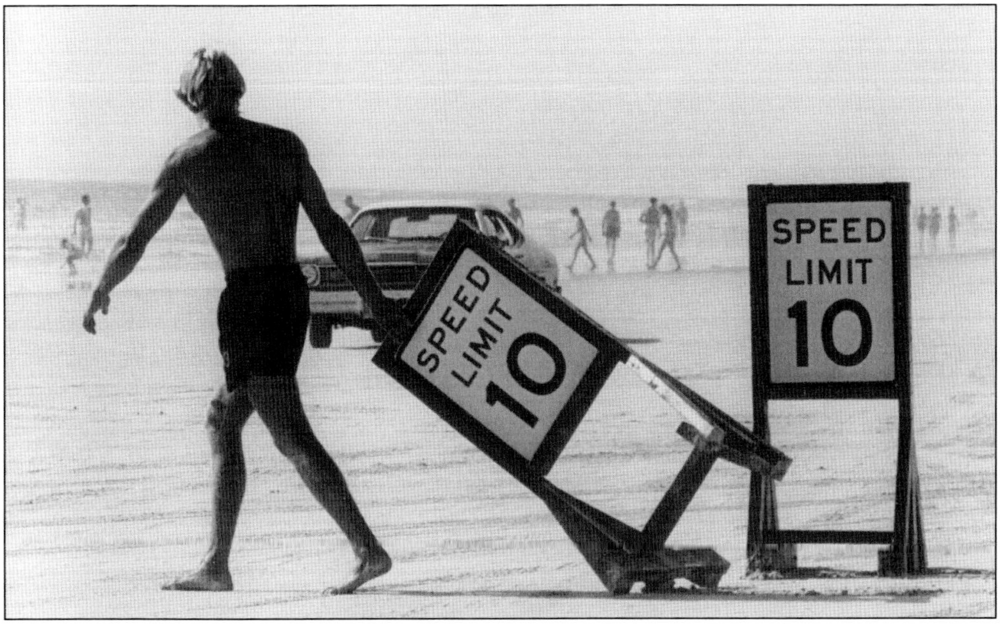

With cars on the beach, lifeguarding responsibilities and potential casualties increase. These signs warn of a 10-mile-per-hour speed limit. Here Paul Rice, now a prominent Daytona Beach attorney, moves the signs in accordance with the advancing tides.

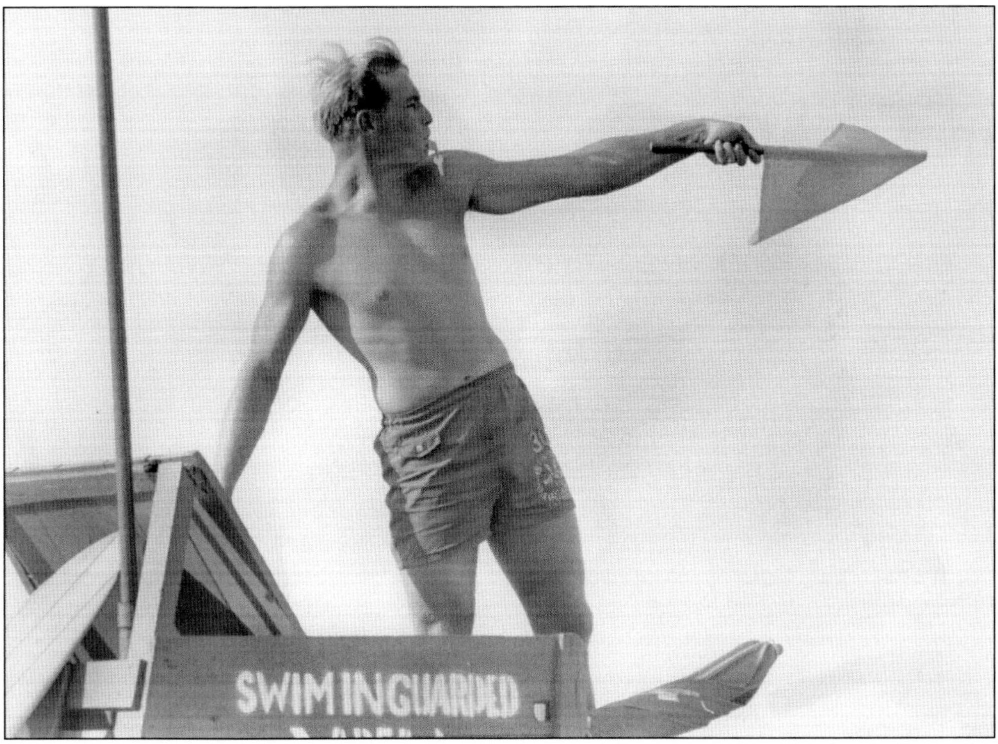

Charles "Rick" Graf waves a swimmer closer to shore in this 1970s photograph. With riptides being a major issue on the beaches of Volusia County, the guards try to spot potential risk areas and prevent problems. Signals involve flags and a series of whistles. (Courtesy of Charles Graf.)

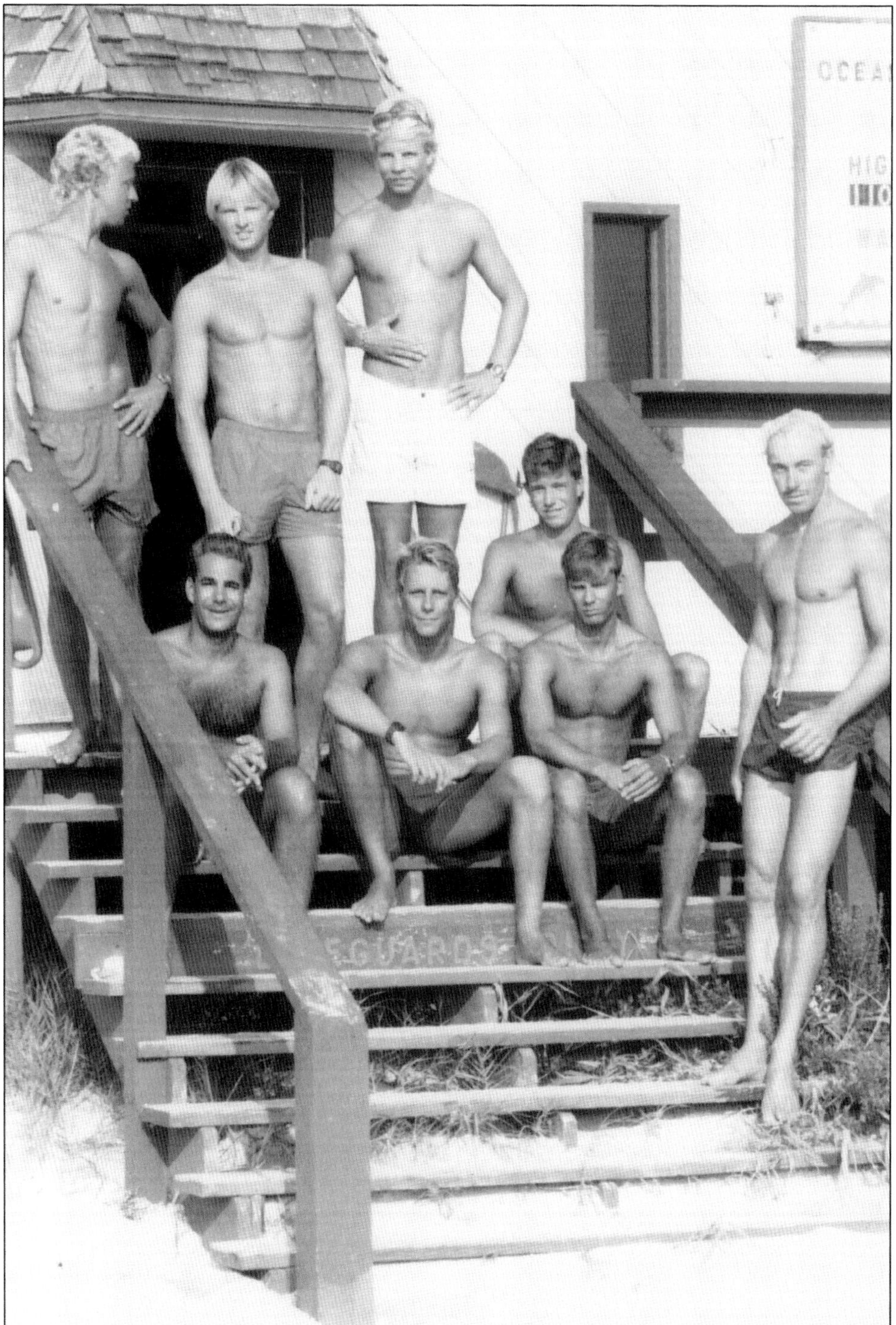

Nominees for 1987 lifeguard of the year gather on the steps of the beach patrol headquarters. They are, from left to right, (first row) Chris Foti, David France, Francis Burns, Jerry Mardquardt, and Daryl Stone; (second row) John Andrus, Pat Cole, and Fred Bauld. Not pictured is assistant chief John Crisp.

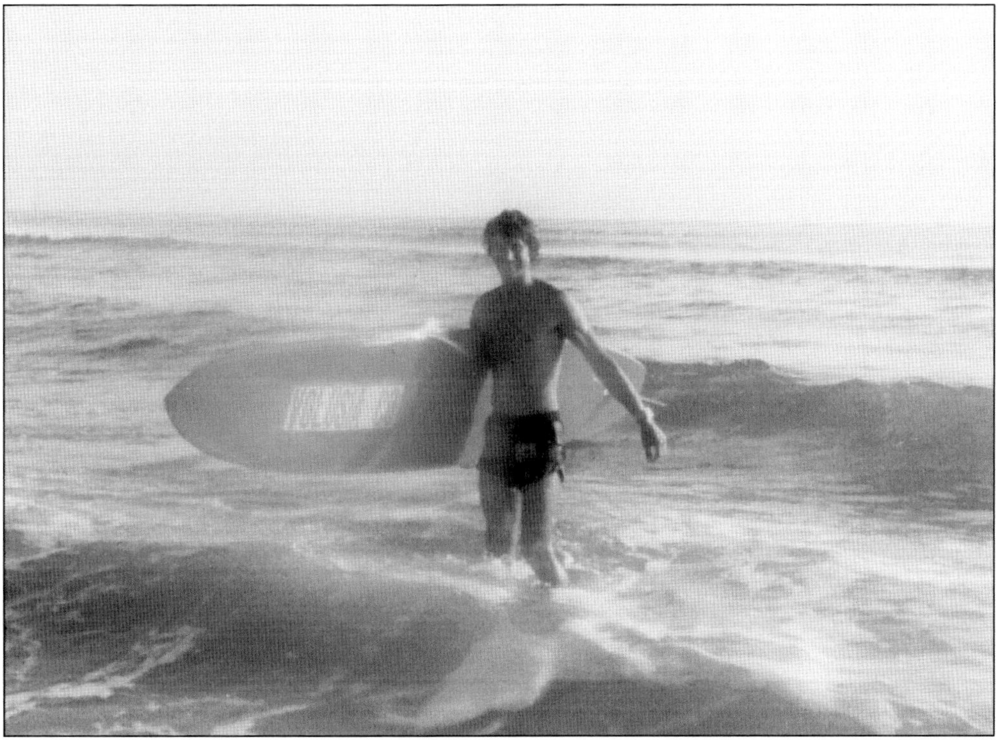

Marlin Poage keeps his surfing chops up. Being adept with a surfboard can make the difference between life and death in a rescue situation.

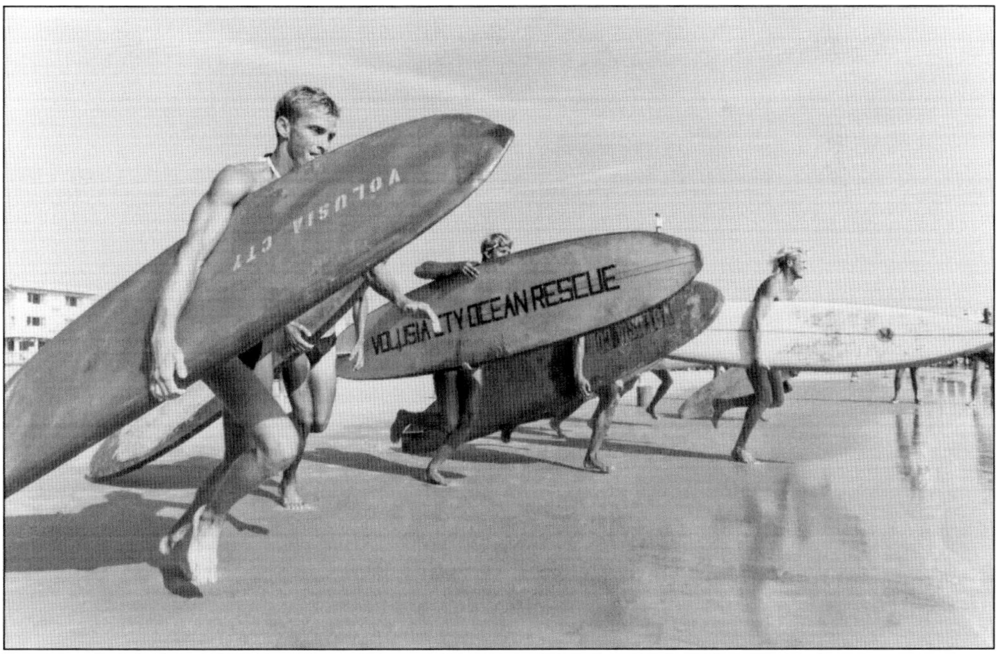

Contestants in the Ironman competition race into the surf.

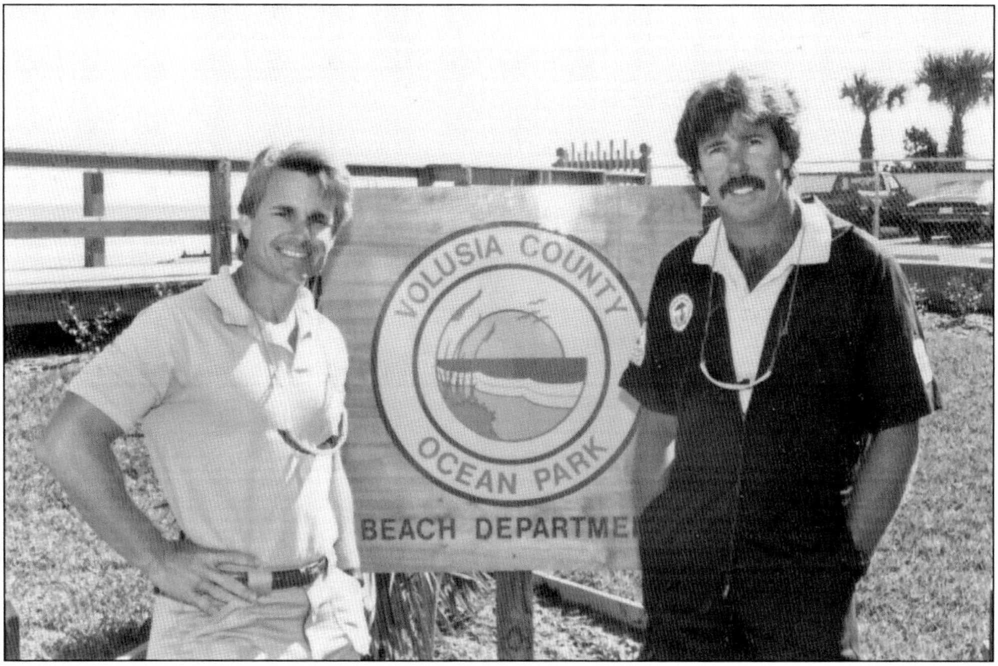

Joe Wooden and Mike Hensler, both career lifeguards with the Volusia County Beach Patrol, stand at the future home of Sun Splash Park in 1988. Now completed, the park provides beachside parking, picnic tables, restrooms, pop-up water sprays, and a playground for children. Adjacent is the new home of the Volusia County Beach Patrol, which consolidated the Main Street and Daytona Beach Shores lifeguard stations and was completed in 2007.

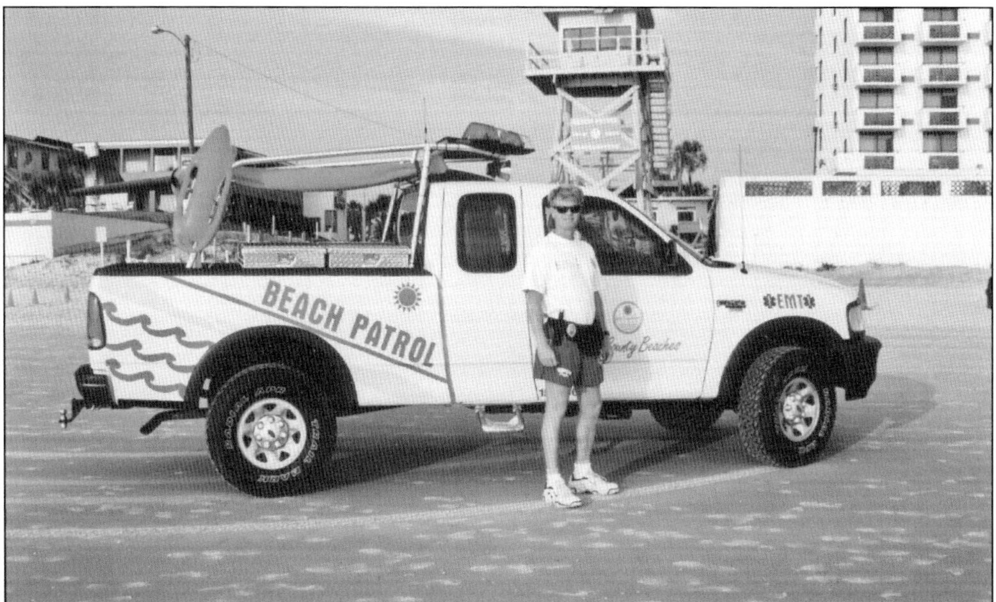

Chuck Alday stands in front of the Daytona Beach Shores lifeguard station, which was taken down in 2009 after the completion of the new facility.

Competition is a big part of the life of a lifeguard. David Schick, 1982 lifeguard of the year, anchored for the swim relays. Now a tax attorney in Orlando, Schick manned the tower at the Silver Beach approach from 1980 to 1984.

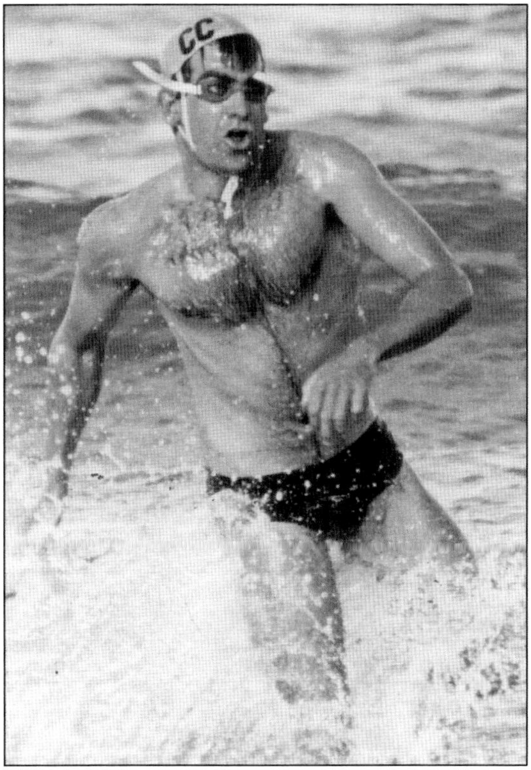

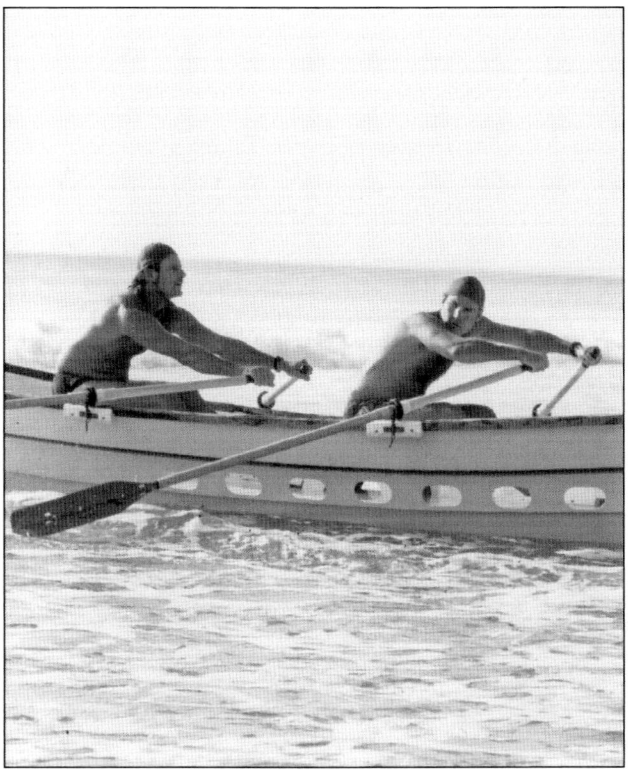

Dave Dickinson and Jeremy Surpin row a dory in a regional competition in the early 1980s. Volusia County has competed regionally, nationally, and internationally.

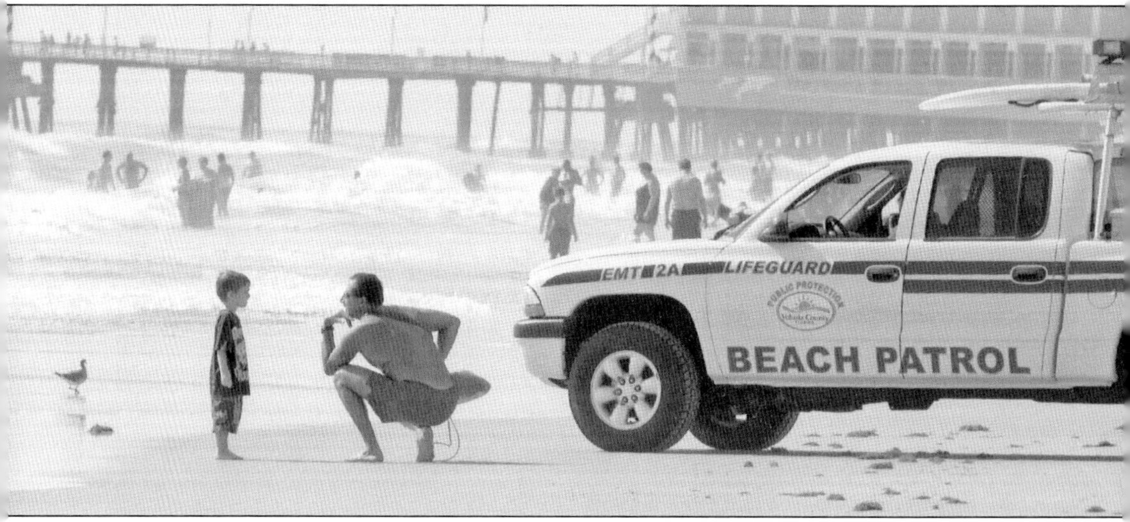

Along with all the other duties of the lifeguard, public relations and finding lost family members are on the list. Here Art Condon befriends a young beachcomber who has become separated from his family. Calls like these are common, and the guards are able to use their bird's-eye views to spot missing children and reunite them with worried parents.

Six

Training, Drills, and Rescues

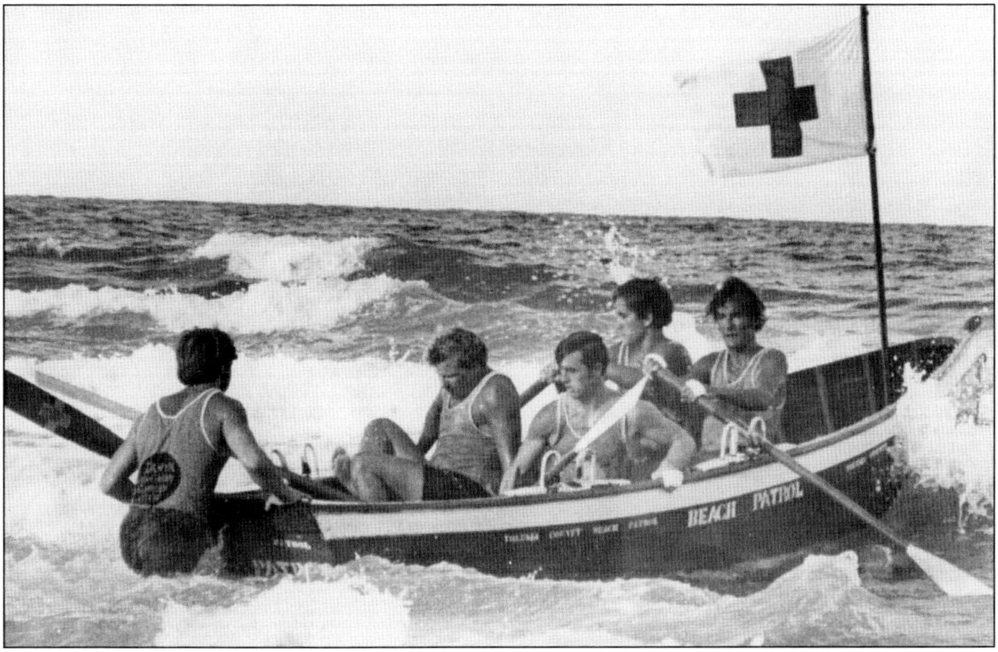

Being a lifeguard may look like a cakewalk. They get to sit on the beach all day, getting a tan, observing the indigenous wildlife, and talking to the beachgoers. But in that split second when someone's life is literally in their hands, the training, drills, and conditioning all come together in the true purpose of the profession—lifesaving. In this September 1971 photograph, from left to right, Mike Hensler, Richard Cherry, Tom Renick, Tony Stellatano, and Josh Phillips launch a lifeboat through the surf for a sea rescue.

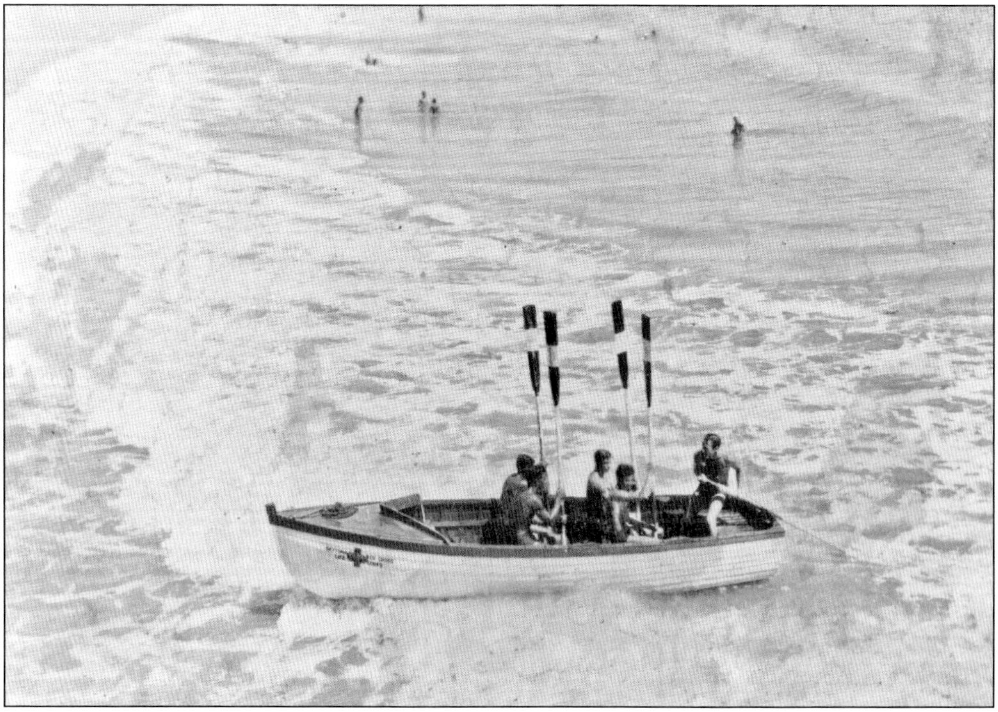

In this late 1950s photograph, a team practices a rescue. If this had been an actual event, the boat would have been backed into the water, but in practice they would "catch a wave" and ride it in. (Courtesy of Bob Wheeler.)

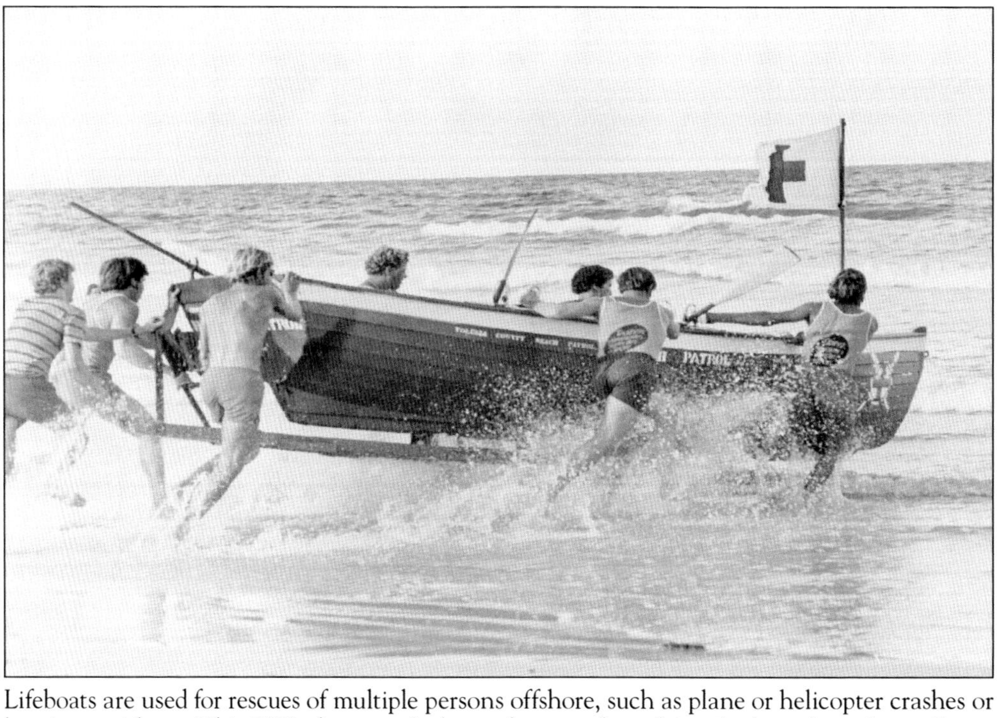

Lifeboats are used for rescues of multiple persons offshore, such as plane or helicopter crashes or boating accidents. This 1971 photograph shows the team launching the boat from the trailer.

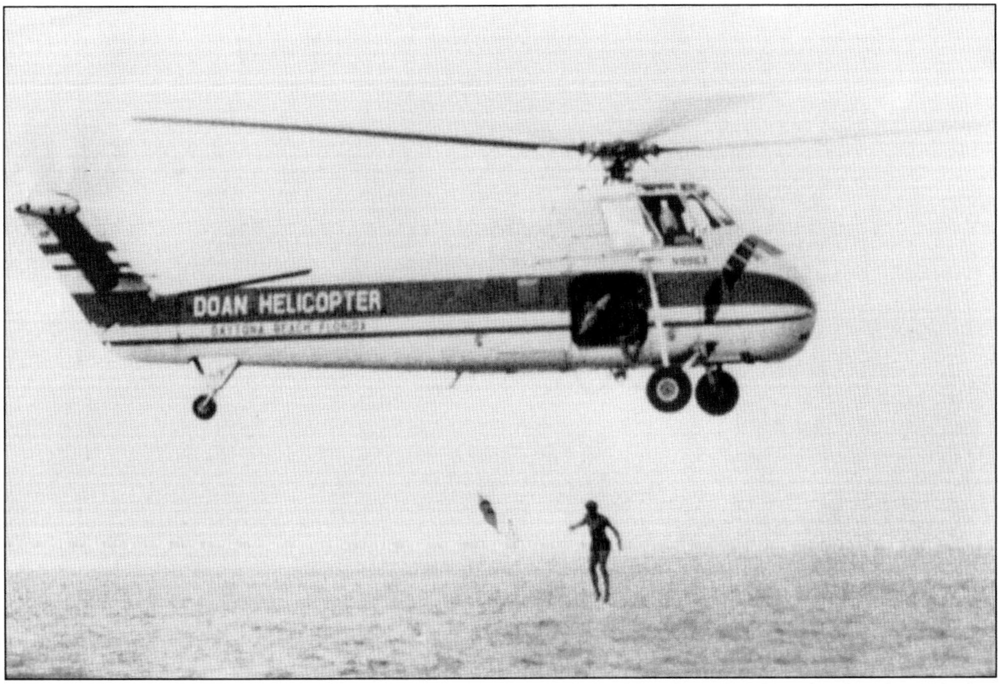

Harry Doan, owner of the Main Street Pier and longtime friend to the beach patrol, made his helicopter available whenever there was a need, including training and demonstrations. This photograph shows one of 60 lifeguards dropping into the water in an exhibit from the 1970s.

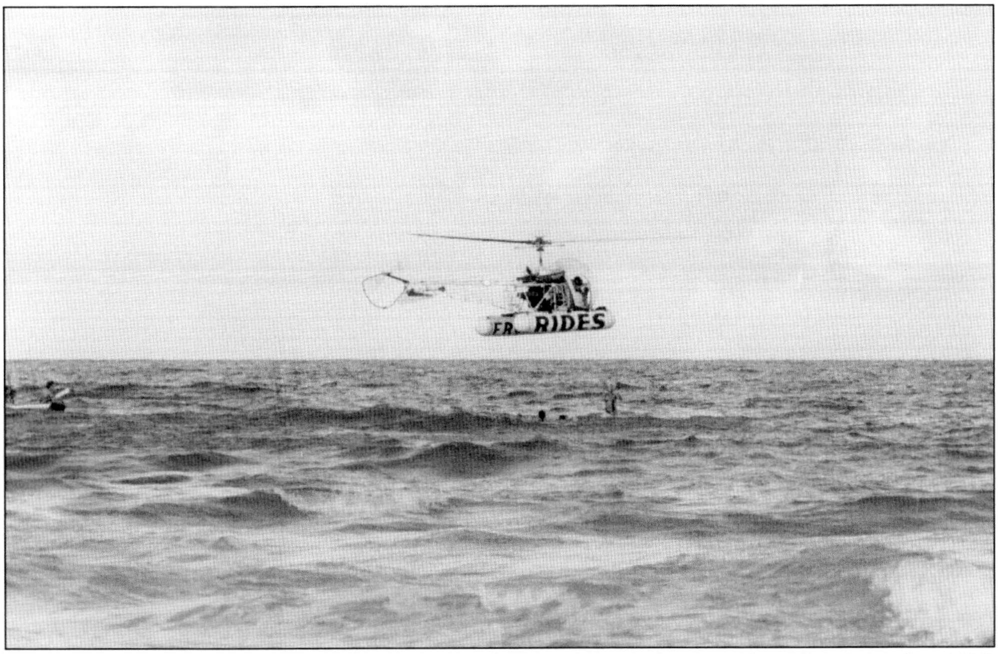

When the rescue involves multiple victims, the beach patrol responds in kind. In this 1973 rescue, lifeguards and coast guard work together, and Harry Doan lends his helicopter to the rescue efforts. Lifeguard captain Bob Wheeler dropped from the helicopter with a torpedo buoy to assist victims while lifeboats were en route.

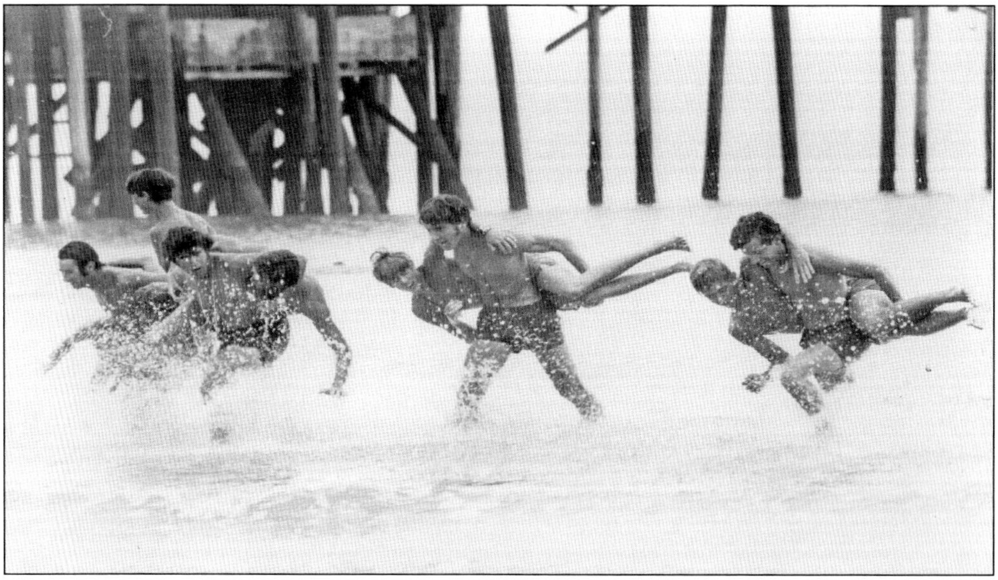

Often the victim must be physically carried to shore. These guards are practicing the saddleback carry, the fastest and most effective way to bring an unconscious or heavy victim through the surf. The fireman's carry, which involves placing the victim over the shoulders, is also used.

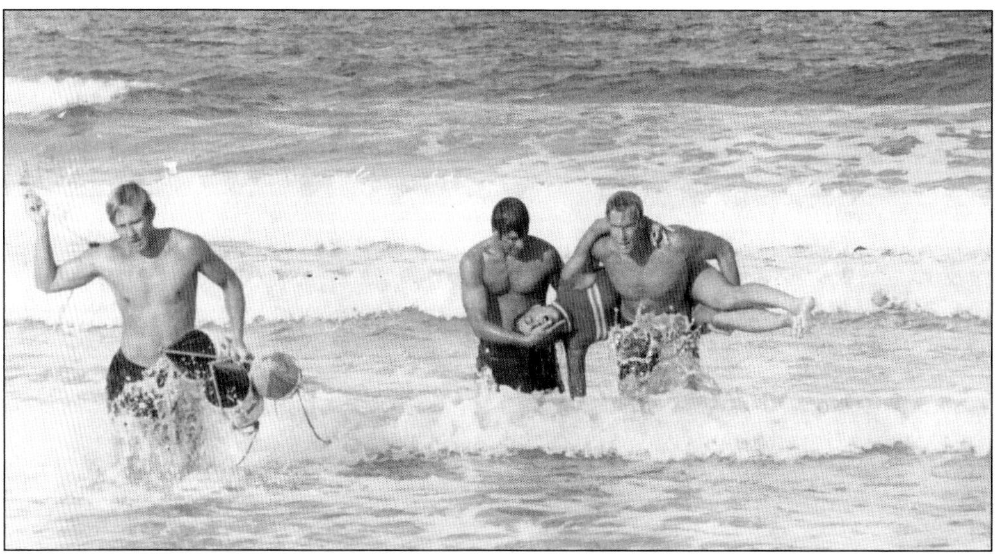

In this drill, from left to right, Jim Willits, Art Hartsell, and Charles "Rick" Graf rescue an unconscious drowning victim using the saddleback carry.

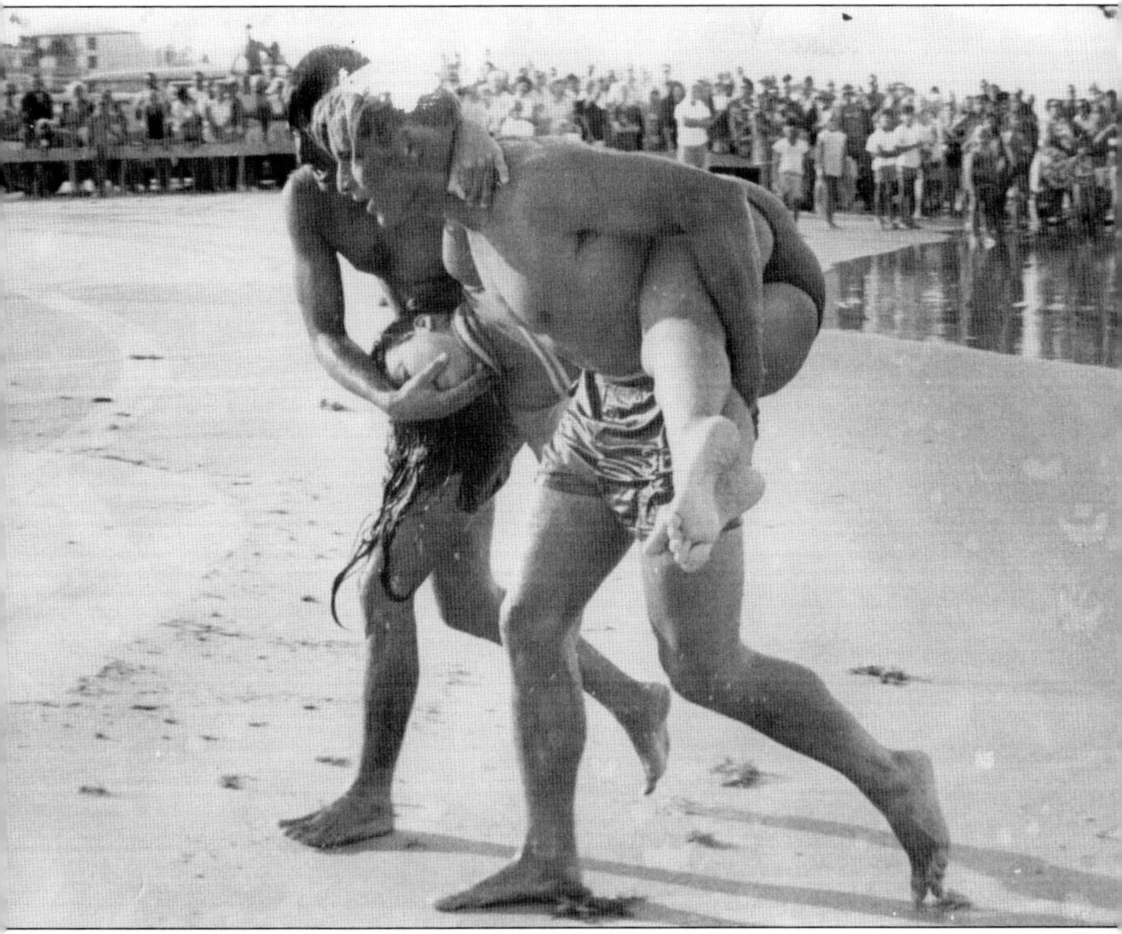

Pictured at the Volusia County Beach Patrol lifeguard demonstration on Labor Day in 1971, Charles "Rick" Graf (front) and an unidentified guard are shown performing a surf rescue demonstration. In 1971, Graf was also nominated for lifeguard of the year.

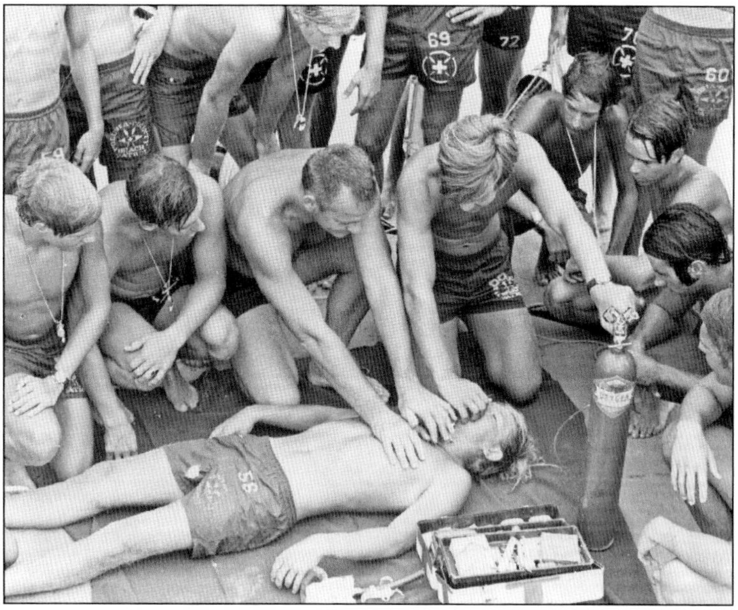

Lifeguards respond to distress calls of all sorts—water rescues, first aid, heart attacks, bites, and stings. But the guards of Daytona Beach have the added responsibility of automobile casualties. Here Bobby Pope, Gene Crouch, Bob Wheeler, and an unidentified guard demonstrate first aid and CPR as they practice resuscitation on Ron Futch in this 1973 photograph.

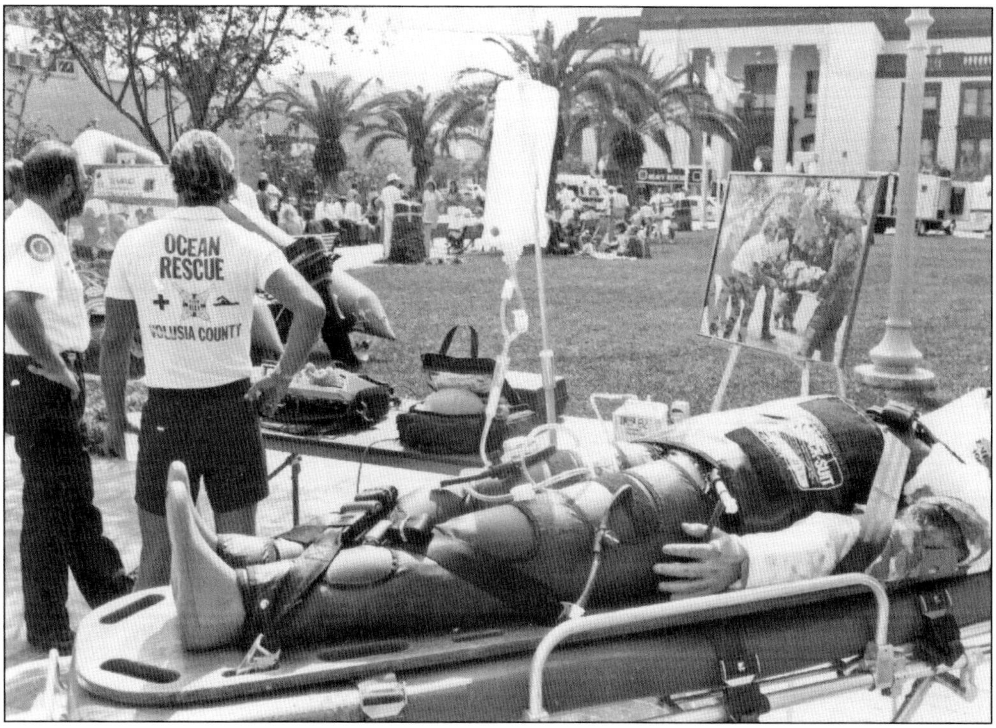

An MCI (mass casualty incident) is an emergency response involving multiple agencies. In recent years, the Volusia County Beach Patrol's demonstrations have included simulating an airplane crash on the beach. In 1991, this public safety display was held in front of the DeLand Courthouse. Visible is the Volusia County fire truck (heavy rescue vehicle). The lifeguard representing Ocean Rescue Volusia County is Darl Bonnema.

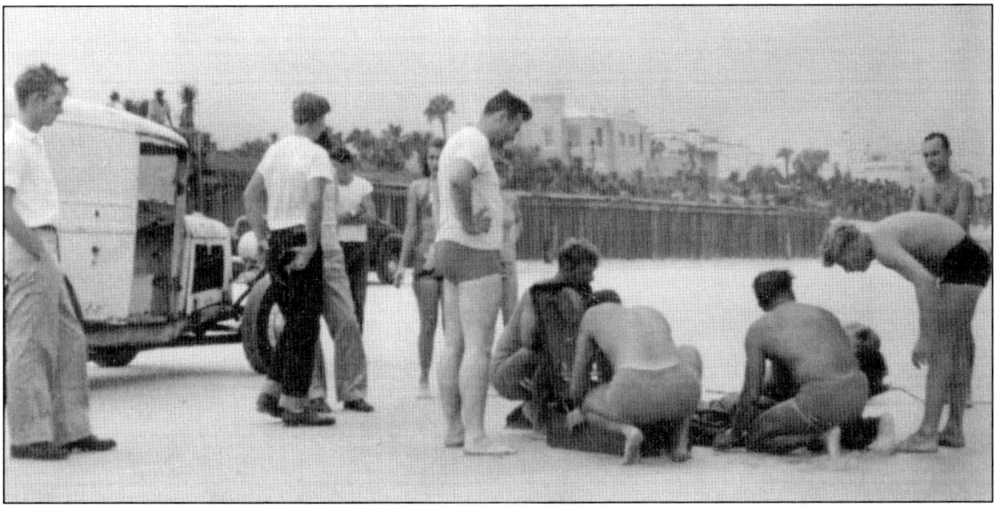

Drills and demonstrations are an important part of lifeguard training and continuing education and practice. But nothing is as intense as a real rescue. This photograph, take in the late 1940s or early 1950s, shows Edgar Pierce (far right) working to resuscitate a victim. Pierce later opened a float stand near the University Beach approach, which was the site of the first lifeguard reunion, a gathering that evolved into an annual gala.

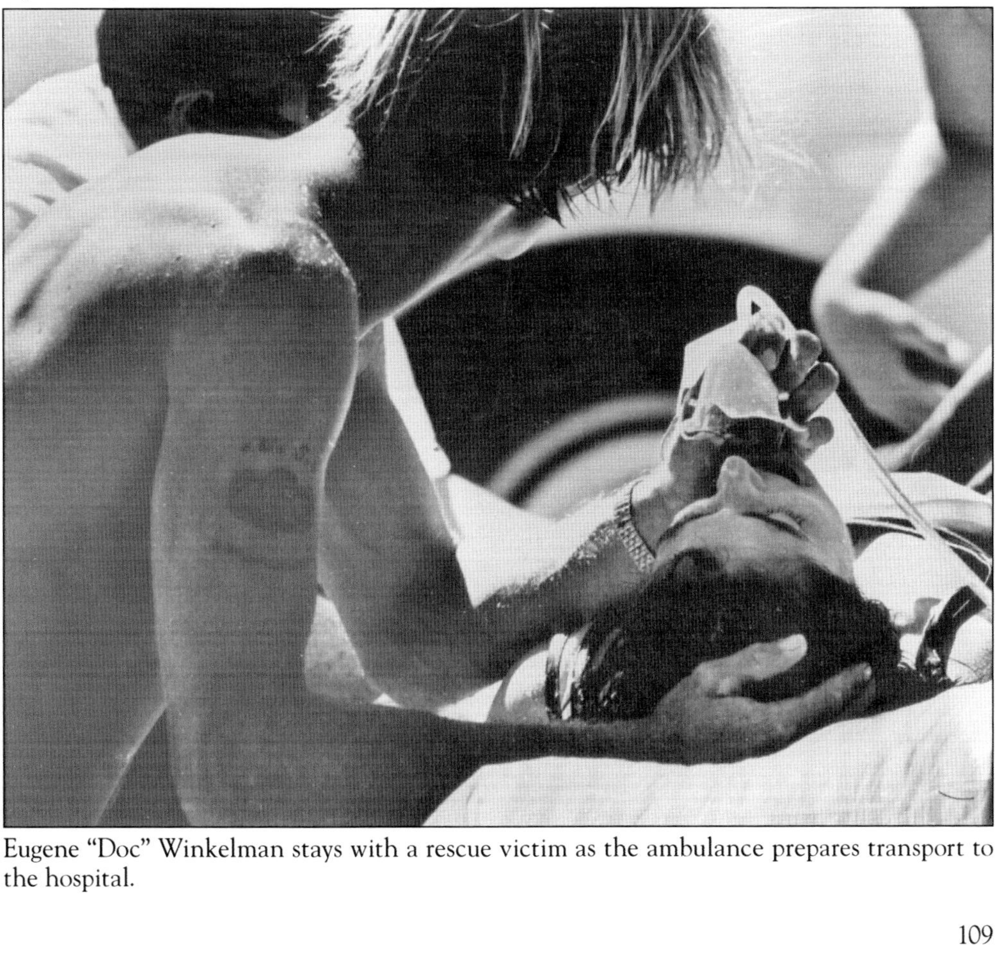

Eugene "Doc" Winkelman stays with a rescue victim as the ambulance prepares transport to the hospital.

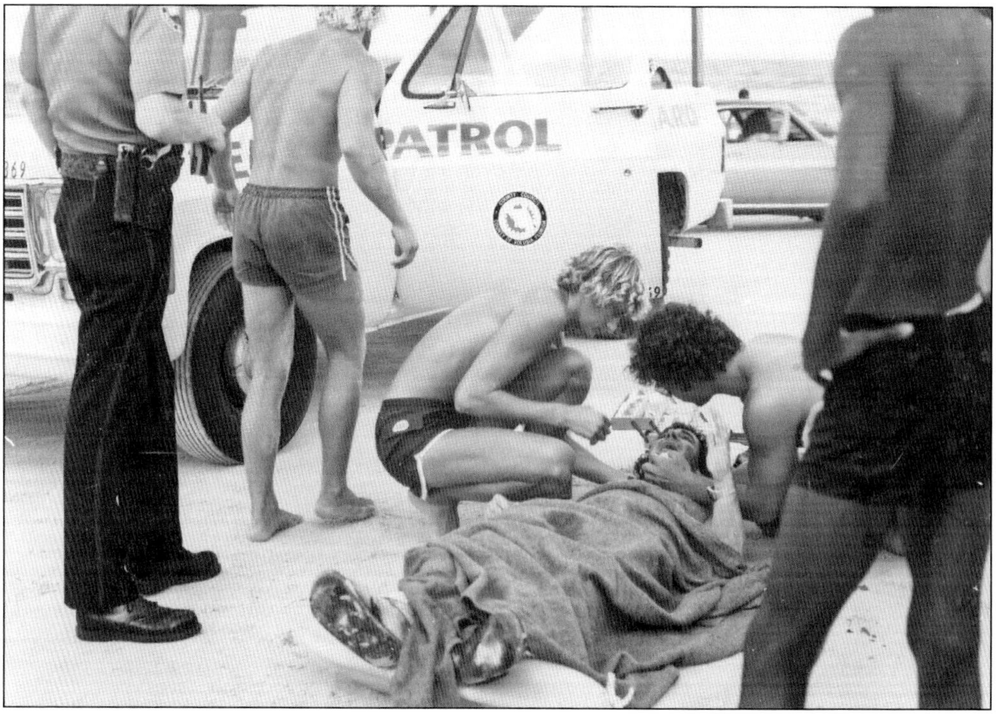

Beach patrol 1A (Daytona Beach) administers first aid, possibly stings from a man-of-war. Guards must be trained in all forms of first aid and CPR, as well as being familiar with the various biting and stinging marine life. And along with all the other calls, Volusia County Beach Patrol also responds to traffic accidents. At the time of this photograph (1975), lifeguards had no law enforcement authority; therefore, police officers were dispatched to the beach as needed.

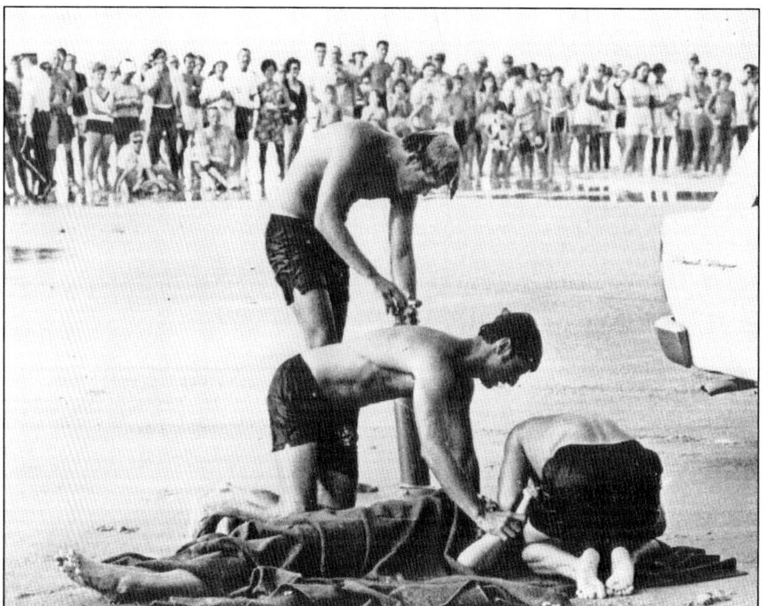

Capt. Bob Wheeler (far right) gives mouth-to-mouth resuscitation as Bill Perry (standing) prepares equipment for CPR. (Courtesy of Bob Wheeler.)

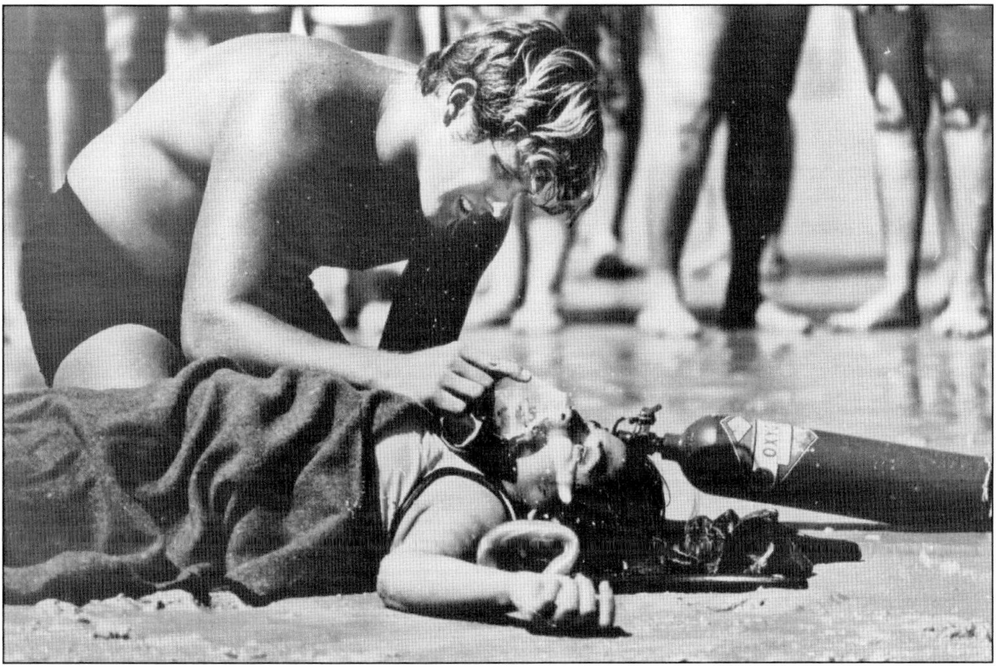

The spring of 1972 was a particularly difficult season. This spring break visitor underestimated the currents between the band shell and the Plaza Hotel near the boardwalk. A tower guard made the rescue and pulled her to shore, where Jim Willits performed CPR. The victim was transported by ambulance, and her fate is unknown.

Unfortunately, not all rescues are successful, as evidenced in this early 1970s photograph. Guards Ron Futch (left) and Scott Swain look on as medics place the drowning victim on a gurney.

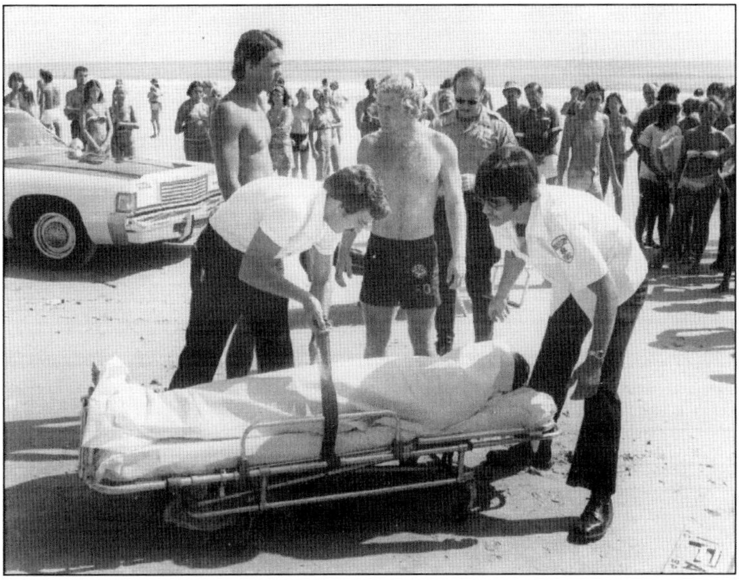

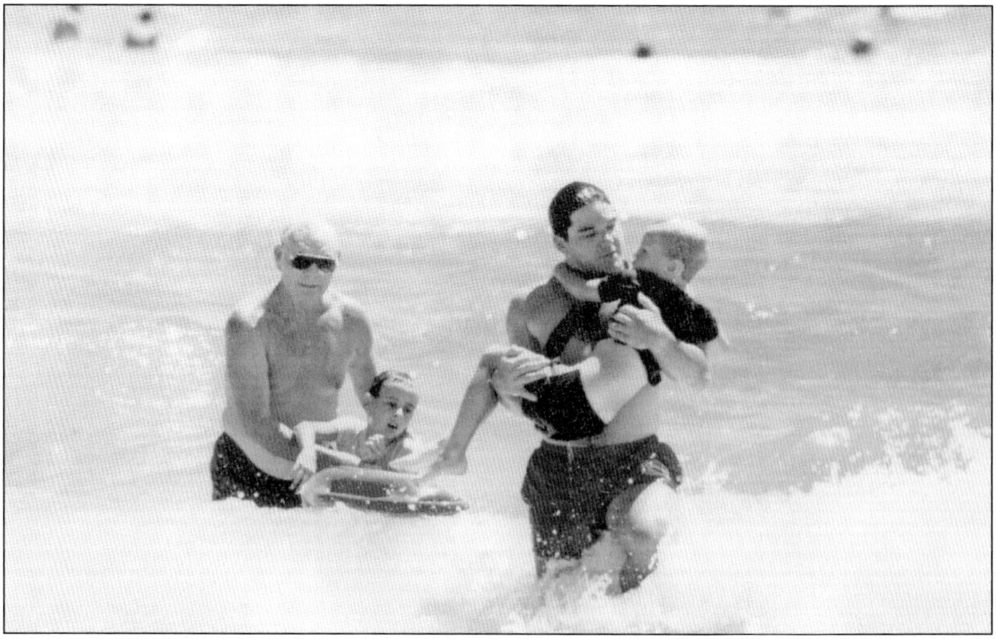

The moments that stay with the guards forever involve successful rescues, where someone's life is saved by their actions. In both of these photographs, there was a happy ending. Here an unidentified guard at the Granada approach in Ormond Beach assists in rescuing two children from the surf. (Photograph by Jim Tiller; courtesy of Volusia County Beach Patrol.)

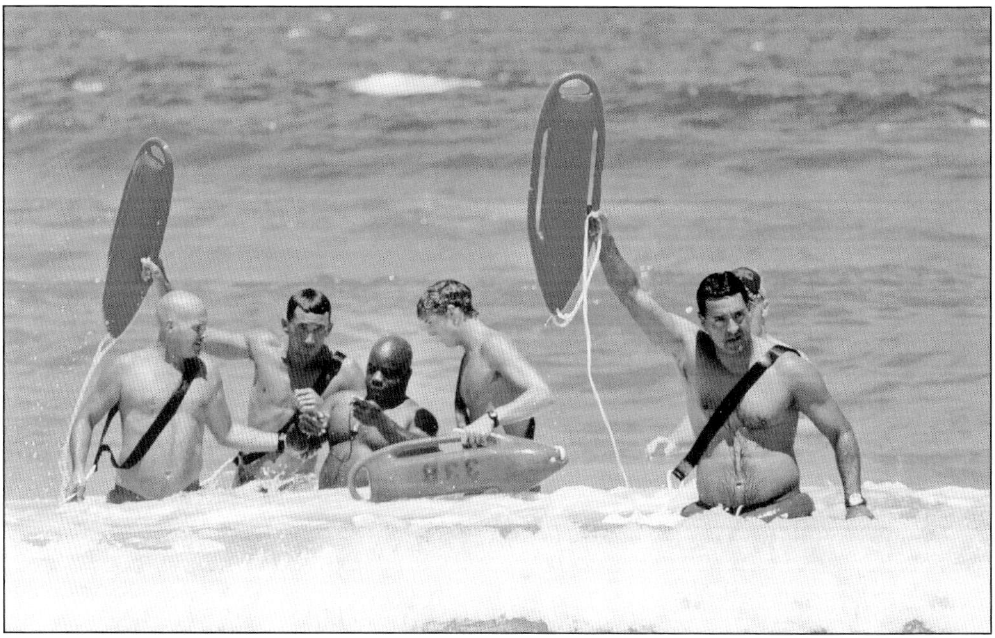

Dave Williams (left) and Ray Cavallo (far right) are among the guards performing a successful rescue in the Daytona Beach area. As backup lifeguards arrive, they immediately assess the situation and make decisions regarding entering the water and assisting. These lifeguards are signaling all clear by raising their buoys. (Photograph by Jim Tiller; courtesy of Volusia County Beach Patrol.)

Seven

Surf Lifesaving Now and Beyond

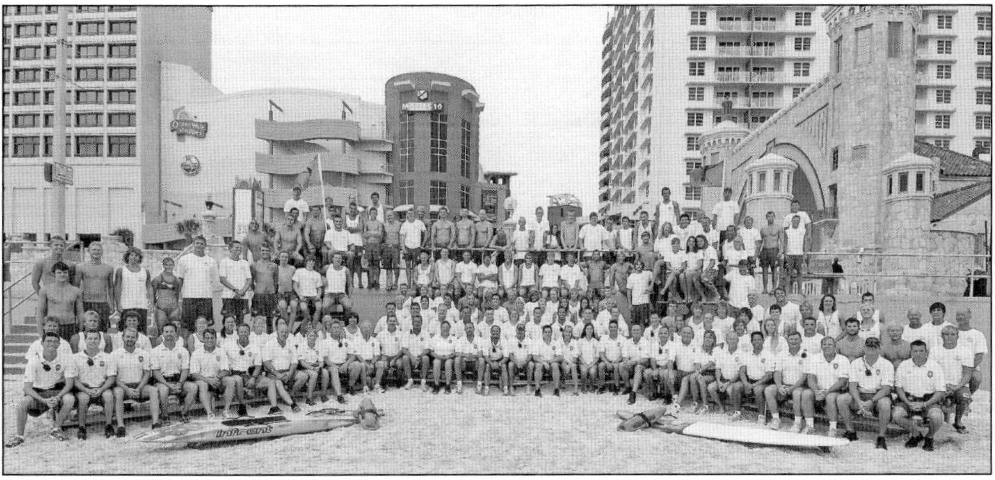

The 2008 Volusia County Beach Patrol assembled for the group photograph in front of the band shell, the site of the original Daytona Beach lifeguard station. Much has changed in the nearly 80 years since the official formation of the corps. Now nearly 250 strong at peak season, it is an exemplary surf lifesaving corps. These men and women compete internationally, and the recruit training and junior lifeguard programs are among the top in the nation.

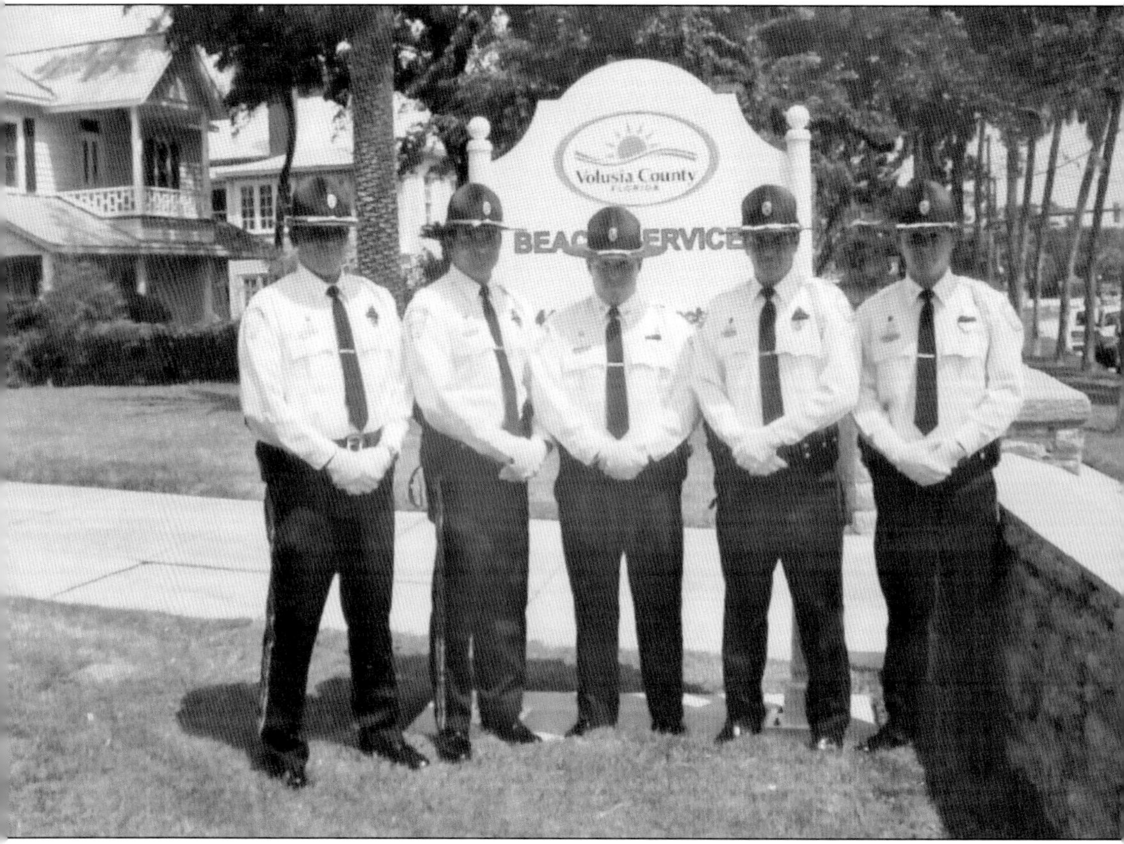

The honor guard was formed in early 2007, founded on principles of honor and discipline with the purpose of representing the state of Florida, the county of Volusia, and the Department of Public Protection Beach Safety Division by attending both public and private events as official representatives. Since its inception, the guard has participated in over 50 events, including funerals and official ceremonies, providing assistance to families of fellow beach patrol members in times of need, and taking part in the annual Tour De Force, a 270-mile bicycle ride from Miami to Daytona Beach to raise money and awareness for the families of police officers killed in the line of duty in Florida. This photograph was taken in 2007 in front of the beach services building at 440 South Beach Street, before the corps moved into the new facilities located on the beach at 515 South Atlantic Avenue. Shown here are, from left to right, Dave Vanis, Jim Conrad, Mark Christman, Kyle McDaniel, and Mike Berard—five of the seven members of the guard.

The majority of those who serve as lifeguards become outstanding citizens, contributing much to their communities. After a brief stint as a lifeguard in 1969, Charles "Charlie" Knight moved on to become a highly successful developer. At that time, Capt. Tom Renick told him if he ever changed his mind he could return to the guards. In 2008, Knight reminded Capt. Scott Petersohn of Renick's words. Petersohn assured Knight that if he could swim the requirement he would have his job. So in February 2009, after a 40-year absence and at age 59, Knight resumed his place on the beach patrol. Here is manning the tower once again in the summer of 2009.

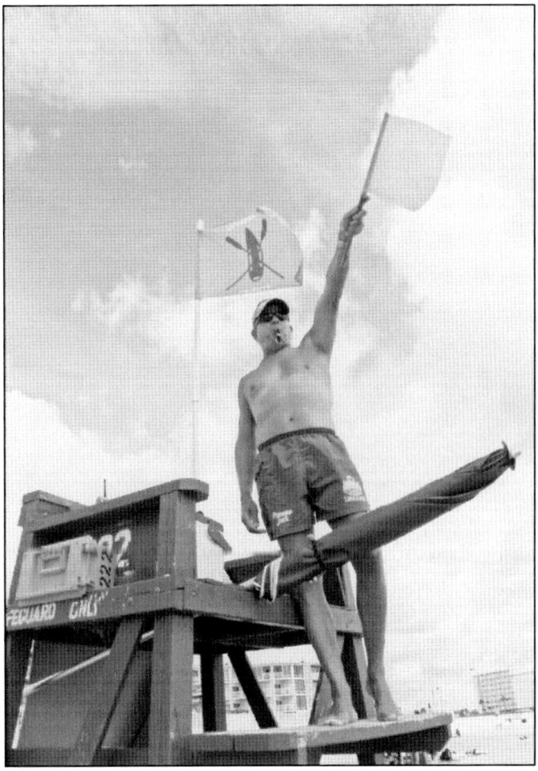

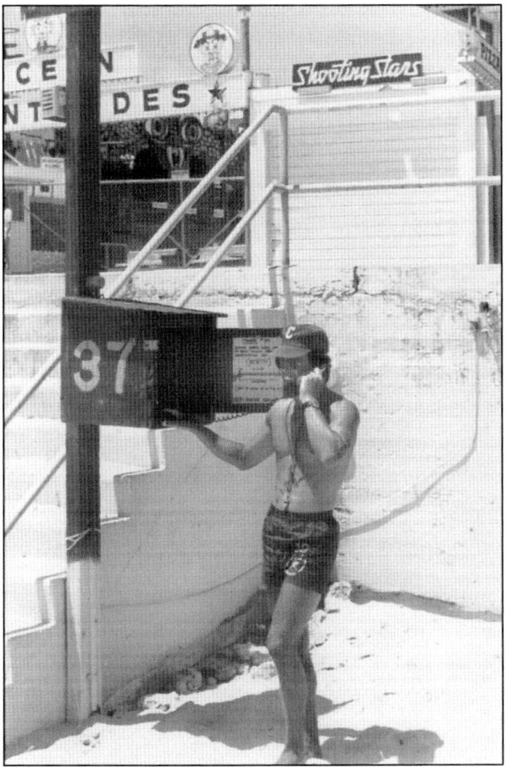

In 1969, communication was limited to signals, whistles, and a phone box located behind each lifeguard tower. This enabled the guards to connect directly to the switchboard in the control tower, which they did each morning for tides, water temperatures, and other information. Dispatchers could provide an outside line as well. This photograph shows Knight as a young lifeguard checking in from the box at the boardwalk.

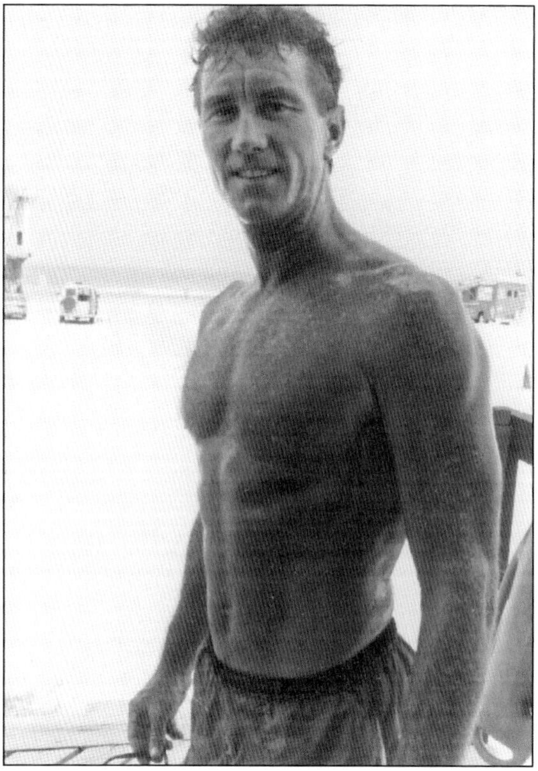

A natural athlete, Phil Brennan was on the VCBP for seven years before entering the county fire service. Brennan's father writes the popular political Internet site *Wednesday on the Web*, and he and his daughter Eryn compete together regularly in triathlons (previous photograph).

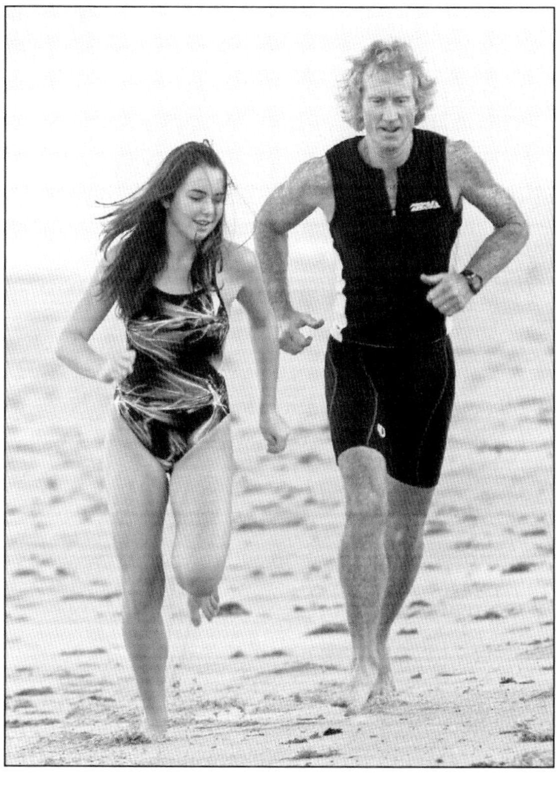

The call to lifeguarding seems to be in the blood—and often runs in the family. There have been numerous brothers and father/son lifeguards throughout the history of the corps. Here Eryn Brennan, daughter of Phil Brennan (VCBP 1982–1989), prepares to follow in her father's footsteps. By summer 2010, Eryn will have participated in 14 junior lifeguard camps, beginning at the age of nine, and will officially become a member of the VCBP, sitting in her own tower for the summer.

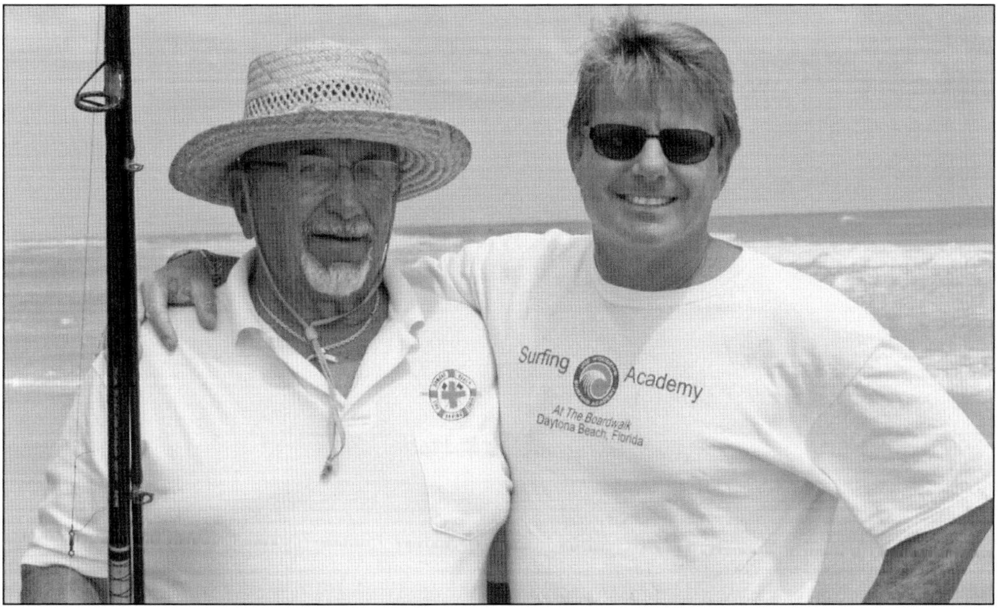

Andy Romano, former captain of the Ormond Beach Life Saving Corps, and Joe Wooden, now retired from the VCBP, remain close friends and still enjoy the wonderful beach lifestyle. Here they fish away a Sunday afternoon in April 2009.

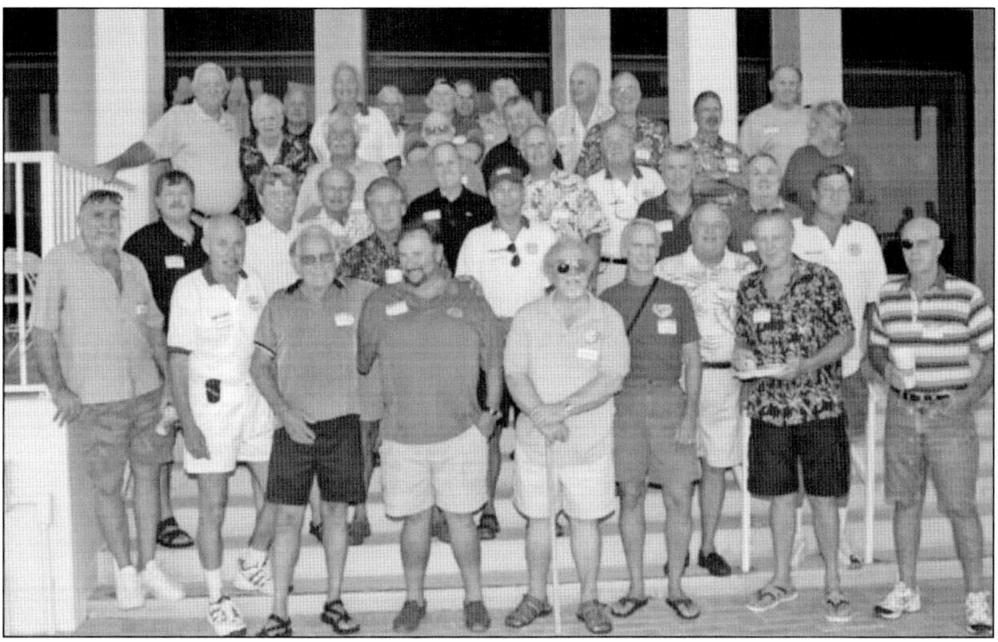

An annual reunion is held for the lifeguards who have retained the membership in the social club—and who have "taken the water cure." The largest number to attend a reunion was approximately 250. Sometimes the gathering is held at a home, such as that of Ron Rice (of Hawaiian Tropic Suntan Oil fame), and sometimes a restaurant is the site. The reunion in 2008 was held at a local hotel. Some years ago, each member was given a mug inscribed with his name, and when a guard passes away, his mug is retired. Today the number of members is dwindling; when the last one is gone, the organization will cease to exist.

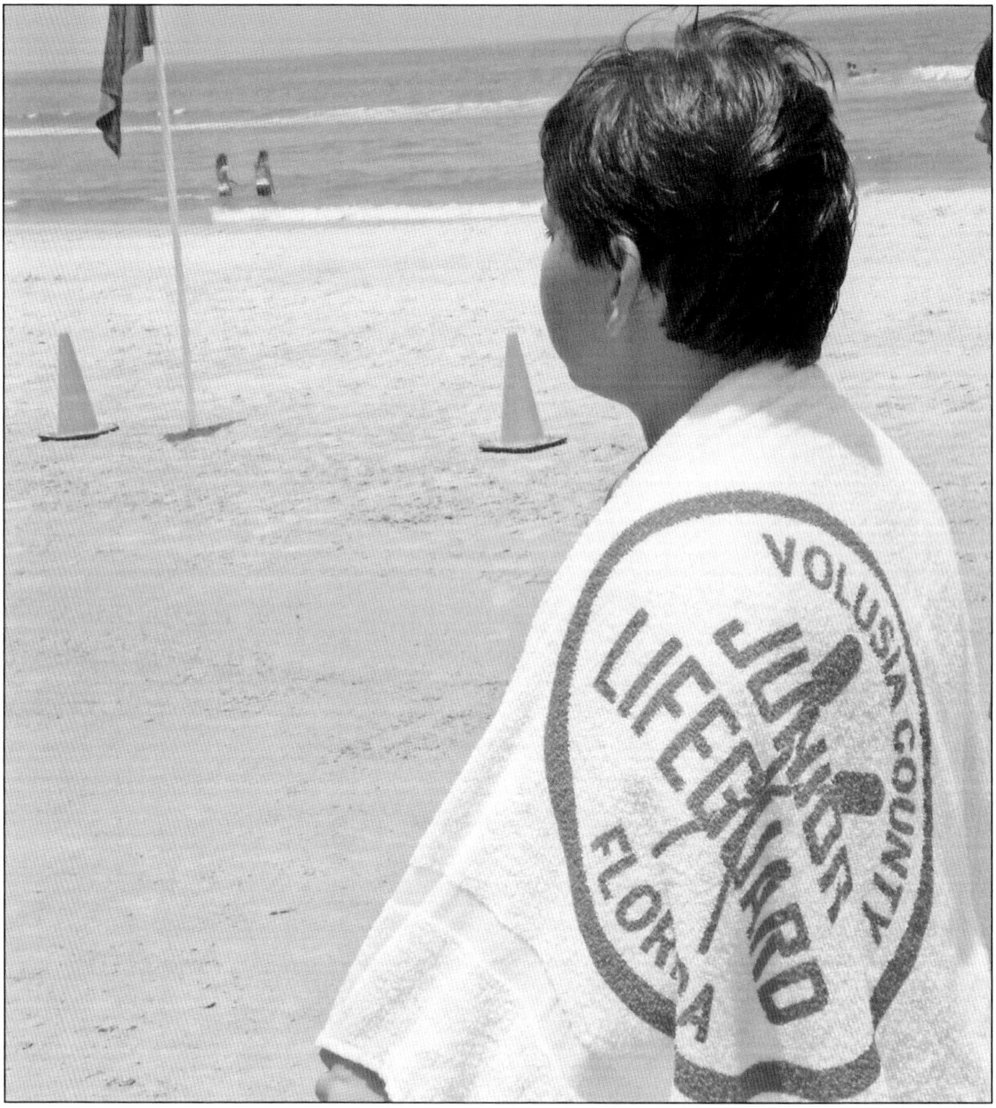

Affiliated with the United States Lifesaving Association (USLA), the Volusia County Beach Patrol Junior Lifeguard Program prepares the next generation of lifeguards. In a weeklong camp setting, youths between the ages of 9 and 15 learn water safety and first aid techniques and develop the athletic abilities to qualify for positions on the beach patrol. (Photograph by Patti Light.)

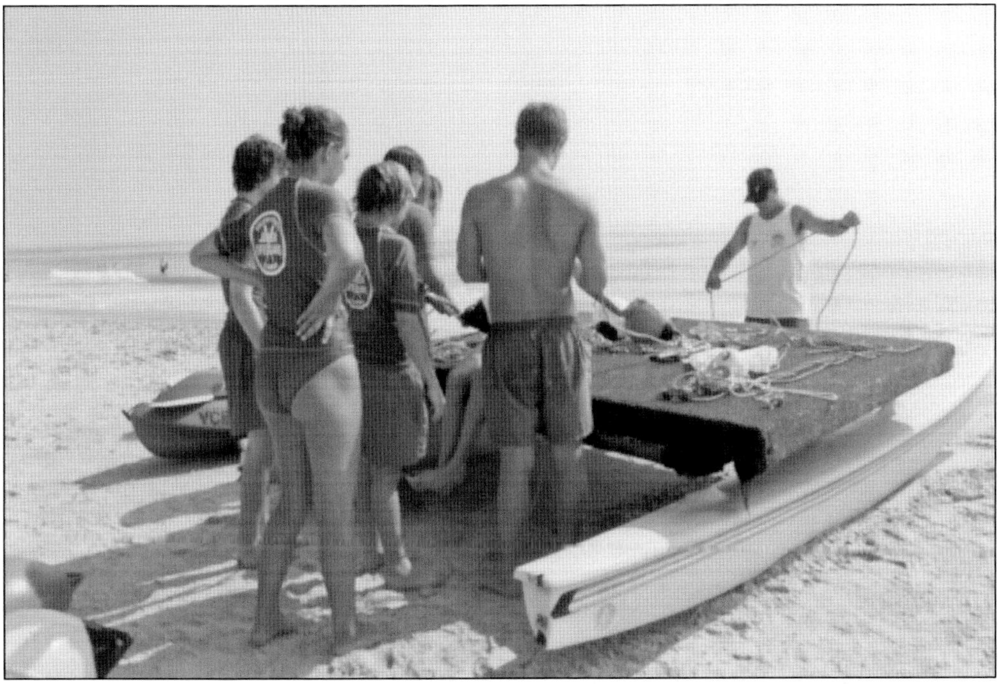

Instruction in the use of rescue equipment includes rigging the catamaran, as demonstrated by officer Chris Nowviskie in this 2009 photograph. Nowviskie is assistant coordinator of the Junior Lifeguard Program. (Photograph by Patti Light.)

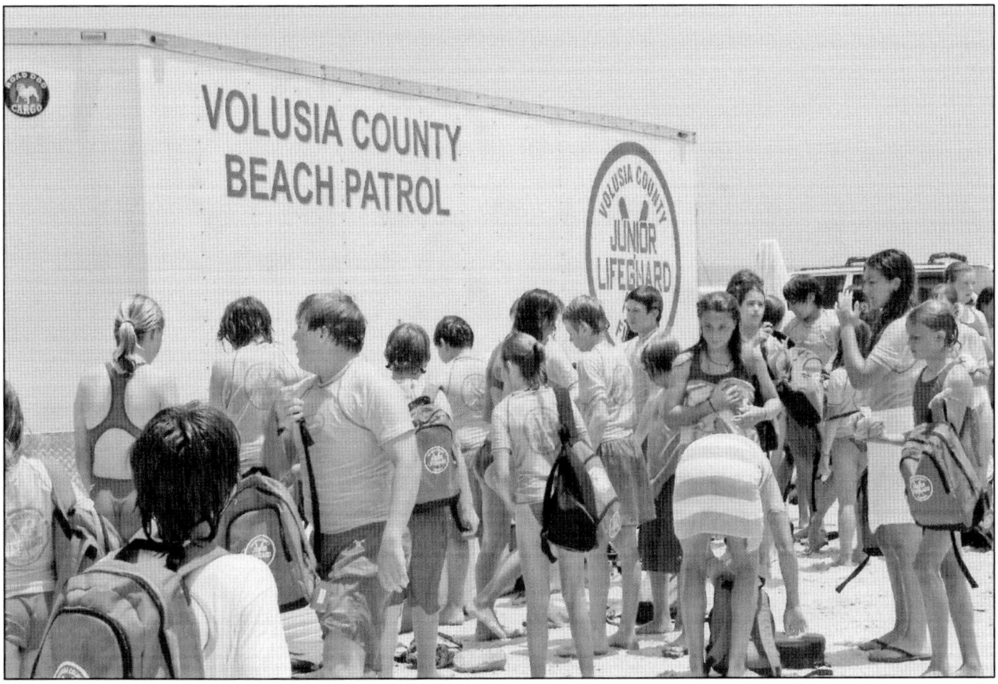

Participants at the camps learn about beach safety in a fun atmosphere. By the end of the week, they will have acquired skills in surf lifesaving, including paddleboard rescues, first aid, and CPR. (Photograph by Patti Light.)

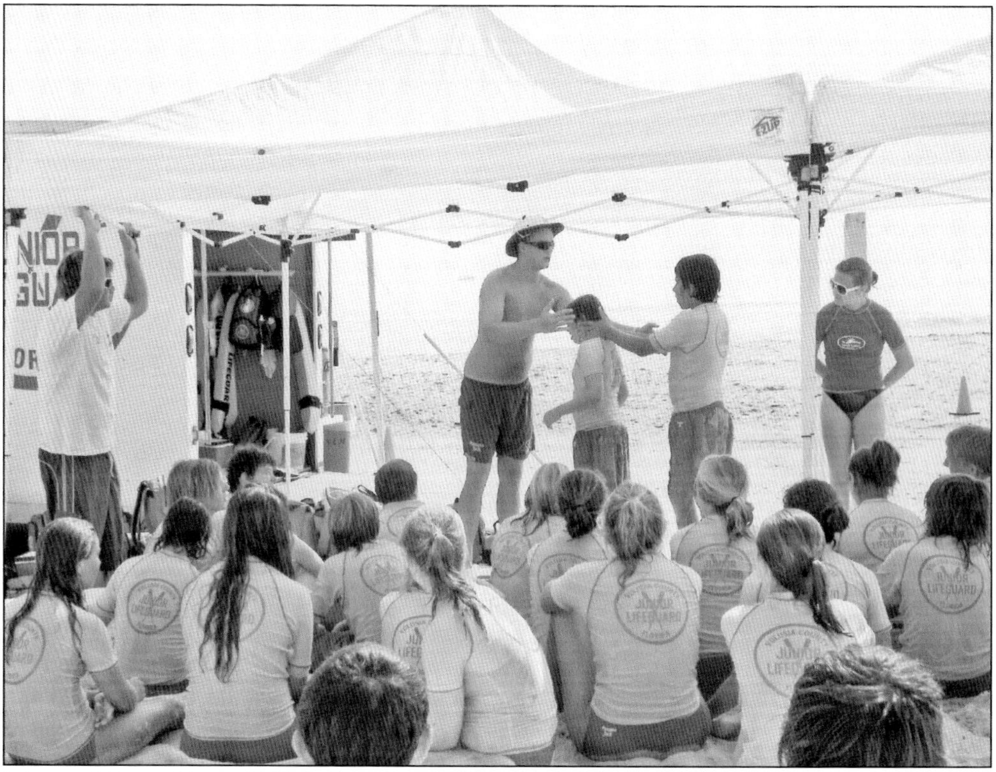

Lifeguard Ryan Shaw (left) looks on as lifeguard Johnny Goode (in white hat) gives rescue instructions to the next generation of lifesavers. (Photograph by Patti Light.)

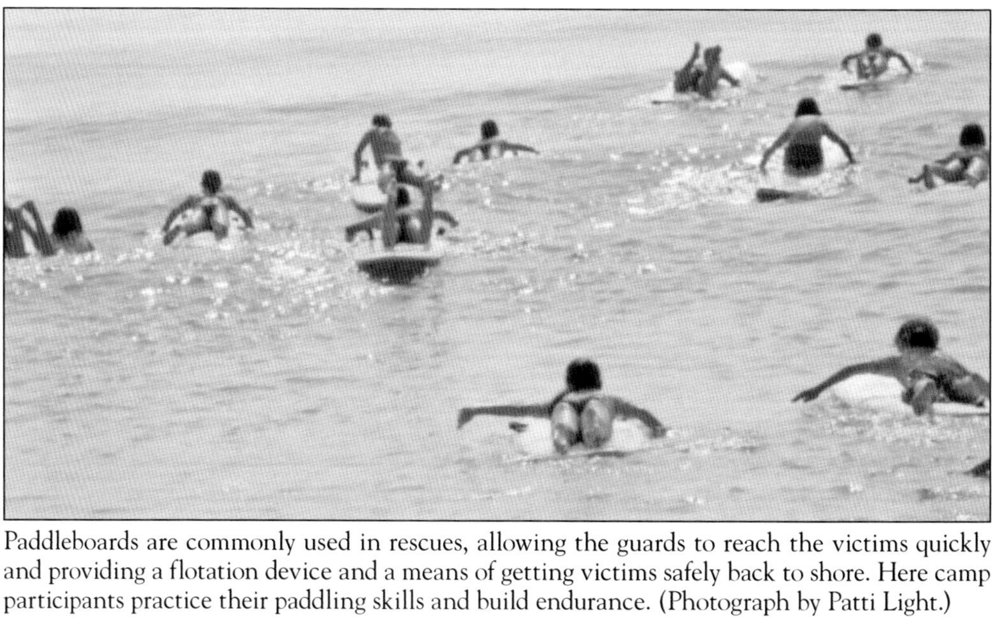

Paddleboards are commonly used in rescues, allowing the guards to reach the victims quickly and providing a flotation device and a means of getting victims safely back to shore. Here camp participants practice their paddling skills and build endurance. (Photograph by Patti Light.)

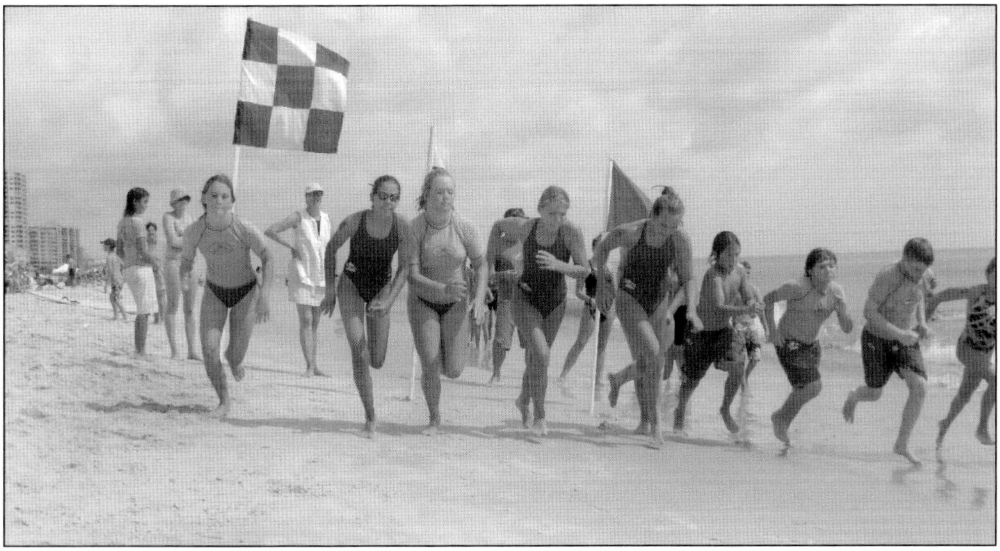

Requirements for enrollment in the program include swimming 100 yards in 2 minutes, 15 seconds, treading water for 5 minutes, and swimming 10 feet under water. Competition events in all age divisions test skills in paddling, running, swimming, beach flags, and rescue relays. (Courtesy of Nancy Gutierrez.)

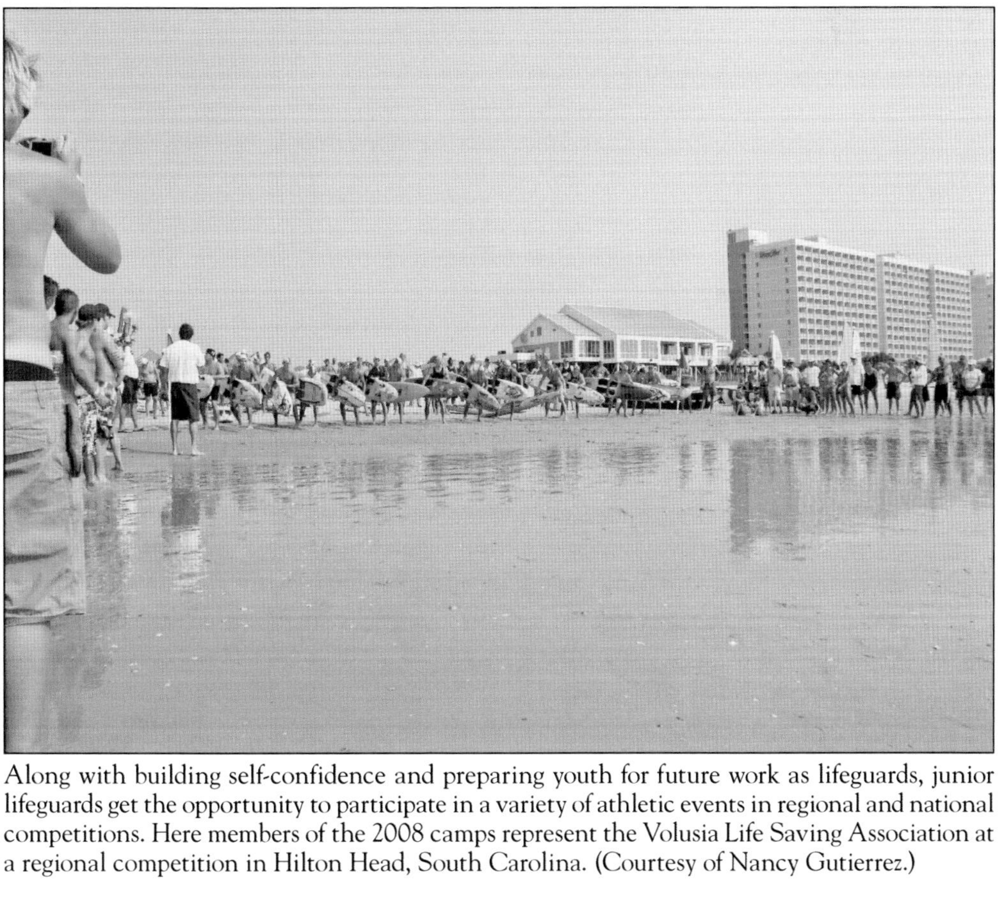

Along with building self-confidence and preparing youth for future work as lifeguards, junior lifeguards get the opportunity to participate in a variety of athletic events in regional and national competitions. Here members of the 2008 camps represent the Volusia Life Saving Association at a regional competition in Hilton Head, South Carolina. (Courtesy of Nancy Gutierrez.)

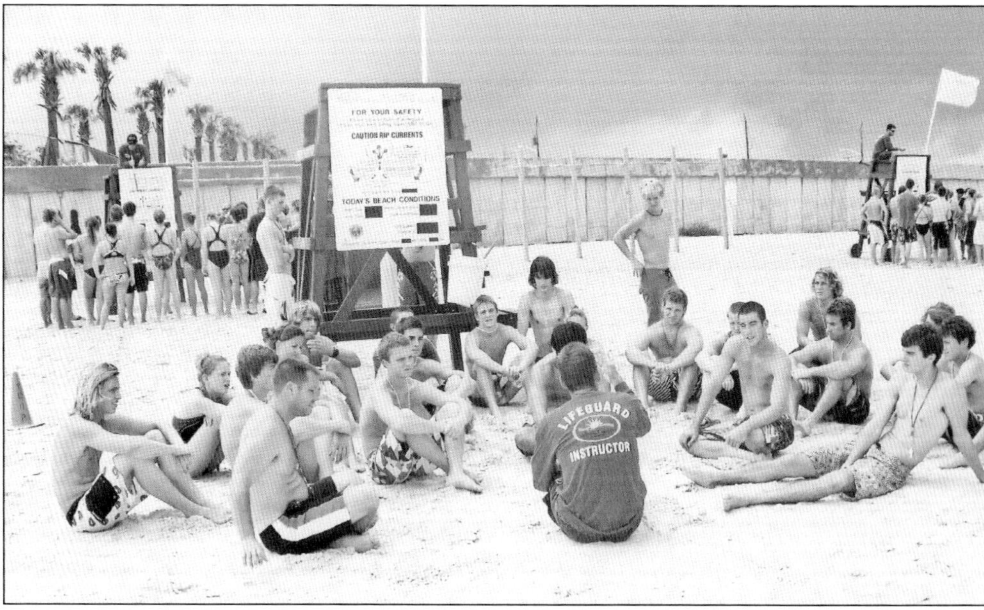

The next step for a junior lifeguard is beach patrol explorer. These 14 to 16 year olds receive advance training to prepare them to become lifeguards. They act as assistant instructors and can even earn community service hours for their high school graduation. Other opportunities include Bright Future Scholarships, and the program satisfies the physical education requirement for home-schooled students.

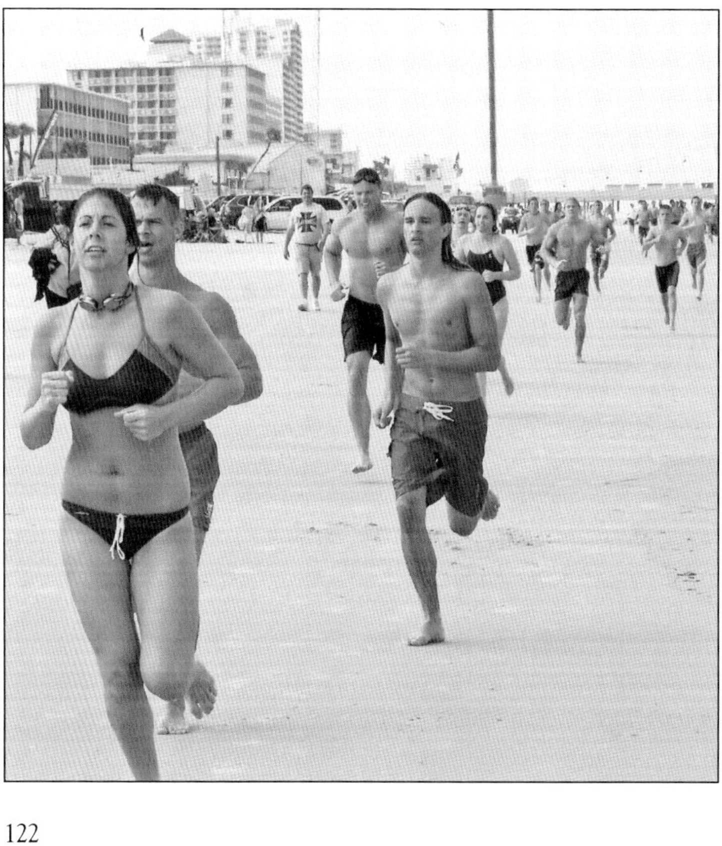

Each year, more than a hundred young hopefuls try out for a position with the Volusia County Beach Patrol. In addition to swimming and lifesaving techniques, running is also a necessary part of lifeguard requirements. Here the recruits attempt to complete their half-mile run in the maximum allotted time of 3 minutes, 15 seconds or less. (Photograph by Jim and Norma Jean Harrison; courtesy of VCBP.)

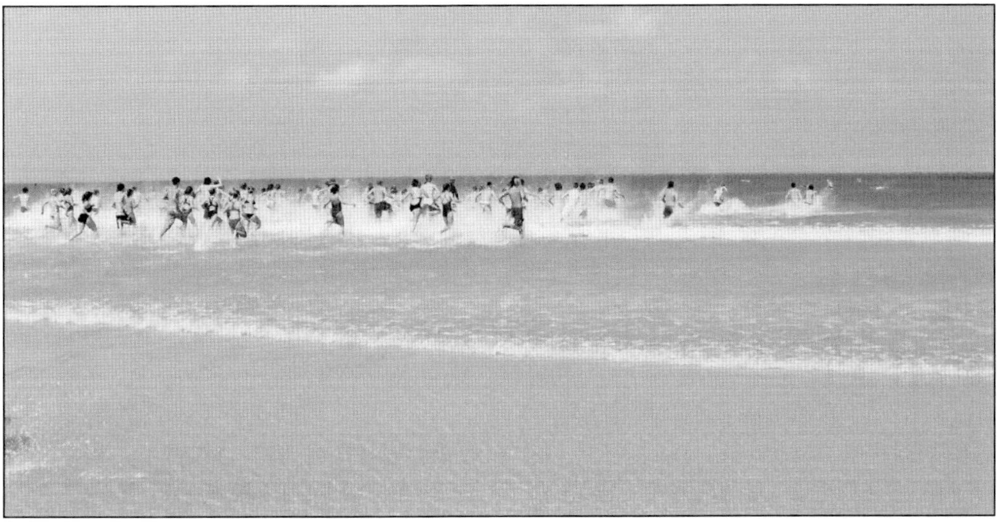

This photograph and the one below, both taken in 2008, show the determination of the recruits as they train and prepare for their exams. Physical requirements include swimming 500 meters in under 10 minutes, either in pool or ocean. Additionally, the recruits must swim 50 yards in 30 seconds or less. These determined hopefuls dash into the surf as the clock ticks. (Photograph by Jim and Norma Jean Harrison; courtesy of VCBP.)

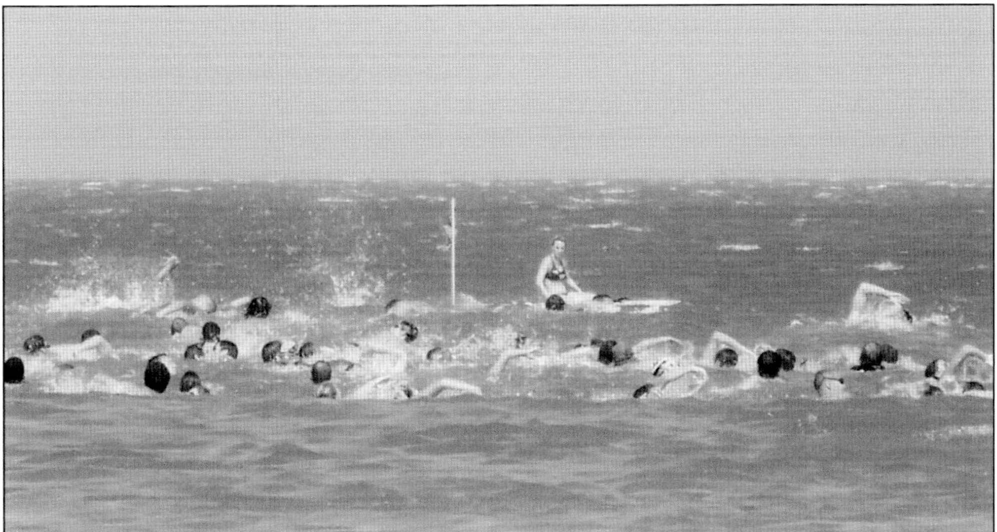

Certified by the USLA as an advanced lifeguard agency, the VCBP's intense recruitment program consists of 44 hours of ocean lifeguard training, both in the ocean and the classroom, plus 44 hours of first-responder/EMS and medical training following the nationally accepted training guidelines of the U.S. Department of Transportation. Finally, there is a required 32 hours of "double-tower," which is on-the-job training with a seasoned veteran for four days. Upon completion of all training and meeting physical requirements, new guards begin their careers in slower areas while they gain experience.

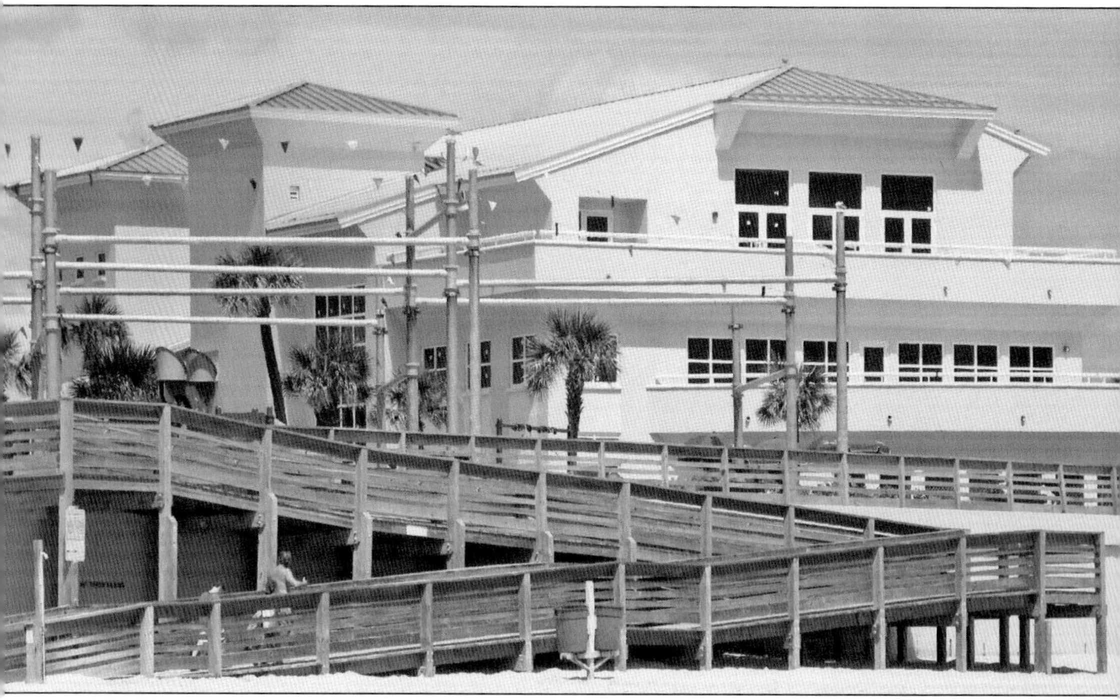

Located at 515 South Atlantic Avenue in the heart of Daytona Beach, the Lifeguard Headquarters and Administration Center is 22,000 square feet of space for administrative support, training facilities, first aid area, and meeting rooms with state-of-the-art audio and visual equipment. The facility, constructed on pilings, is built with concrete masonry and designed to withstand hurricane-strength winds and beach erosion. The building features a display of memorabilia from the Daytona Beach Life Saving Corps and Volusia County Beach Patrol from as early as the 1920s. (Photograph by Patti Light.)

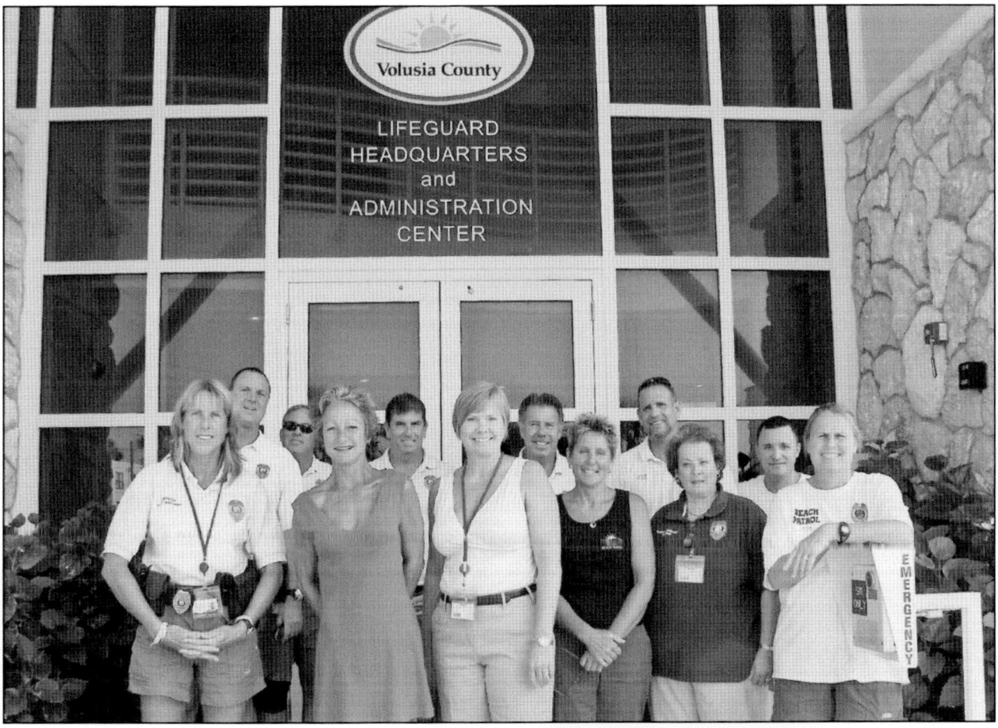

Some of the beach patrol officers and staff are represented here, standing in front of their headquarters in June 2009. They are, from left to right, (first row) Kathy Shulzinsky (officer), Tami Andrasco, Nanci Nolin, Judy Hallock, Pat Sinuk, and Liz Johnson (officer); (second row) Rich Gardner (captain), Rob Horster (captain), Kevin Sweat (director), Mike Hensler (deputy chief), Pat Casey (officer), and Chris Dembinski (accreditation manager). (Photograph by Patti Light.)

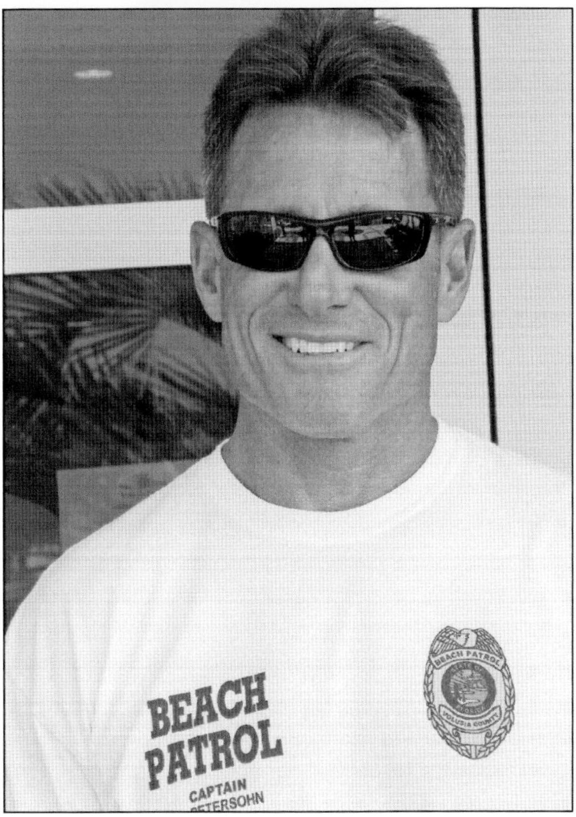

Capt. Scott Petersohn, a 25-year veteran with the Volusia County Beach Patrol, is the official public information officer for the organization. Formerly with the fire department, Petersohn also works with recruits and is active in training.

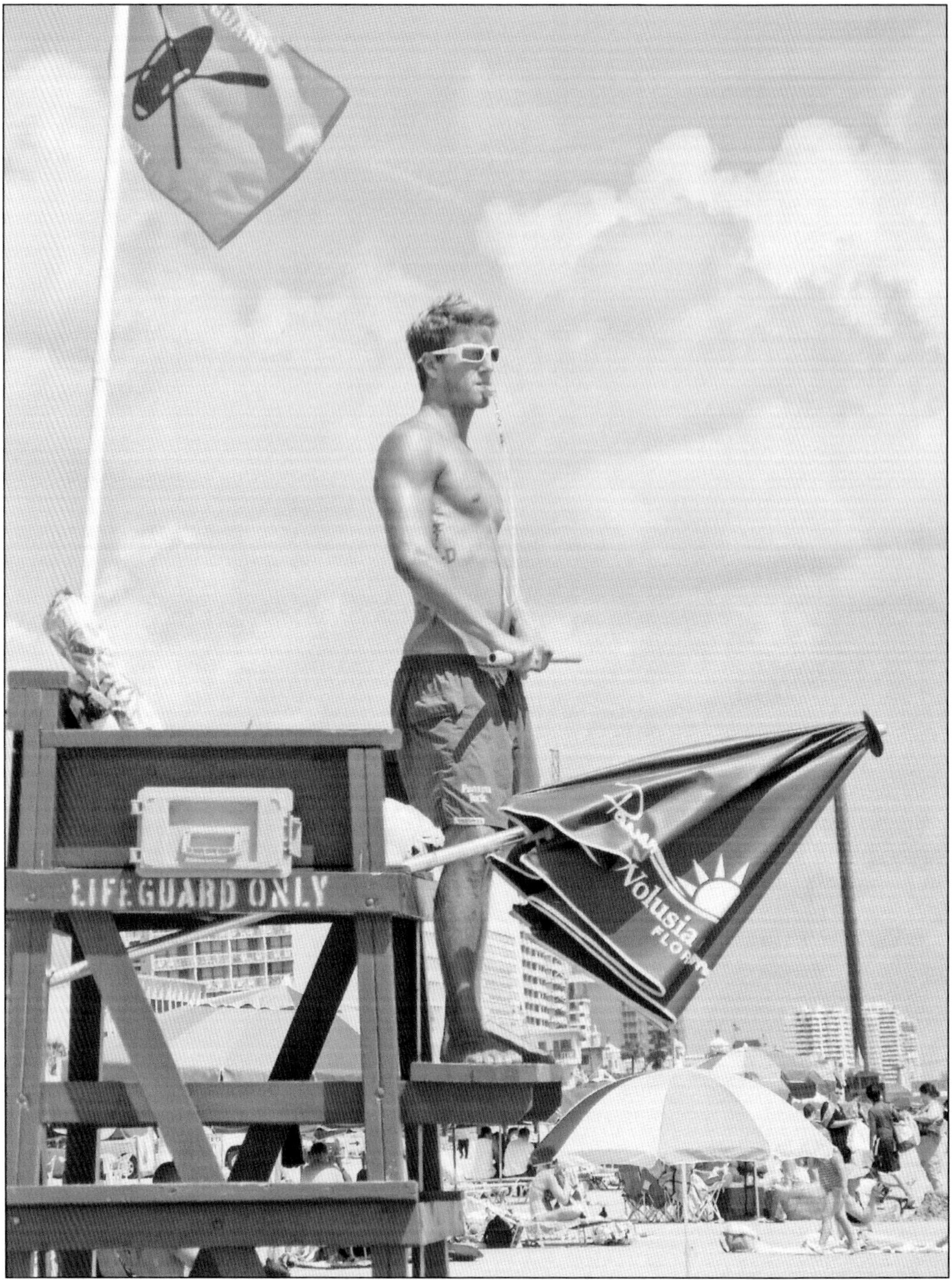

Ben Manganaro is an example of the future of the beach patrol, manning a Daytona Beach tower in the spring of 2008. After attending junior lifeguard camps as a youth, he became a beach patrol explorer, a program where selected individuals aged 14–16 receive advanced training to prepare them for positions as lifeguards. They also act as assistant instructors at the camps. Explorers are eligible for community service hours needed for graduation, Bright Future scholarships, and may satisfy their physical education credit requirements for Florida Virtual School, a home-schooling program. (Photograph by Patti Light.)

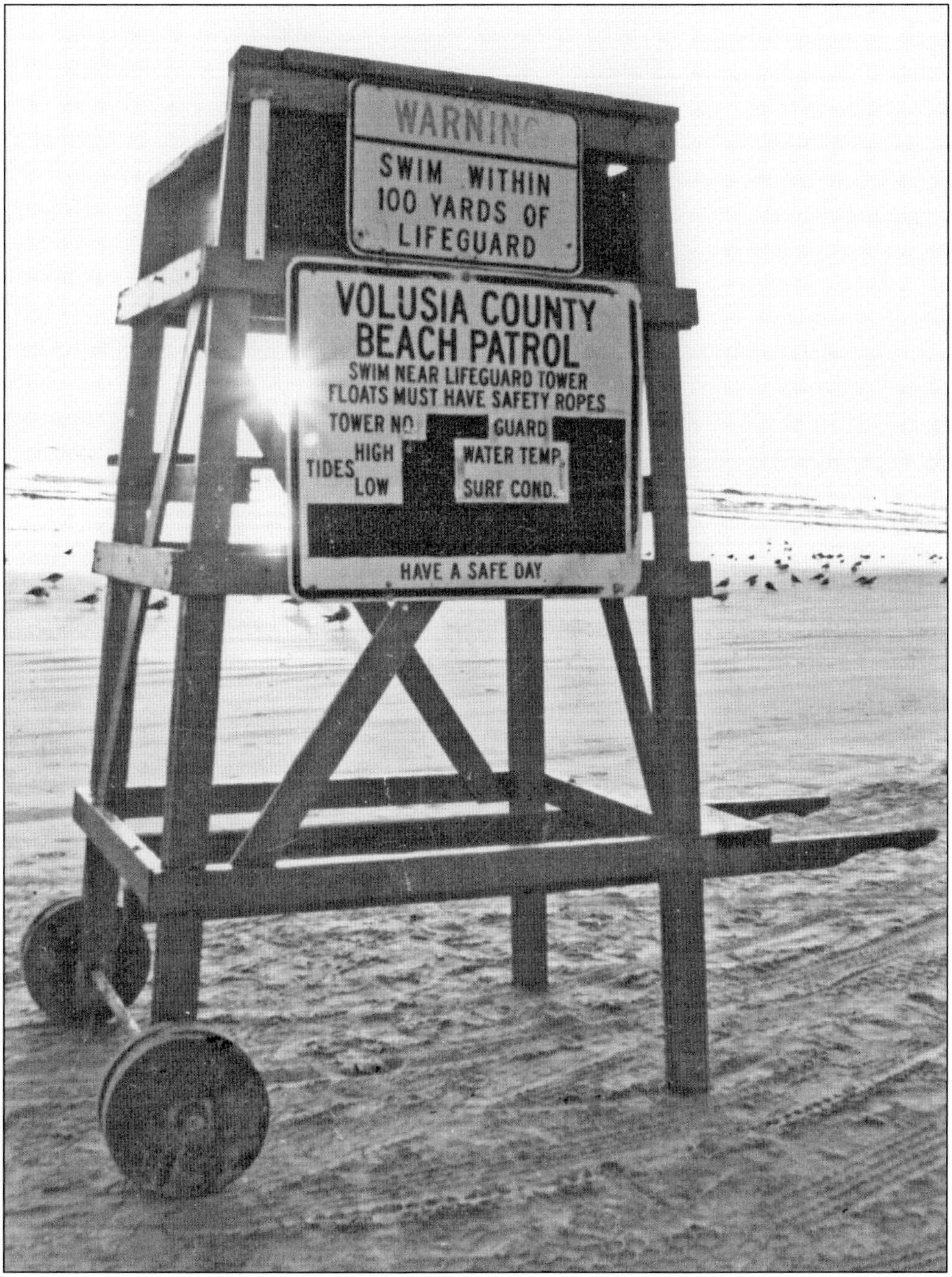

The sun comes up on another day in Daytona Beach, and the tower awaits the man or woman who will attend it. Some days are quiet, even boring, sitting on the tower watching over calm waters and occasional bathers. Some days are nail-biting, when the rip currents are wild and the crowds are thick. But no matter what the day brings, the public—locals and visitors alike—can enjoy the incredible freedom of frolicking in the ocean, knowing that a highly trained individual is on guard. And should something go wrong, world-class assistance is just a shout and a buoy line away. "Only the Lord saves more than the beach patrol."